A Charter for the Church

A Charter for the Church
Sharing a Vision for the 21st Century

GEORGE CAREY

Introduction by
RICHARD HOLLOWAY

MOREHOUSE PUBLISHING
Harrisburg, PA

Text © 1993 George Carey
Introduction © 1993 Richard Holloway

First published in Great Britain 1993 by

Darton, Longman and Todd, Ltd

First published in America 1993 by

Morehouse Publishing
P.O. Box 1321
Harrisburg, PA 17105

Scripture quotations
are from the Revised Standard Version of the Bible,
copyrighted 1971 and 1952 by the
Division of Christian Education of the National
Council of Churches of Christ in the USA

Library of Congress Cataloging-in-Publication Data:
Carey, George.
    A charter for the church : sharing a vision for the 21st century / George
Carey.
       p.   cm.
    Lectures and sermons delivered 1991-1992.
    ISBN 0-8192-1612-7 (paper)
    1. Christianity—Great Britain—20th century—Sermons.   2. Church of
England—Sermons.   3. Anglican Communion—Sermons.   4. Sermons, English.
I. Title.
BR759.C36   1993   93-26327
252'.03—dc20   CIP

Printed in the United States of America
by
BSC LITHO
Harrisburg, PA

Contents

CONTENTS

MISSION IN A QUESTIONING WORLD

CHALLENGES FACING A CHANGING CHURCH

Preface

The addresses and sermons assembled in this book were all designed for particular gatherings of people – ranging from congregations in English cities to political assemblies in the Council of Europe. I am generally uncomfortable about using addresses to talk over the heads of such gatherings to a wider audience beyond. Nevertheless, most things said by the Archbishop of Canterbury are available to the media and are of interest to a wider public also. In the preparation of this book some editing has been necessary to make these addresses accessible to a wider audience but the substance of what I said has not been changed.

This collection is meant above all for two groups of people. First, ordinary worshipping Christians, both of the Anglican Communion and of other traditions. I hope they will derive some encouragement and nourishment from it in their spiritual pilgrimages. Secondly, I have in mind a much wider range of people who, whether or not they worship God regularly, are searching conscientiously for a sense of purpose in life. In all I do, it is these two audiences that matter most to me. It is my hope that all those who care about the deeper things of life will feel that I am addressing issues that are important to us all. My dearest wish, of course, is that through this book God's Holy Spirit in some way may touch their hearts and lives and enrich their vision.

This book contains only a sample of a constant outpouring of addresses and excludes contributions made in media interviews and newspaper articles. It is not therefore a fully representative cross section of my ministry, but it does show the great variety of issues with which I engage as Archbishop of

Canterbury at a time of challenge in the Church and the wider society, both at home and abroad.

On a recent visit to Korea I learnt an apt Korean saying: 'A monk cannot shave his own head.' It illustrates something we all know well – that we owe our wellbeing to others. My thanks go to the staff of Darton, Longman and Todd for their work in helping to edit this book. I acknowledge too my debt of friendship, fellowship and the sharing of ideas with my own staff at Lambeth, with my fellow bishops, the staff of Church House, and many others in the wider Church. I also offer grateful thanks to Richard Holloway for writing the introduction and, finally, and especially, to Eileen whose enthusiasm, support and encouragement I value more as each year progresses.

✝ George Cantuar

Introduction

Offering someone like me a subscription to a news agency is like inviting an alcoholic to join a wine society. I already read too many newspapers, but when our church office suggested that we ought to subscribe to a religious news agency I was unable to resist the offer. It means that every week they dump an enormous pile of press cuttings on my desk. Every news item that could conceivably be linked to a religious theme is clipped by the agency and sent to us in great bales. I am agreeably surprised by the level of coverage of religion in the British press, but I am depressed by much of the tone. Some of it is straightforward reporting of religious news, but certain predictable themes appear again and again in a ritualistic way. The tabloids, in particular, are fascinated by clergy who fall foul of the British public's hypocritical code on sexual morality, but the broadsheets are just as interested in this theme, though they express their fascination in silkier prose and with an occasional stab at sympathetic interpretation. Another enduring topic is the imminent disintegration of the Church of England. This one has been around for at least twenty years and shows no signs of abating.

The third major topic in recent months has been the Archbishop of Canterbury himself. The broadsheets, and some of the weeklies, have published articles patronisingly dismissing George Carey or praising him with faint damns. There are several elements in this fascination of the media with the present holder of the See of Canterbury. The first is the insatiable need of the communications media for enduring themes. Manufacturing news is a chancy and inexorable process, so it's not surprising that themes are sought that will have the dynamic of popular soap operas that just run and run, and the private lives of famous people provide one of the enduring staples of journalism. Daniel Boorstin described celebrities as people who are well known for being well known. Certain offices and public roles in our society confer immediate celebrity status. But the consequent regard of the communications media is a dubious blessing. It raises up and it casts down, it creates instant heroes whom it can just as suddenly turn against. Few people can survive the relentless surveillance of intrusive journalists, which is why public leadership in our electronic society is much more difficult than it used to be. There is no longer a protective mystique that guards monarch, prime minister or archbishop. Though there has been gain in accountability to the public, there has been loss as well. No human being can long survive the glare of publicity that falls upon celebrities today. W H Auden pointed out years ago that writers should be assessed on the quality of their work not their biographies and Dr Johnson made the same point when he wrote:

It has been long the custom for oriental monarchs to hide themselves in gardens and palaces, to avoid the conversation of mankind, and to be known to their subjects only by their edicts. The same policy is no less necessary to him that writes, than to him that governs; for men would not more patiently submit to be taught, than commanded, by one known to have the same follies and weaknesses with themselves. A sudden intruder into the closet of an author, would, perhaps, feel equal indignation with the officer, who having long solicited admission into the presence of Sardanapalus, saw him not consulting upon laws, inquiring into grievances or modelling armies, but employed in feminine amusements, and directing ladies in their work.

There is unlikely to be a return to the days when a conspiracy of silence protected our leaders from the gaze of the public. Now they have to prepare for the attentions of the press the way the police prepare for riot control.

But a second element in these media preoccupations is clearly metropolitan self-absorbtion. London is still the main headquarters of the British press and London gossip inevitably, if wearyingly, predominates in our newspapers. More depressingly, some clergy are easily lured into colluding with this system of metropolitan self-dramatisation. They can be flattered by the attentions of the press and ambitious or frustrated clerics can be used by it for its own ends.

That is why the publication of this book is important. It will give the British public an opportunity to make up its own mind about George Carey. I hope that he will not allow the fickle preoccupations of the British press to deflect him from his work or depress him in its execution. The best way to handle these unwanted attentions is to treat them the way a driver, speeding through the country on a summer night, treats the insects that end up coating the windscreen of the car – as unpleasant concomitants of a necessary journey. Nor, I hope, will the Archbishop pay much attention to the PR industry's equivalent of plastic surgeons who have offered to operate on his image. I suspect, anyway, that he is not interested in reinventing himself, as opposed to learning from his experiences. In fact, there is considerable evidence that George Carey is a secure and strong-minded personality, who is doggedly sticking to his script in spite of the sniggers of the sophisticates in the front stalls, because he knows the people at the back of the house are gradually getting the message.

But what is his script? What message is he trying to get across? On the evidence of the addresses gathered in this book, four consistent themes dominate his thinking. The first theme came as something of a surprise to me and it reveals one of the major ironies in British society at the moment. One of the consistent complaints of the Conservative Party about the Church of England is that it is failing to offer moral leadership to the nation. Personally, I am dubious about the value or efficacy of public figures offering moral exhortations of the sort that is clearly desired by some. On the evidence of this book, however, the concern that lies behind these complaints is close to the Archbishop's own heart. In addresses up and down the country, George Carey has been hammering away at the necessity of having a set of common values, if our society is not to disintegrate into moral anarchy. One of his most consistent themes, as reflected in this book, is the danger of moral relativism. In pluralistic societies like modern Britain, where a variety of views are tolerated, the danger is that moral emotivism or subjectivism confines morality to the private sphere, individualises it. This means that society itself ends up with no set of common values or moral purposes, except, perhaps, the task of refereeing the endless debate on moral priorities that characterises a pluralistic society. Archbishop Carey affirms many of the values of modern plural societies, but this book shows that he is constantly pleading for the recovery of a common moral vision in our country; a vision that, while it affirms the value of personal freedom, also acknowledges the need for a core of objective values and standards, because without them society can scarcely be said to exist at all. On the evidence of this book, Archbishop Carey can be described as a moralist, one who practises and teaches morals. In moral debate the tone is almost as important as the content. The tone here is firm, but compassionate, and reflects the rootedness and security of a man in possession of a set of robust principles. This theme in his recent addresses shows that Archbishop Carey is very English in his preoccupations. The English, while they conspicuously lack the tragic sense of life, have a genius for the empirical, for the adjustments, compromises and disciplines that are the mark of stable societies. There is no dominant moral tradition in Britain at the moment, but there is evidence of an increasing desire for a new moral vision that will reinforce common purposes and mutual relationships. Instinctively, George Carey has tapped into that emerging consciousness and may one day be seen as one of its most significant guides.

The second major theme in his recent utterances is a message to the Church rather than to society as a whole. He insistently calls for a new and more positive attitude within the Church about its own achievements and strengths. He accepts the need for self-criticism and he is as aware as anyone of the Church's flaws and failures, but he has clearly set out to counter the mood of defeatism that prevails in certain quarters. In several of the addresses in this book he steadfastly catalogues the Church of England's contribution to the life of English society in all sorts of areas. I suspect that this theme will resonate with many people beyond the metropolitan gossip belt who are aware of the strength of life in the parishes. They know that the record of the Church of England, in responding to the needs of individuals and society, is one that is worth celebrating.

But there can be no doubt that the Christian cause in Europe is facing severe difficulties, of which consistent numerical decline is one of the major symptoms. Archbishop Carey's third insistent theme addresses this situation. He is clearly wanting to use his office as an instrument of mission, both directly, by preaching and teaching, and indirectly, by energising and emboldening the Church to find new ways of sharing the Faith with the people of late twentieth-century multi-cultural Britain.

The fourth element in the working out of his vision for the Church of England is one that balances the previous theme. All expressions of Christianity have their strengths and weaknesses, their brightnesses and their shadows. Broad national Churches, like the Church of England, tend to lose their evangelical cutting edge by reason of the responsibility they feel towards society as a whole. Again and again George Carey applauds the intrinsic magnanimity of the Church of England in its approach to the stumbling faith affirmations of people who use its presence in their midst to add some spiritual significance to their lives, however undefined. He emphasises the pastoral opportunities offered by this national role, rather than the theoretical danger to the integrity of the sacraments as defined by more rigorist consciences. Indeed, he informs us that had the Church in the East End of London imposed the kind of baptismal disciplines that are now called for by many in the Church of England, he himself would never have been baptised or come to faith. Insistently, therefore, he reminds the Church of England that it has the breadth and open-endedness of the Church Catholic and not the narrowness and clearly defined nature of the sect. This, he believes, is something to celebrate about the Church of England and not denigrate. To me, one of the most interesting subtexts in the book is the way he constantly reminds Evangelical audiences, with whom he is obviously at home, that they belong to a Catholic Church and not a Protestant sect, and must learn to affirm the breadth and comprehensiveness of Anglicanism. He constantly tries to demonstrate why the different elements and emphases in the Church of England need and ought to fortify each other. This is a message that is of tragically urgent importance today.

To call for the recreation of a set of common values and moral purposes for society as a whole, to be affirming and celebratory about the record of the Church, while exhorting it to be active in mission and evangelism, without undermining its comprehensive and Catholic nature, seems to me to be a significant vision for the future of the Church of England. It is clearly one which the Archbishop of Canterbury has thought through and decided to own as the theme of his ministry. These are long-term goals. My hunch is that this Archbishop will be judged by history on his strategic achievements in persuading Church and society to follow the vision he himself is compelled by, rather than on the basis of the transitory preoccupations of the chattering classes. I suspect that he knows that being Archbishop of Canterbury is more like the steady trudge of a marathon than the flashy excitement of a sprint. On the evidence of this book, he is getting into his stride and is settling down for the long haul.

Richard Holloway

Prologue: Enthronement

> Wherever a saint has dwelt, wherever a martyr has given his blood for the blood of Christ, there is holy ground, and the sanctity shall not depart from it.

That sentence, from T S Eliot's play, *Murder in the Cathedral*, is about the death of a former Archbishop of Canterbury, whose manner of dying made Canterbury holy ground. My own enthronement, as successor to Thomas à Becket, falls on the anniversary of an earlier martyr bishop, St Alphege, who in 1012 was beaten to death with the bones of an ox. Martyrdom is usually messy, often humiliating, never romantic, whatever we make of it later. This is certainly what another Archbishop would tell us – William Laud, the only other Bishop of Bath and Wells to move to Canterbury, whose blood was shed on the scaffold. Such predecessors make me wonder – a little uneasily – about what may lie ahead, though it is not the particular circumstances of history which occupy my mind but the very nature of the calling to be Christian and a leader of Christians.

The clue lies in that word 'martyr'. It originates from a word meaning 'witness', a word which Christians use of anyone who tells their story of what God has done for them in Christ. It expresses the fact that Christianity is about proclaiming good news and expressing it in joyful worship and service.

Archbishops do not exist for their own sake. They too are witnesses – called to be preachers, pastors, teachers and evangelists. St Paul's words are directed at me today, and every day – 'Necessity is laid upon me; woe to me if I preach not the gospel'.

Enthronement Sermon, Canterbury Cathedral, Friday 19 April 1991.

Necessity is laid upon me – or as another translation puts it, 'I am compelled ... woe to me if I preach not the gospel'. Knowing and loving and living within the grace of Christ, the Church must so tell of its Lord and Master that others are brought to his allegiance. Like Paul, I see this as central to the role of Christian leadership. The Church is duty bound to call people to the living God; and it is the Archbishop's duty and joy to lead that call.

Let none think that I say this in disregard of the doubt and secularism of much of our nation. I know there are many voices raised in disbelief that anyone can still think there is a God who loves, who hears our prayers and whose will is our good. They point to the bloodstains of human history, not least in the Church, and ask, in anger, contempt or amusement, for evidence of this good and gracious God. They suspect that faith is simply a shelter for the weak in mind and spirit against the storms of life or nostalgia for a bygone age.

To such sceptics I ask: Is Mother Teresa weak? Is Desmond Tutu weak? Is Terry Waite weak? Are the Christians of Eastern Europe weak, especially those who have been persecuted or exiled for their faith? Christians from all over the world who have courage and tenacity in the face of hatred and hostility compel our admiration. We must remind ourselves that there have been more Christian martyrs this century than any other of the previous nineteen. Ours is an age of martyrs. God has not left himself without witnesses. Nor does he now. Among those witnesses are my brother Archbishops and bishops of the Anglican Communion, many of whom bring to our Communion a faith that has matured in terrible adversity and triumphed over suffering.

Other witnesses are from different Christian bodies, and there has been a slow but steady movement towards greater unity which has been one of the remarkable gifts of God to us in these times. And yet there remains a sadness, for as the 103rd Archbishop of Canterbury I stand in a succession which directs us back to the one undivided Church of Christ, a long way away from the 360 member Churches of the World Council of Churches. If necessity is laid upon us to preach that God reconciles, then we cannot rest content with our

2

scandalous divisions. 'The love of Christ compels a burning desire for unity', Archbishop Benson declared years ago. Indeed it does, for that love requires of its messengers the love of Christ for each other.

And we must face that sober truth within the Church of England. Over the centuries we have faced many issues that deeply divided us. Each has tested our commitment to the God who reconciles. In our own time there are other challenges that will test us deeply – not only the ordination of women but also the challenge to live with and accept gratefully the diverse traditions that make up the breadth of Anglicanism. I ask that we set above our divisions the urgency of witnessing to our nation that there is a God who cares and loves all people. We shall only be able to do that if we stand together even when decisions are made that cause us terrible pain. Our witness to the God who unites divided humanity is always more important than our pain. That is true witnessing. This helps us to understand why true martyrs, who suffer in order to witness to the God who reconciles, are always a gift and a blessing. For there will be many for whom simply staying and serving within the Church may feel as costly as the service of those martyrs with whom I began.

This is our main challenge: to be the kind of Church that puts God first, the people we serve next and ourselves last. It will be woe to us if we preach religion instead of the gospel; woe to us if we seek to live off the inheritance of the past and fail to build on those foundations for the future; woe to us if we preach a message that looks only towards inner piety and does not relate our faith to the world around.

And that earthed gospel takes us directly into the market place of the world. No Church can or should avoid political comment when freedom, dignity and worth are threatened. The cross of Jesus Christ firmly roots us in human concerns and needs, and places us alongside the oppressed, the dispossessed, the homeless, the poor and the starving millions of our planet.

And all this must be held together within a Church in which worship and service go hand in hand! Yet we hear from time to time the cry that the Church is irrelevant. But how can that

3

be when the life and traditions of our Church are woven into the fabric of English life and community in many unseen ways? We are there with thousands and thousands of children in Church schools and youth organisations; we are there with the sick at home and in hospital; we are there among prisoners; we are there in universities, the forces, in industry and commerce; we are there in the struggles of farming communities and in needy inner-city areas.

And all this is applicable to another group of people who are among us; people of goodwill who are unable to accept all or most of the doctrines of the Church and especially those who belong to other faith communities. It is good to have you among us. You pose an important question to those of us who follow Christ: 'We recognise that we live in a land that is Christian by heritage and predominant culture. But do we have a place with you?' Part of the answer lies in that shared texture of life I have just described. But deeper than that is the issue of integrity as persons and believers. I would want to put it this way: 'The faith that I have in Christ and his good news is so important that I am compelled – necessity is laid upon me – to share it with all people. But I trust I can listen to your story and respect your integrity even though having listened I may still want to offer to you, as to all, the claims of my Lord.' Through such listening, sensitive dialogue and mutual sharing I believe that our Church may express its faith, while always learning from the very breadth of the nation we serve more of its full meaning.

As my new ministry begins, I am aware that I enter into an office graced by many distinguished men – Robert Runcie, Donald Coggan and the 100 other faithful servants of Christ going back to the nervous Augustine who nearly 1400 years ago landed on a wild Kentish shore. He came with the desire to make Christ known as the light of the world. I too enter into that mission with my hopes and vision; a vision for a Church, renewed and invigorated, growing in faith and increasing in number; a Church united in its ambition to draw out a living faith in the young as well as in others and to involve lay people fully in its mission; a Church eager to join other Churches in maintaining and deepening the Christian heritage which is at the heart of our nation's traditions, culture and morality.

And we can be confident in our mission. In spite of what we sometimes hear, the Church of Jesus Christ will never die. But the local manifestation of it has no guarantee of success. We depend on the grace and power of God and our faithfulness to his call.

Such faithfulness will take many different forms. For the majority of us death by ox bones, the sword or scaffold will not be part of our pilgrimage. Our journey of faith will involve most probably sharing the love of God in many ordinary ways in our homes, communities and churches. And that way may be just as hard. It will require commitment if you and I are to fulfil our ministries. I hope that today might mark a fresh step in your journey. Perhaps it might be a step of commitment to a more authentic profession as a Christian; a greater confidence in the claims of the one who calls us to follow; it may simply be a willingness to explore the claims of the Christian faith once more.

And commitment is the word. As someone who has an undisguised affection for football, I love the words of Bill Shankly of Liverpool Football Club who on one occasion said to his players: 'Football is not a matter of life and death – it's far more important than that!' So is our Christian faith; far more important than life and even death, as our martyrs have witnessed. And woe to us if we fail to hand on to future generations the unsearchable riches of Christ which are the very heartbeat of the Church and its mission.

Alphege and other martyred Archbishops of Canterbury were burning and faithful witnesses in their day. Our time is now. Will you join me in the mission and ministry of our Church? And may I invite you also to join me in a joyful witness to our world that God has revealed himself in Jesus Christ and there is life, hope and peace in him. A hymn puts it in memorable words:

> Lord, for ourselves in living power remake us,
> Self on the cross and Christ upon the throne,
> Past put behind us for the future take us,
> Lord of our lives, to live for Christ alone.

VALUES
IN A CONFUSED
WORLD

I

Christianity and the New Europe

Behold, I am doing a new thing; now it springs forth, do
you not perceive it? ISAIAH 43:19

The prophet Isaiah is speaking here of God working his
providence through the events of the secular world. The
exploits of Cyrus, the Persian King, herald a new order.
The prophet senses the beginning of more than a political
reordering. Isaiah believed the return of the people of God
through the wilderness was imminent, that God was doing a
new thing. We cannot claim Isaiah's prophetic assurance, but
we sense that we too are approaching more than a new political order in this continent, that God is doing a new thing in
Europe today. That is why we can allow ourselves to have
fresh hope.

As we consider the future of Europe in the light of the
gospel, we must ask what contribution the Churches can make.
The first Malvern Conference, over which my predecessor
William Temple presided like a giant among men, was held in
1941. That was one of the bleakest years in the history of
modern Europe, yet the war failed to stop that Conference
from being full of hope. It was a realistic gathering because
Temple and others did not believe, despite their optimism, that
the Kingdom of God was just around the corner. He did not
believe that you simply had to rearrange the social furniture
to achieve it. The Kingdom of God is already here in Jesus
Christ. The eye of faith can see it. But all our eyes can see the
Kingdom has not finally come. We live in an interim time,

*Sermon at the Opening Service of the Malvern Conference, Wednesday 17
July 1991. The 1991 Conference was held to consider the crisis
confronting civilisation in the light of the Christian faith.*

where God has made his purposes known, but they remain to be fulfilled. This basic theological truth is worth remembering as we contemplate the future of Europe.

How should the Church offer guidance as the new Europe emerges? Let me suggest four Christian principles.

First and foremost, Europe needs a body of common values and public doctrine. I know that our Western society today is diverse, with people living alongside one another with different religions or none. We must not, however, fall into the trap of thinking that every belief and religion is of the same value – that would be to ignore the claims of truth. Pluralism without common values is individualism run riot, and carries within itself the seeds of its own decay. Without public doctrine there is nothing to hold a community together. It collapses like the tower of Babel, which fell because the people simply could not understand one another. But the biblical image of a confused world in that story is matched by the image of a united world on the day of Pentecost. The gift of the Holy Spirit was not the gift of a common language: diversity remained. Yet within the languages, the people heard a common theme, a message which, according to Luke, so 'amazed and perplexed' them that some reckoned the disciples had been over-indulging in their equivalent of Beaujolais Nouveau.

And yet Christianity copes with complexity. In this alone it may offer Europe a model. There is a terrific diversity in European Christian culture; sometimes little seems to unite us. The icon of the Orthodox and the Thirty-nine Articles of the Anglicans are certainly the products of such different traditions that it might seem to observers that we have created an ecclesiastical Babel. But this simply adds to the storehouse of Christian treasures. And in every tradition there is a single loyalty – *to Jesus Christ*. In a person rather than in a philosophy Christianity finds its common values. And because Christ was a person, Christianity's values are personal – compassion, peace, long-suffering, self-control: those fruits of the Spirit about which St Paul speaks with such eloquence. From that person has emerged the complex web of Christian culture created over the years – a mixture of theology, faith, moral thinking and worship. It would be a tragic mistake to seek to

simplify it, to reduce Christianity's diversity in seeking uni-
formity. That would be to undo Pentecost.

This leads me to my second theological principle – the
unique identity of every human being. Each of us has been
made in the image of God. Each of us has a unique identity.
In the eyes of God, everyone is literally irreplaceable. This
principle and truth is reinforced by the incarnation, because
in Jesus Christ we are reminded that we are all children of
God, that God's interest in and care for us is greater than that
of even the most loving of human parents.

We believe as Christians that the process of finding ourselves
cannot be complete until we are found by God. We need to
know who we are in the ground of our being. But to realise
ourselves we also need to belong. We would find it hard to
feel we belong to a Europe so large that it dwarfs us. If Europe
is to strengthen its bonds among its member states, it may
reduce a person's national identity and offer only a continent
too large for finding a new identity. If this is the case, we will
need to strengthen people's links with their region and locality.
But if we wish to encourage local, regional and even national
loyalties, within these loyalties we must retain a sense of proportion. We have all seen how the demise of totalitarian
oppression has also released yet another seven demons. The
spirit of nationalism is volatile and in some places its flashpoint
is extremely low. It can work against common values, against
respecting diversity, against a larger vision of human identity.
The tragedy of the Balkan conflicts and the renewal of anti-
semitism in Europe are two stark reminders that Europe is
not yet properly welded by common values rooted in human
identity. And our European partners look on with some apprehension lest British, or even English, nationalism or jingoism
should itself keep frontiers barred.

We are less likely to bring down the shutters against the
outside world if we uphold the third of my theological principles – to see ourselves as stewards of God's world. The
terrible spoliation of Eastern Germany, Poland and Czecho-
slovakia, and the menacing legacy of Chernobyl remind us of
our own responsibilities. The Jewish tradition out of which
Christianity grew knew well that we had been placed on earth

as God's stewards, which meant not exhausting or exploiting the land. The year of Jubilee was a reminder that all belonged to God; the seventh part of a field left unplanted was a reminder that the soil was his. So the prophet Isaiah says, 'Woe unto those who build house upon house till there be no more place'.

Europe is not such a conspicuous consumer as the United States; but we come second. It is because of the conspicuous consumption of the West that the planet is faced with diminishing non-renewable resources and increasing world pollution. Here the European Community has already shown that in some respects its standards of conservation and its determination to become pollution-free are greater than in Britain. But there are important areas, such as the drainage of phosphates into the oceans, which still remain to be tackled. Europe needs to show that its increasing production is compatible with decreasing pollution and renewable resources.

The Christian theological tradition has much to contribute to the outworking of those principles, for Christians do not seek only limiting prohibitions. We seek instead to work with the natural creation that we may stand again to overlook the Eden which has been left far behind. As Edwin Muir says in his poem:

> One foot in Eden still, I stand
> And look across the other land.
> The world's great day is growing late . . .

Looking across to other lands brings me to my fourth and final principle – a plea for open frontiers. The common values with which I began suggest that the divisions within Europe should not be the only barriers to be broken down. Europe's own frontiers should remain healthily open to the rest of the world. Our prosperity, our technology, our cultural riches must be shared with a world desperately craving for fairer shares. This is a reminder of our common humanity and of the gospel imperative to stand with the poor. That is its theological base. Like Jesus, we must identify with the marginalised, the outcast, the alienated. That is a clear Christian duty. Ways forward need to be agreed with Europe so that the rich do not get richer at the expense of the poor, so that help to the needy is not just left to private charity and so that there are means of securing justice for those who are powerless and not in a position to defend their human dignity.

The scriptures are strong on remission of debts. That is why the Church must always sound an uncomfortable reminder to our political and financial leaders not to prevent poor countries from developing their potential through charging excessive interest on loans which they took out in their necessity. Europe must share its bread with the hungry, instead of continuing its present practice of building bigger and bigger barns for its agricultural surpluses (and because the rate of building is not fast enough, in some cases surplus grain is stored in ships). This does nothing to promote common values, or honour human dignity. It is not good stewardship of God's creation and it closes rather than opens frontiers. Those four principles hang together.

William Temple said, 'the art of government is the art of so ordering life that self-interest prompts what justice demands'. If we can see that the four principles above are all built into the new Europe we will make it stronger, more useful, more just, and more pleasing to God. God is doing a new thing amongst us. The prophet challenges us: 'Do you not perceive it?'

2

Education: Commitment, Co-operation, Challenge

Why does the Church of England keep so quiet about its schools? That is a question I ask myself time and time again. Our Church schools provide one of the major ways in which the Church of England makes contact with the people of this country. They represent its most significant investment – both in money and in people – in the young. They are in demand by parents – there are long waiting lists and over-subscribed places. So why doesn't the Church of England proclaim the good news about its schools more loudly?

Partly, I believe, it is because of the Church of England's natural reticence and modesty. We are more conscious of our failures than our successes. An over-weaning arrogance is always unpleasant in a Christian church, but we must not allow a realistic appraisal of our shortcomings to blind us to our strengths. There is such a good story to be told about the Church of England – about lively worship in vigorous parishes, about ministry in the most demanding and unpromising of situations, about clergy who live amongst the people they care for and so experience their problems for themselves and not simply from the vantage point of a desk in an office, about our youth organisations and the thousands of people who voluntarily give their time to them, about the Church Urban Fund and the revival of our work in the inner cities, about the witness and ministry of cathedrals to thousands of visitors and pilgrims, and the care offered up and down the country to the sick, bereaved and house-bound, and so I could go on. And part of that good story is told in our Church schools.

*Address to Anglican Secondary School Heads, Chester,
Thursday 19 September 1991.*

The impression is often given that the Church of England's involvement in education stops at the age of eleven. The statistics seem to bear this out. A quarter of all primary schools are Church of England. By contrast only one in twenty-five of all secondary schools are Anglican. This means that many Church people scarcely know of their existence. It is compounded by their very uneven distribution over the country as a whole. Outside the Dioceses of London, Southwark, Blackburn and Manchester, an Anglican secondary school is a very unusual sighting indeed.

The impression that the Church of England should be intensely involved with children's education only up to the age of eleven mirrors too uncomfortably the feeling that a little Christianity does not do young children any harm, but it is better that they do not take it too seriously when they get older. One of the tasks facing us in the Decade of Evangelism is to overcome the view that adulthood is achieved by throwing off childhood dependency, especially dependence on God. Being human is largely defined by what we do with our dependence. A mature recognition of our dependence upon God is the best means of living with generosity, compassion and a capacity to love others.

I suppose that the Church of England's long and historic involvement in education may be one of the reasons for our being so quiet about it. It's simply that it's always been there. The Church of England, not the state, took the initiative in building schools and providing an education for the generality of young people. I doubt whether many of our population realise that the National Society, still active today, began its work sixty years before the 1870 Education Act created Board Schools. And I doubt too whether many know that, before that, the Sunday School movement provided the very first means of access to any education at all for young people whose weekdays provided nothing but grim toil in the meanest of labouring jobs. Yet the voluntary principle in education, most notably expressed in Church sponsorship, could not do everything. The creation of those first Board Schools was due in no small measure to the need to fill gaps in educational provision which the Church of England simply could not meet.

I begin with this historical perspective since the Church of England itself may benefit from a reminder about why it is involved in education at all. That involvement did not begin because the Church simply wanted to create and nurture good Anglicans, although I believe that is an aim which should not be ignored. The primary aim was to improve the possibility that ordinary young people might aspire to a life which was more satisfying – morally, spiritually and physically. We worry today – and rightly – about the alienation of some of our young people, such as those who were involved in the recent riots in Newcastle. But 200 years ago similar problems were endemic, in the country as well as in the cities. Robert Raikes, founder of the Sunday School movement, wrote in the *Gloucester Journal* in 1783:

Farmers and other inhabitants of the towns and villages complain that they receive more injury to their property on the sabbath than all the week besides: this, in a great measure, proceeds from the lawless state of the younger class, who are allowed to run wild on that day, free from every restraint.

The same worries can be found expressed in newspapers in the great cities, in letters from bishops, in speeches made in Parliament at the time. The children were generally employed in the factories, the mines and the mills six days a week, but, as the Bishop of Chester wrote in 1785, 'On Sundays they are too apt to be idle, mischievous and vicious'.

The Bishop was right to recognise the presence of our sinfulness, but he no doubt ignored the fact that human wrongdoing is inextricably linked to social deprivation, poverty, poor housing and illiteracy. The story has a familiar ring about it – the events we saw on our televisions of the recent riots in Newcastle occurred where people were socially deprived. The answer then was perceived by some to lie in education, not that the mobs were clammering to be taught. Education, as the very derivation of the word (from the Latin *educare*) implies, is a 'leading out'. Education fails when young people feel the only place they are being led to is a blind alley, when they become convinced that a better and fuller life cannot be attained. Education should lead to the opening up of wider horizons. It might lead, but not inevitably, to better prospects of employment, prosperity and travel. It should certainly lead to the opening up of the imagination so that adverse circumstances can be transcended and spiritual and moral resources built up. But it would be mistaken to suggest that this has always been the aim of those who have supported the educational enterprise. Not all education was intended to change the settled order of things. In *Lark Rise to Candleford*, Flora Thompson describes the Rector's daily visit to her village school towards the end of the last century:

Every morning at 10.00 o'clock the Rector arrived to take the older children for Scripture. He was a parson of the old school; a commanding figure, tall and stout, with white hair, ruddy cheeks and an aristocratically beaked nose, and he was as far as possible removed by birth, education, and worldly circumstances from the lambs of his flock ... His lesson consisted of Bible reading, turn and turn about around the class, of reciting from memory the names of the Kings of Israel and repeating the Church catechism. After that, he would deliver a little lecture on morals and behaviour. The children must not lie or steal or be discontented or envious. God had placed them just where they were in the social order and given them their own special work to do; to envy others or to try to change their own lot in life was a sin of which he hoped they would never be guilty.

There we hear the unmistakable voice of education as a means of social control. But we cannot ask of education a means of solving problems which wider society chooses to ignore. What schools can do, however, is make a most significant contribution in preparing pupils for their future citizenship. A school should be a secure environment in which a child can learn, grow and develop. There should be a predictability and a reliability in its life. Routines are not to be dismissed. Many children come from homes where there is little routine, little sense of security and who may live on estates where the whole social fabric feels fragile. In our schools we should strive to create a secure, caring and stable environment where a child might find some sense of belonging. And all the signs are that this is well achieved in our Church secondary schools.

There are three things that I look for within our Church

schools themselves and within the Church of England more generally in its relationship with them.

The first is *commitment*. For the Church of England, this means being committed to its role in education. Essentially this commitment is anchored deeply in a Christian concept of education in which spiritual and moral values are paramount. The point about Christian education is that it offers a holistic framework which takes people through life and prepares them for a destiny with God. But we are often told that such talk in a secularised world is unfashionable and out of date. We are told that this is a 'climate of unbelief' and that materialism rules. And it is that kind of talk which is driving Christians to set up protected schools in which the Christian faith can be taught in an atmosphere of tolerance and love. It is the same driving instinct which is behind other faith communities wanting to start their own schools in which the religious values they believe in may be protected from the harsh and cold winds of an indifferent and secular world.

However, I do not believe that we should concede the case so readily. The vast majority of the people of this land are not unbelievers who, having considered the case for God, have turned away from him in favour of a godless, cruel and indifferent universe in which no absolute and eternal values reign. On the contrary, most of our fellow citizens do believe in God, do pray and do believe that Christian morality is important – however tenuous their links may be with the local church. We have only to look at the myriad Christian, sub-Christian and non-Christian religions and superstitions and spiritualities all around us. We look abroad and see the collapse of an atheistic regime in the Soviet Union and millions of Christians returning to worship. Adrian Thatcher arguing against Donald Cupitt's point that the 'Christian era is finished' argues in return: 'An alternative hypothesis, equally consistent with the sort of evidence Cupitt is interested in, is that if there were a period of secularisation, it is over, not in a linear progression into some post-Christian spirituality, but in a recovery or rediscovery of elements of the religious past.'

However, the kind of education I am interested in is not only the rediscovery and repossession of a Christian world-view but the breadth of vision in which the individual's growth is physical, intellectual, moral and spiritual. And we are not talking about brainwashing or indoctrination, but an open system in which doubt, questioning, argument and enquiry are allowable and essential ingredients. That is why, in my opinion, the desire on the part of some Christians to send their children to tightly protected Christian schools, in which no alternatives to the Christian faith are known, is socially divisive, educationally damaging and spiritually unsatisfying – because the time will come when unpalatable realities have to be faced – and that often comes about when there is no structure of support to see the student through the threat of collapse. I remain convinced that the Anglican pattern of open education, rooted in a firm Christian base and a loving Christian environment is a better context for growth. Certainly this kind of openness is deeply appreciated by many non-Christian parents who would like to send their children to Anglican Church schools. I realise that the comparatively small number of Anglican secondary schools with over-subscribed places means that many such parents have to be disappointed. But what is it they are after for their children? They know that in a Church school their children's spiritual progress will be respected, even where Christian worship and teaching is explicitly and clearly given. And I think we can be quietly confident that such a theistic approach to education is not without its academic and scholarly support. George Steiner in his intellectually stimulating and deep book *Real Presences* makes a powerful case for the argument that literature, art, music and other things that enhance and inspire the human spirit are essentially spiritual and religious in pointing beyond themselves to a real presence beyond.

A second level in our commitment should be, I believe, to raise the profile of the Christian teacher and to set before our young people the prospect of teaching as a Christian vocation. Compared with a generation ago I sense that teaching (and perhaps nursing as well) has begun to lose its vocational basis. The more managerial and administrative responsibilities are given to teachers, the more likely it is that this vocational aspect will be eroded. But it is partly the responsibility of the

Church itself to ensure that amongst the options of a satisfying life of Christian service, the vocation of the teacher is not ignored.

And yet I want to share my concern that we need to do more to affirm the worth of our teachers and boost their morale. I have seen enough schools over the last ten years to recognise what a battleground the classroom has become. An ideological battleground in which educational theories have exhausted and depressed teachers; a moral battleground as parental irresponsibility in securing a moral framework for their children has meant that teachers have had to bear the burden of that demand too. Add to that problems of discipline, long hours, low pay, and the constant questioning about the future of education, and we are not surprised at the depressed state of many teachers. Perhaps the wonder is that so many still manage to believe in what they are doing, that so many are still so dedicated and alive, so many are still inquiring and eager to learn themselves. I believe that our government, local government, and governors of our schools all need to share in the task of affirming the worth of teachers whose work is so integral to the future of our land. In our classrooms sit tomorrow's political leaders, medical experts, lawyers, bishops, generals, to name but a few professions. Personally speaking, I was not educated in a Church school, I am sorry to say, but a state school, and two Christian teachers were of major influence upon me. I recall them well. Mr Kennedy, a Scot and a Presbyterian, who gave me a love for literature. And Mr Bass, the headmaster, who was the first to trust me with leadership. I am sure the seeds of faith were sown in that school and through their quiet and consistent witness. But to return to my main point; the vocation of the Christian teacher must be re-emphasised. Of one thing I am sure, the Christian teacher is on the frontline of mission and we need to encourage more young Christians to find their calling within the teaching profession.

The next level of commitment comes from the local church. The links between parish churches and Church primary schools are often strong and mutually beneficial. I read in the National Society's magazine, *Crosscurrent*, that there is evidence of a beneficial link between Church schools in villages and the mission of the Church there. Their closure may therefore be detrimental, not simply to the community life of a village, but to the witness of the Church there too. Yet the links between local churches and our Church secondary schools are less frequently as close. Some of these schools perhaps feel that local clergy neither sympathise with, nor understand, their aims. Rarely are they identified with a single parish, and often they draw their pupils from a wide catchment area. This inevitably diffuses the links between the school and the local parish, its clergy and congregation. I think that, where this is the case, it is a serious disadvantage to the school and to the local churches. Many schools have vigorous programmes of Christian education. Within many there is imaginative worship. But sometimes little of this touches the parishes which surround them and that cannot be good. So I hope for a renewed commitment at the local level between clergy, the parish churches and our Church secondary schools.

But having said that, there are already many clergy who are giving a great deal to our schools. The 1988 Act has made enormous demands on clergy and lay people. One incumbent told me recently that 40% of his time is taken up by school duties as Chairman of the Governors. But, he went on to tell me, he does not grudge a minute because his contact with children, staff and parents is the stuff of pastoral work and the seed-bed of his growing and caring church.

There are however some clergy who are a little fearful of the world of the school and they need encouraging. In my last diocese one enterprising headmaster has a day when he invites clergy of all denominations in his catchment area to meet the staff, to see some of the work of the children and then to discuss with him and a few selected senior staff the role of the school in the community. No wonder that school has such a visible presence in the area, and it is not surprising that in that part of Somerset the clergy feel valued and confident to enter and support the school.

You may have heard about the Cambridgeshire Village Colleges. There comprehensive schools have been built deliberately in villages with a role which extends beyond the education only of their pupils. Those schools are centres for adult education; their sports facilities are open in the evening and at weekends; their resources, whether in books or in buildings, are used for the community as a whole. I'm sure I'll be told that there are problems in giving a school such a wider community role. But I cannot but think that the vision is a sound one, and I dream of every Church school having that same sort of easy and open relationship with the wider community which is the village college ideal.

Schools' primary commitment is to their pupils and, as the 1988 Education Reform Act puts it, to their 'spiritual, moral, cultural, mental and physical development'. This commitment is shared by every school in the land. But Church schools should demonstrate and support Christian values and exert Christian moral influence. They should do this in their own community life, which should reflect the values expressed in their worship and religious education. The statutory requirements for acts of worship in our schools is, I know, unwelcome to many teachers and headmasters outside the Church school system, but Church schools should be exemplars of how it can be done, just as they should be exemplary in the quality of the religious education they offer. As part of the Basic Curriculum, religious education remains as a statutory subject, but since it is not part of the National Curriculum, it suffers the dangers of marginalisation in the timetable and in the resources given to it. But that should not be the case with you.

As well as commitment, I look secondly for *co-operation*. For the Church of England generally, this means a spirit of co-operation with central government, local education authorities, with other Churches, especially the Roman Catholic Church, and with all other agencies involved. The best statement I know of the place of the Church in education was written by Bishop John Trillo more than twenty years ago:

[In education] the Church is privileged to work in partnership with the State. The significance of the part we have to play is not based on the contribution we have made in this field in the past, great as it was. Nor is it based on our vested interests in existing schools and colleges, nor in any desire to capture the young by indoctrination. *We are in, and will remain in, education, because that is where we belong.* The pursuit of truth and the imparting of it are very much our business, as are the healthy enlargement of men's minds and personalities and the creation of truly human relationships and communities.

Co-operation, however, is never satisfactory when it is simply unilateral. The Church of England rightly looks for co-operation on its side from the Department of Education and Science and from local education authorities. By and large, I believe that the relationship is constructive, but it is worrisome, at the very least, that some major educational proposals and decisions are made without any consultation at all by the DES with the Church. For example, the decision by Government ministers to encourage a large scale move to grant-maintained status was made without any prior consultation with the Church of England, even though it may substantially affect the Church of England's own educational planning. As a Church we are not opposed to seeking grant-maintained status where this seems appropriate, but it is disturbing when, as in some cases, it seems that a school is pushed in the direction of opting out simply because this is the only means of getting cash from the DES for new buildings. Indeed, aided schools seem to be suffering from an increasing degree of financial strangulation. The likelihood of getting a grant to replace a condemned classroom at an aided school is decreased if the pupils can be accommodated in empty places in a nearby county school. That seems little reward for excellence and popularity, both of which are so well illustrated in the reputation of Church schools. In the Diocese of London, for example, recent statistics have shown that four out of five of its primary schools are over-subscribed, some of them more than 100% over-subscribed. All but three of its secondary schools are heavily over-subscribed, one to the tune of 430%. Parents want their children to go to Church schools. About that, there can be no doubt. Yet instead of a wholehearted welcome for the Church of England's current contribution in education, a good many teachers and diocesan directors of education tell me that they are given the feeling that they are an administrative nuisance. That is why I call for a renewed spirit of co-operation between all the providing bodies in our educational system.

Third, a spirit of commitment and co-operation must be complemented by a spirit of *challenge*.

In our schools we must challenge some of the prevailing assumptions of our culture. When all levels of society become blind to the spiritual dimension of life, despair and disorder flourish. A concentration on prosperity as the real goal in the pursuit of happiness is deeply flawed. It marginalises those who will never be prosperous. It gives a false picture of the good life and so deludes rather than educates. As I have noted earlier, the Education Reform Act of 1988 places the spiritual development of pupils before the 'moral, cultural, mental and physical' development that should also be the aim of the curriculum. Yet this can often be ignored, not deliberately, but simply by marginalising the spiritual dimension of reality.

Let me offer two challenges which the Church of England and other Christian Churches make to contemporary assumptions. First, we resist an undercurrent of opinion which assumes a philosophical model of education wholly dependent upon commercial criteria – competition, excellence expressed in terms of utilitarian worth, education circumscribed by training. Such ideas are around and become prevalent when a nation is aware of the harsh realities of having to compete in world markets. Yes, we understand and sympathise with the motivation. We warn against reductionism.

Secondly, we resist forms of reductionism which see science as the only way of interpreting the world. For example, the consultative documents of a working group set up to advise on the content of science in the National Curriculum included in one of its early drafts the staggering sentence, 'Science is *the* means of explaining reality'. I do not suppose its authors would have seen this as a statement of faith but, of course, that is what it is, and a mistaken one at that. To suggest that there are no other means of understanding reality, and so to dismiss humankind's religious quest down the centuries in a single sentence, is scarcely the provision of a good education as such. It is good to note that the sentence did not survive in that form, but it does illustrate the way in which no subject can be taught which does not at the same time teach a world-view and a realm of values. Yet the delusion that education can be value-free persists. It must be challenged most forcefully and this can best be done by a Church school illustrating the linkage between subjects. The spiritual development of any child is not limited to acts of worship or the time given to RE, but by the way in which the spiritual dimension of life is seen to be integrated with the physical, moral and mental development in the teaching of all subjects.

A second challenge, intimately linked with the first, is to reject as inadequate any view of education that seeks to limit it solely to preparation for work or even for a vocation. The current emphasis on vocational training may prove to be very short-sighted. Education does not consist in the acquisition of skills. It is a preparation for life. The unique importance of each person is not derived from our capacity to contribute to the gross national product, important though that might be, but derives from the fact that we are created in the image of God and are loved by him. And so our approach to special educational needs, equal opportunities and multi-cultural issues must be informed by our theological understanding of them. One London Church secondary school gives pupils with special educational needs second priority in their admissions policy. Five others include that amongst the first five categories in their admissions policy. That is part of the Christian vocation expressed in those schools. Yet in an age in which it is proposed that schools' examination performances should be published in the form of league tables, it is unlikely that such a high priority to children with special needs could continue without affecting adversely the reputation of the school. As the headmaster of Haileybury School commented: 'The only thing that an examinations results league table tells you is what the academic admission policy of the school was in the first place.' It is telling that the heads of independent schools see the weakness of such a crude method of comparison.

Finally, Church schools must issue a challenge to the Church of which it is an important part. Does it keep quiet about its schools because it doesn't really want them? That, I know, is what some might suspect. The grounds for being an aided school come from the continued relationship with the Church which it implies, but it would be understandable if the schools felt that they did more to generate links with other parts of the Church than the Church did to generate links with them.

As I indicated earlier, I know that grant-maintained status is likely to become more prominent in Church schools. Without wishing to come down on one side or the other, I want to caution that if giving grant-maintained status leads to an even lesser degree of corporate identity amongst Anglican secondary schools, I think the loss to the schools, to the Church and to the children whom they serve would be considerable. I offer the assurance that our schools are not isolated and unsupported in their work, and that the Church of England *does* value all that they contribute. May God bless them in all that they do.

3

Do We Need God to be Good?

The title of this chapter is deliberately provocative. Does the Archbishop think God himself does not need to be good? No, I am not going to suggest that God is evil, although the source and origin of evil in our world demands attention. Instead, I intend to look at the relationship between our goodness and our godliness. Does morality remain when God disappears? This question is deeply relevant to the nature of our society and to the problems we face today. All I can hope to do is to explore some of the ethical and philosophical issues that lie at the heart of our moral instincts.

I want to begin with a most important premise. I would not suggest for a moment that only believers can be good. This would be to disenfranchise atheists, humanists, agnostics and many others whose goodness is real, deep and admirable; it flows from their understanding of what it is to be human too.

But what is the basis of our goodness if ethics is separated from its roots in theism? If religion no longer provides the nourishment for our ideas of right and wrong, what then? Let me illustrate this with a dilemma taken from Gore Vidal's fascinating novel, *Washington DC*. The novel focuses on an ambitious Senator, James Burden Day, who is one day offered a bribe. If he were to accept this bribe, with all that it entails in compromise, intrigue and partnership, the Presidency of the United States would be his. The Senator goes off into the country to think about it. He reflects along these lines: If the country's best interests are served through the Presidency of James Burden Day and that Presidency could come about only as a result of taking Mr Nillson's money, ought he not to take the money? After all, a defender of the Constitution

Address to the University of Kent, Friday 25 October 1991.

who has taken a bribe is morally preferable to an unloved President whose aim is to subvert the Republic. Then, finally, he poses himself the familiar black question: What difference does any of it make? He has already been shown plans for his tomb in the State Capital. 'There will be room', said the architect comfortably, 'for four people. Naturally Mrs Day will want to join you and perhaps your daughter will too.' So, Senator Day reflects, 'in time no one would know or care which dust was Bill's and which dust was Joe's'.

The key moment was the 'black question'. Does anything have lasting relevance? Does anything have meaning? If life is ultimately pointless then surely whatever you can get away with can be justified. All objectivity is removed from the moral life. All external reference points have gone.

This is a modern problem. It would have been foreign to the ancient mind, and even to those who lived in Britain up to the middle of the last century. It would have been to question the natural source of morality; God is, and from him flows the destiny of human nature.

I think it was the German, ex-Lutheran Nietzsche who was the first to point out the problem. 'For the Englishman', he wrote in 1899, 'morality is not yet a problem.' The English, he said, believed that religion was no longer needed as a 'guarantee of morality', that morality could be known intuitively. But, remarked Nietzsche, that illusion was itself a reflection of the persistent strength and depth of the Christian ascendancy. Forgetting the religious nature of their morality, they also forgot the 'highly conditional nature of its right to exist'. Nietzsche was implying, of course, that once religion lost that ascendancy, then morality would be a problem. In her book *Marriage and Morals among the Victorians*, Gertrude Himmelfarb argues that a generation after Nietzsche, morality was very much a problem in England. Not that it was much of a problem for the mass of English people. But then Nietzsche was never concerned with the masses of people of whom he was totally contemptuous. The decline or enlightenment, depending on one's perspective, is traced through one writer, E M Forster, who in his own family united two influential groups of people: the Clapham Sect, a group of well-known Evangelicals, including Wilberforce and others, and the Bloomsbury Group centring on Virginia Woolf and Lytton Strachey. The moral distance between the two groups is immense. The former based their good works, their lifestyles, their political thought and personal behaviour on the reality and nearness of God. The other group was just as consistent – its morality was based on the absence of faith. E M Forster, in an essay, remarked that if pressed on his own belief he would be obliged to invoke 'personal relationships', the only good and solid thing in a world of violence and cruelty. Here was the one article of faith he could unequivocally affirm: 'I certainly can proclaim that I believe in personal relationships.'

The residual basis of truth and morality in personal relationships had already been invoked by Matthew Arnold. Aware of the shaking of the foundations by Darwin's discoveries, Arnold had, in his disturbing yet beautiful poem *Dover Beach*, felt that all he could rely on was the nearness of the one he loved. You may recall the poem:

> Ah, love, let us be true
> To one another; for the world, which seems
> To lie before us like a land of dreams,
> So various, so beautiful, so new,
> Hath really neither joy, nor love, nor light,
> Nor certitude, nor peace, nor help for pain;
> And we are here as on a darkling plain
> Swept with confused alarms of struggle and flight,
> Where ignorant armies clash by night.

And all the time he hears the 'melancholy, long, withdrawing roar' of the sea of faith. Arnold is stressing the implications of the loss of faith; it is much more serious than most people realise – it involves the loss of everything. All that one can cling to is personal love.

But even though personal relationships may be the only things we can trust when the chips are down, they are an insufficient and inadequate basis for morality; insufficient since they are rooted in an uncritical individualism, inadequate since they appeal to emotions alone.

How have moral philosophers dealt with the problem? If there is no God, where do we locate the source of our moral sense? Let us briefly consider a number of different approaches to the question. The first can be labelled subjective humanism. As the word suggests, the implicit assumption is that the absence of God means that there can be no objective grounds for morality. Morality is located in the individual's response to the question: 'How shall I live?' As the philosopher Basil Mitchell points out, this approach centres around two components – questions about fact and questions about value. Disagreements about fact are in principle soluble. Let me offer one example directly from an official visit to Papua New Guinea – although I hasten to add that this particular problem has not come my way! The issue is that of cannibalism. Does it harm you if you eat the brains of an ancestor? Medical science has been able to answer that question. There is a virus known in Papua New Guinea as *Churu* which, similar to 'Mad Cow' disease, passes through families, paralysing and eventually killing the victim. But even once the question of fact is answered there is no rational way of settling the moral question which in the illustration I have chosen is: Is it right or wrong to kill and eat other human beings who invade your tribal space?

The essential problem of subjective theories is that different people will give different answers and, to make matters worse, different people will give different answers at different times. A J Ayer, of course, attempted to argue that morality is no more than this. Each of us chooses our own response and it is rested in our subjective choice. We invent our own morality. Here is pure emotivism. Thus, unless there is some criteria to control the explicit individualism of this approach it is difficult to find any unifying framework that will be acceptable to a group, tribe or nation.

A second approach can be described as objective humanism. This begins very directly by arguing that there has to be a basic social framework if a civilised society is to survive and to flourish. Therefore there has to be an objective morality which all citizens acknowledge. The indications of this we should doubtless all agree. Any tolerable form of social life requires that there should be rules governing relations between persons in respect to such matters as property, sexual relations, care for the young and elderly. We are not surprised to find a common pattern in the codes and conventions of most peoples.

However, that is not the issue. Rules of behaviour are the 'small change' of morality. Most people take it for granted that they should not cheat, steal, lie or be promiscuous. What few of them will be able to tell you is why it is or why it is not a sacred obligation to be honest, law-abiding, good and faithful.

One distinguished proponent of liberal humanism is Sir Peter Strawson. As with a number of moral philosophers, he distinguishes between morality and ethics. *Morality* has to do with the observance of such rules as are necessary for the wellbeing of society. *Ethics*, by contrast, refers to these pro-found truths which may be incompatible with one another – these could be rested in religious belief, in a form of humanism, in Marxism or whatever. In the academic context of a univer-sity the most natural illustration is that of the difference between an agreed syllabus and optional subjects. The agreed syllabus of society is the conventions, norms and rules that we invent over a period of time for the uniform security, peace and harmony of the community. The optional subjects are the self-selected philosophies which work for us; which Strawson calls 'profound truths and general statements about man and the universe'. These are then added by their proponents to the basic core of agreed moral rules accepted by the majority of people in society.

This argument has a familiar ring to it; it is the vision of a liberal society in which there is diversity. Listen to Strawson again:

What will be the attitude of one who experiences sympathy with a variety of conflicting ideals of life? It seems he will be most at home in a liberal society, in a society in which there are variant moral environments but in which no ideal endeavours to engross and deter-mine the character of the common morality. He will not argue in favour of such a society that it gives the best chance for the truth about life to prevail. Nor will he argue in its favour that it has the best chance of promoting a harmonious kingdom of ends, for he will not think of ends as necessarily capable of being harmonised. He will simply welcome the ethical diversity which the society makes possible, and in proportion as he values the diversity he will note that he is the natural, though perhaps the sympathetic enemy of all those whose single intense vision of the ends of life drives them to try to make the requirements of the ideal co-extensive with those of common social morality.

A fine statement, but one that I would suggest is weak when examined closely. For example, it is doubtful whether Strawson's rather idiosyncratic definition of the distinction between 'moral' and 'ethical' can be maintained. It returns us to the agreed morality of general platitudes, to use platitudes in its technical philosophic sense. The 'agreed syllabus' is drawn up so tightly as to make morality uncontentious, so that even sexual morality is placed in the area of optional rules agreed only by some. That, of course, would please certain people; how pleasant it would be, they would argue, if promiscuity, chastity, sexual freedom and so on were but matters of choice in a totally free society. But the fact is that although there are wide variations between societies with respect to sexual codes, there is no society which regards sexual morality as of no social concern. Secondly, Strawson's statement will not satisfy those whose experience of life binds them to a 'single intense vision of the ends of life', such as the Christian or the Marxist. They would reject the inference that such a philosophy of life, with its binding principles, was simply optional. Indeed, in spite of the eloquence of the liberal ideal, I suspect that few liberals would be happy with a definition which seems so definite, so comfortable and so costless.

Indeed, this criticism goes to the heart of the weakness of such a liberal humanism because it fails to answer the question: Is there such a thing as ultimate care and concern? Why should anyone worry about fundamental human rights, the plight of the starving, the rights of those who do not as yet share the rights of the liberal community? It would seem then that the distinction between a basic social morality and personal ideals is untenable simply because most of the major decisions of life have to do with ideals. Furthermore, most of these ideals have not arisen from the agreed will of the group, but from the struggles of individuals and minorities who have seen values and ideals long before others.

A third approach is to be found in the writings of Iris Murdoch, who offers a form of non-theistic objectivism. Her Christian roots are well known, but she has rejected these as a basis for ethical thought. For her, human life has no external point or 'telos': 'We are what we seem to be, transient, mortal creatures subject to necessity and chance.' She rejects, on the one hand, subjective humanists for whom morality is culturally and historically conditioned. On the other hand, she rejects Christian thinkers for whom God provides the givenness of morality. Nevertheless, for her morality is discovered and not invented. She is convinced that goodness issues from a transcendent demand which has authority over humankind. It is this transcendent goodness which gives to life its inspiration and transient goal. She acknowledges the complexity of life with its shades of grey and blue, black and white, but

... there is something in the serious attempt to look compassionately at human things which automatically suggests 'there is more than this'. The 'there is more than this', if it is not to be corrupted by some sort of quasi-theological finality, must remain a very tiny spark of insight, something with, as it were, a metaphysical position, but no metaphysical form. But it seems to me that the spark is real, and that great art is evidence of its reality.

But is it possible to have the transcendent spark without the form which creates the spark? Is it possible to hint at such Platonic forms of art and goodness without implying so much more? So George Steiner argues in his book *Real Presences* in which he claims that art, beauty, music and the good things of life are 'real presences of the transcendent'. Indeed, Steiner effectively implies the necessity of a God to underpin 'moral seriousness'.

Starting from the other direction, we can express the problem from the viewpoint of the Christian, the Jew, the thinker of any religious community. The sincerity of those who do not believe in God must be respected and honoured. No one can be coerced into belief and there are those for whom the religious dimension appears to be pointless, meaningless or impossible. Such people still try to make sense of a morality which takes into account the ultimate pointlessness of it all. So Basil

Mitchell argues that: 'Where selves as such have so little significance, there is no more warrant for altruism than there is for egoism.'

But where *does* the Christian seek the validation for morality? A number of points spring to mind.

Christianity recognises that morality and moral sense are not simply gained from society, but are intrinsic to what it is to be human. Moral standards and moral codes are familiar to us all. Most have been shaped by value systems from our childhood, and are part of our lifeblood. We in the West have been profoundly influenced by the Judaeo–Christian ethical system that embraces the Ten Commandments and the teachings of Jesus Christ; elsewhere in the world, other moral codes have given people a sense of worth and purpose. There are striking variations, of course, in the codes but there are correspondingly impressive similarities and identities. What is common to all shared moral codes is an assumption that we are moral and spiritual beings who are answerable to a claim which lies behind the particular codes which speak to us and inform our moral sense. That is to say, such moral codes speak of a 'telos', a journey towards something else and invite us to grow into a dignity and humanity of which we are but dimly aware. In these they point towards the fullness of human nature, nature formed in the image of God. Christianity implies a natural morality.

Secondly, Christianity and other world religions resist limiting moral codes to the level of utilitarian theories. Such theories suggest that morality is nothing more than 'the greatest good for the greatest number'. Others limit morality to preserving society from disorder, anarchy and disintegration. It is true that many values have clearly been shaped by the community and its changing needs and interests, but it is manifestly wrong to say categorically that community alone should determine moral values. It seems very clear that the sense of moral obligation has deeper roots than our own social advantage. We seek to do good because it is right and not usually because it is to our advantage. There is plenty of evidence to suggest that qualities such as bravery, courage, goodness, honesty, faithfulness and so on have been chosen, not because they coincide with the benefit of tribe or individual, but because they represent deeper values which transcend life itself. Furthermore, the 'nothing but' approach limits morality to the relativising and conditioning of individual societies. It does not show why murder, pillage, rape, dishonesty, molesting of children ought to be regarded as 'sinful' or wrong, irrespective of time and place. The result of these reflections is that we find ourselves almost unexpectedly and surprisingly postulating objective standards of right and wrong.

This discussion was at the heart of the debate a generation ago between Bertrand Russell and Thomas Copleston. Russell had declared that there are no absolute values as such; all we may say is that there exist values we deem to be important. We are returned once again to emotivism and subjectivity. In response to this Copleston referred to the Nuremberg trials in which Nazi criminals had been convicted of crimes against humanity. If there was no objectivity, no absolutes, he argued, what was the conceptual basis for the trials? Crimes against humanity suggest that there exists a moral standard that all would agree the Nazis contravened. Many of those accused could and did claim that they had carried out the edict of the State or that they followed the orders of their superiors. Yet the trial expressed the unanimous assumption of the nations of the world that those condemned had broken a moral law that was objective, absolute and eternal.

A further assumption for the Christian is that life is lived *sub specie aeternitatis*; from the viewpoint of the eternal. For some this may be a most unfashionable view but it is one which should not be dismissed too easily. The story from Gore Vidal's novel and the 'black question' presses this point home. For Christian morality is based, as I said at the beginning, on the character of God and the character of humankind as made in his image and likeness. Every human life is therefore of infinite worth. This Christian belief in the fundamental worth and dignity of human beings is a foundation stone of Christian moral thought.

What, then, does this imply for humanity and the moral life? We must ask this question in terms of our culture, our society and our human needs. What shall we say of morality as it relates to the individual, to society and to the world we live in?

First then, to the individual. At the beginning of the 1990 Reith Lectures, Jonathan Sacks stated his aim clearly. It was to show that moral values are still active within our frame of moral reference. They have been eroded but not absolutely eclipsed. They lie at the heart of some of our deepest commitments: to the worth of the individual, to society as a covenant rather than as a contract, to morality itself as a community and as a communal endeavour, and to the family as a crucible of personal relationships.

As a concept, the absolute worth of the individual derives from the Judaeo–Christian tradition of men and women created in the image of God. It means that for all their contingency and frailty, human beings reflect the divine character in their ability to think, in their ability to form personal and enduring relationships and in their ability to act as moral people. Without this theological underpinning the value of an individual will soon become relative. As we have seen, agnostic humanism simply cannot supply the validity for this concept, even though it is a theme frequently found in humanist thought. The denial of God means that the absolute worth of another human being has to be extrapolated from what we feel about ourselves. But an emotivist morality based on feelings or hunches supplies us with no objectivity. It leads nowhere.

Of course, the role of the Church and churches with respect to personal morality is widely appreciated. Douglas Hurd, when he was Home Secretary, told General Synod in 1988 that: 'What society desperately needs from the churches today is a clear, definite and repeated statement of personal morality.' The objective morality for which we have argued would support this affirmation most firmly. But Christian morality cannot be separated from Christian faith. Morality is not a body of 'Do's' and 'Don'ts' which somebody orders another to obey. Rather it is the living personal and social expression of a relationship with God. So Jesus in John's Gospel says to his disciples: 'If you love me you will obey my commandments'; obedience flows from commitment. The same point is made by St John later in the New Testament but this time it is the other way round: 'We love, because God first loved us' – that is, social morality flows from God's commitment to us. To insist that the Church first teaches morality is to put the cart before the horse. We can do so only when people feel called to follow the Christian faith, when they desire to root their lives in its teaching and when they wish to worship God in Jesus Christ. Without this the exhortation to the Church to teach and uphold morality is to attempt to make bricks without straw.

This then leads me to reflect on the family which some have called 'a crucible of family relationships'. I envy the traditional Jewish home with its regular pattern of Festivals and Friday meals. Jewish children grow up to be members of the covenant; they grow up to feel the strength of the tradition, and to feel themselves to be part of a historic and enduring family. That tradition when expressed in a mature and loving home will undoubtedly provide a moral base, and a guide and support for life. Something similar still exists in some Christian homes. The tradition of daily prayer, regular bible reading and knowledge of the Catechism as the pivot and mainstay of many homes is, however, no longer familiar.

There are many reasons for the disintegration of this pattern of family life. Arguably this century has included the fastest ever period of social change. Two terrible World Wars, a revolution in travel and information technology, a revolution wrought by broadcasting and television, and the startling mobility of the individual made possible by the motor car: all these, and much more, have disrupted the Western family and weakened the cohesiveness of traditional bonds of social accord. Of course, we cannot ignore the many beneficial effects of these momentous changes, but we must also note the deleterious effects upon the fabric of our society. A decline in moral standards has sometimes been blamed on the churches because they were once at the heart of community life and therefore were central to the formation of the moral person. I suspect, and suggest, that the reasons have more to do with people's deliberate choices and changing patterns of social behaviour, than to the Church's neglect.

But whatever the reasons for it, one cannot be sanguine

about the moral effects of this social upheaval. Secular authorities will call in vain for a renewal of family life and will equally vainly appeal to the Church to be active in that endeavour, without a reaffirmation of the person as essentially a spiritual being and the family as the God-given womb for the individual's growth into moral maturity.

So we should go on to widen the circle to speak of society as a *moral community*. In all theories of morality the community is the context in which the person discovers for herself/ himself the meaning of 'right' and 'wrong'. We are formed in community. We are formed more than we realise by the interlocking network of relationships which enrich or damage our lives – the family, the school, the peer group, the university and the unseen world of books through which reality and unreality is disclosed, embraced or rejected. If the doctrine of the absolute worth of the individual is ignored or forgotten the community becomes potentially demonic. *Racism* may develop where the superiority of one colour is asserted; forms of *elitism* may result where the superiority of aristocrats or meritocrats is the measure of human worth. Every society and community has to resist attempts that ignore the powerless or which threaten the weak.

The Church has a clear role in assisting the wider community to recognise the obligation of moral demands which confront it as well as us all. In the Old Testament the notion of covenant is a crucial concept which expresses the responsibilities a community has towards God and towards one another. Within both Old and New Testaments it is clear the communities have moral responsibilities towards their members. Communities cannot be morally neutral; they have a beneficial or deleterious effect on their members. Following from this, in our present pluralist society there has to be an agreed base of common values for a community to function properly and for it to cohere harmoniously.

In a recent lecture to Anglican Secondary Head Teachers, I referred to the Newcastle disturbances. My brief comment was reported out of context as suggesting that such disturbances are caused only by social deprivation. That was not my argument. I also referred to individual sin and to our personal responsibility and culpability for our own wrong doing. But the point I wished to make was that human wrong doing also has a social dimension. I still believe that to be the case, and it is for that reason that we ignore the nourishing of common values in a pluralistic society at our peril.

But the problem of communication lies deeper than the misquotation of my words. It lies in an implicit, unspoken notion that the Church's role and ministry relates to the individual and to the area of personal morality alone, and that it is the role of others in society to deal with social problems. It is true, of course, that we all have our own areas of expertise, and that consultation between experts is essential. The Church, however, must resist attempts to confine its remarks to the personal, since the Christian faith is incorrigibly social and it cannot be relegated to the domain of the individual person. William Temple once remarked, after one of his speeches was criticised: 'When I talk or write theology they say I am irrelevant; when I talk or write about social issues they say I am interfering.' But the Church is never interfering when it is fulfilling its proper role of applying Christian moral truth.

Central to that task is its duty to remind everyone within society that we form a moral community responsible for the welfare and wellbeing of all citizens. The Church, then, in partnership with other groups, must point to areas of life where there are clear wrongs that have to be righted. It must stand alongside those who have no voice or who feel trapped by structures not of their making. A moral society will respond to the dilemmas of those within it who are especially vulnerable. This includes a variety of groups: children, the elderly and the long-term unemployed. In my experience, the Church's relationships with those who lead our nation are cordial and warm, in spite of what some would have us believe. Our work in the inner city is respected and the level of co-operation is very great. But it is also recognised that the Church can never be treated as a department of government policy and neither government nor Church would wish this to be so. A healthy, critical yet affirming relationship is desirable if the Church is to bear witness to truths which it has received and which it regards as eternal.

Finally, *if God is*, then all peoples are called to co-operate in discovering a global ethic to confront our common problems. In his book, *Global Responsibility*, Hans Küng faces this issue. He outlines the urgent need for partnership. Such partnership will require, he argues, a wholly new attitude towards creation which has more to do with humility and service to nature and less to do with exploitation and greed. We must learn to think of 'progress' as more to do with inner contentment, personal fulfilment, deeper human relationships and spirituality, and less to do with affluence, acquisitiveness and material possessions.

If God is, then a new creation lifestyle is required which depends less on materialism and what we have, and more on the spiritual side of our humanity and what we are.

Such a morality will respect the needs of our fragile, precious and much-abused planet. We know that we have done incalculable harm to the life forms and the delicate eco-systems of the world. We are aware of the despoliation and destruction of the rainforests. We know too that the world population is daily exhausting the resources of the earth. There are those who will tell us that we are too late. Some will argue that if this life is all there is, then care for the environment and concern for the future of humankind is a waste of time and effort. Many will reject such attitudes. The theist will wish to go further still: *If God is*, then all things have value and are here for a purpose. Therefore, conservation and environmental care are obligations which are demanded by our position before God and our position on the evolutionary ladder. We have no right to lord it over the rest of creation but rather our proper role is to be stewards of it.

In all this, religion has the opportunity to play an enormous part. At the beginning of this century, materialism seemed to be in the ascendant. When Communism toppled Christianity in Soviet Russia in 1917 it seemed that the age of religion was over. Today, we can see how mistaken that view was. It is often said that we now live in post-socialist, post-capitalist, post-modern, post-ideological societies. No one, however, has argued that we live in a post-religious society. We have seen how Christianity has reappeared in great strength in Russia and in China, and the prevalence of faith suggests that there is something in us which reaches out to God and will not be satisfied with anything less. But *if God is*, as I have suggested, then we need to establish a world ethic which encompasses all people and has the agreement of all faith communities. The term 'global village' has become a cliché but embodies a truth. Technology has made us all neighbours. As neighbours we can now see the vast inequalities and gross injustices which separate us; the affluence of the First World as distinct from the Third World; the exploitation of two-thirds of the world by a third of its population. Only a moral solution, a repossession of primary ethical principles which start by reminding us that we have an obligation to 'pay now, spend later', can help reverse the current drift towards a growing ecological crisis.

The great religions of the world share important ethical principles which are regarded as unconditional and binding on all people. These can be the starting point of a significant step towards a more moral world.

Let me now return to where I began. Does morality remain when God disappears? If God is not, can morality be unconditional? What is not in dispute is the fact that people who reject God can and do live honourable and good lives. But their dilemma may be like that of Sigmund Freud when he confessed: 'When I ask myself why I have always behaved honourably, ready to spare others and to be kind whenever possible, and why I did not give up doing so when I observed that in that way one harms oneself and becomes an anvil because other people are brutal and untrustworthy, then, it is true, I have no answer.'

Perhaps Christianity may be pointing to the moral character of human nature, to the divine spark which enlightens all of us. Professor Oliver O'Donovan may have been right when he remarked that: 'No earthly good can be worth dying for unless there is a heavenly good that is worth living for.' It may also be the case that because God is, we are – and that the absence of God may lead to the loss of everything. That may seem a very gloomy note to end on, but I am an eternal optimist and I believe that God always has the last word. As David Jenkins, the Bishop of Durham, would say: 'You can't keep a good God down!'

4

Universities: The Grit in the Oyster

When I graduated from King's College, London, as a Bachelor of Divinity 30 years ago, little did I think that I would one day go back as the College Visitor. I am not sure I knew then that King's had one, and I certainly didn't know what the Visitor's duties were. As it turns out, they appear to be onerous only when things go badly wrong, and my staff tell me that King's College has caused no trouble in recent years, unlike (they mutter darkly) some other institutions they could mention. King's, however, is taking no great risks. It has appointed me for just five years. Even College Visitors these days have limited tenure, and so, for that matter, do Archbishops.

Being asked to become the College Visitor at King's and my involvement with other universities and colleges made me think afresh about what a university is for. I cannot begin to answer this adequately here but I would like to explore within the context of prayer the question of how a university's worth can be measured. Is it in the number of firsts obtained or the starting salaries of its graduates? Or is there something which a university offers wider society which is scarcely quantifiable but very precious?

I want to suggest that a university is *one of the means by which society transcends itself*. In an inaugural lecture in Cambridge, David Ford, the new Regius Professor of Divinity, coined this phrase. He was looking particularly at the role of theology in a modern university, but I want to apply this idea of society transcending itself in a university more widely. How does it do so? First, by extending the boundaries of what we

Address as Visitor to the College, King's College, London, Thursday 13 February 1992.

know. New knowledge is often greeted by fear. It threatens established thinking. It unsettles dull conformity. Universities should be an irritant, the grit in the oyster that may become a pearl. Universities remind us that our knowledge and experience of the world is always provisional. That is why they are among the first places to be targeted by totalitarian regimes of whatever political colour.

Secondly, a university is always concerned with educating the next generation. It is where knowledge is passed on. It is a repository of tradition – traditions of thought, analysis and speculation rooted in the accumulated wisdom of the past. Although a university naturally looks to the future, since it forms the minds of the future, it is always building upon the mind of the past. No one going to a university is expected to start their physics, history or even their theology from scratch.

Thirdly, a university analyses the past afresh. It is always revising its judgements, changing its mind, discerning what has ceased to have the claim of truth and recognising blind alleys for what they are. A university generates this sense of detachment from history. It is not a slave to tradition, but always reflects critically on the past.

These three things – the exploration of new knowledge, the education of the next generation, and the fresh analysis of the past – blend to create an institution in which society may transcend its limits. All this has its parallels in the life of the Church.

You may find that statement surprising. Surely the Christian faith is given once and for all? What new knowledge can be gained? But that is to forget the gift of the Spirit. 'The Spirit of Truth, whom the Father will send in my name, He will teach you all things, and bring to your remembrance all that I have said to you.' (John 14:26) So says the writer of the Fourth Gospel. And at the end of John's Gospel there is that other testimony of the incomplete nature of the record of the things Jesus did.

But there are also many other things which Jesus did; were every one of them to be written, I suppose that the world itself could not contain the books that would be written. JOHN 21:25

The very testimony of scripture itself is to a record which is incomplete. There is always much to learn.

Our knowledge of God is finite. The Christian revelation recognises that it has a sort of incompleteness this side of the establishment of the Kingdom of God. So, although Christianity has not always seemed to welcome new knowledge – Galileo springs to mind – it has, by its true nature, always encouraged it. In discovering more about our world – God's world – we discover more about God.

The Church also has an interest in passing on its traditions of thought, devotion and reason to the next generation. Worship is not only an offering to God but it instructs and socialises as well. In this way too, Church and university share common goals. Each has its eye on the future.

In itself, that causes a re-examination of the past. Christians look back today and, analysing Church history, wonder how it was that slavery and anti-semitism could have been thought consistent with the gospel. Only by analysing its past can the Church avoid corruption. The difference between tradition and traditionalism has been explained in this way: 'Tradition is the living faith of the dead; traditionalism is the dead faith of the living.'

So there is much that binds Church and university together. Each must possess a capacity for transcendence – whether of itself or society. In that transcendence the Christian glimpses something of God himself – able to incarnate himself in the world, yet never submerged by it, never incapacitated by it.

This is one of the reasons why I have been glad to spend so much of my career in higher education. Yet much of what I have written for publication has been deliberately non-academic, because my strong desire is to reach people who are turned off by an academic approach to knowing God. I do not doubt their capacity to understand and to know him. What I do sometimes doubt is our capacity to explain him. But that is no surprise: I have always seen my task as not only conveying the doctrines, history and traditions of Christianity but also kindling that freedom of thought and spirit of inquiry which lead to true knowledge and conviction. For understanding is not created simply by communicating facts. There is a spiritual side to the way we receive and use learning. A spirit of understanding is what every teacher yearns to create.

I say this especially to all those in tertiary education, regardless of what subject they may be reading or teaching or of what religious beliefs they may hold. The spirit of understanding is what they all seek. It is, I believe, enhanced by attention to the connections made between each branch of study. Courses are often so arranged that students can study the ethical or theological dimension of almost any subject. It is important to take advantage of that, whether by studying formally or simply by browsing in the library or discussing with colleagues some of the moral dilemmas of life. There is, alas, no shortage of them. I will continue to pray in the words that are recited daily in the chapel of King's College, London, that 'the seeds of learning, virtue and religion, may bring forth fruit abundantly to thy glory and the benefit of our fellow creatures'.

5
Industry: Burying its Talents?

Industry. The word may sound unspiritual. Yet we celebrate the industrious, the diligent, those who apply themselves to the care of others. The very word industry refers to *diligence* as well as to the *organisation and production of goods and services*. Without both of these, we cannot have a civilised society. Deny the need for industriousness and organisation and we cannot feed the hungry, clothe our children, preserve our health or heal the sick. God gives us our unique gifts as human beings so that we can work hard in serving him and our neighbours – not so that we can sit back and leave it to him, or even to other people. That is the meaning of the parable of the talents: we must use our human ingenuity positively, actively, lovingly, tirelessly and account later for what we have done. Complacency spells the end not just for a commercial company – it is death to Christian discipleship too. Doing God's Will requires ceaseless effort in his service.

Somehow a myth has circulated that the Church of England is hostile or indifferent to the making of money, but that simply is not the case. These days it is essential that the Church of England knows all about creating wealth, for there is no pot of gold supporting its life and ministry. Financial backing has to be created, earned, attracted by the vibrancy of its Christian faith and life.

Followers of the Lord who told the parable of the talents could scarcely be critical of applying human skills and intelligence to the resources given us by God, in order to create things of value and use to other people. Unless we want to create greater poverty and destitution, we must honour and

---

Address at the CBI (Confederation of British Industry) Service, Derby Cathedral, Sunday 10 May 1992.

encourage those who use their God-given talents to help produce goods and services for others. Without them we cannot
have a planet with plentiful resources and the human adventure will end with the same wailing and grinding of teeth that
awaited the servant who failed to use his talent.

Biblical scholars will know that in the New Testament the
talent is a sum of money – a large sum, reckoned to be about
fifteen years' wages for a labourer. But – and it's a big but –
the story of the talents is *not* intended to mean that the more
money a person makes, the better God is pleased! It is a
parable, about using the gifts given us by God *for his purposes*
– not for any old purpose. It is about being creative with our
lives, with what God entrusts to us, but also about not being
surprised when God calls us to account. It is immediately
followed by Jesus explaining what God will be looking for at
the time of judgement:

Then the King will say to those on his right hand, 'You have my
Father's blessing; come, enter and possess the Kingdom that has been
ready for you since the world was made. For when I was hungry,
you gave me food; when thirsty, you gave me drink; when I was a
stranger you took me into your home, when naked you clothed me;
when I was ill you came to my help, when in prison you visited
me'.

Jesus goes on to explain that 'anything you did for one of my
brothers here, however humble, you did for me'. (Matthew
25:34–40) These, then, are the kind of ends to which God
calls us to use our talents. And each of us has talents, make
no mistake about that. We may not have fifteen years' wages
stored up, but we can take that unit of money to represent
our skills, abilities and diligence. Up and down the country
the talents of people in our inner cities have been released by
projects they have started and which have been helped by the
Church Urban Fund. Ends as well as means are important.

This brings me to the question of what are the ends sought
in British industry. What is the fundamental purpose to which
those in industry put their talents?

The ultimate purpose of industry is, I believe, to serve our
fellow human beings by creating goods and services to meet

their needs. It is not to make money for its own sake. It is not to make profits for shareholders, nor to create salaries and wages for the industrial community. These are necessary conditions for success but not its purpose. Nor can the purpose of industry be to serve the market, as if the market were the master instead of the servant of human need. No, industry's *purpose* is surely to serve people by creating things of use and value to them. British industry, like the Church, has plenty of critics, but it has excelled in creating things of use and value which have brought enormous benefits to many people's lives. I have great admiration for many industrialists and industrial workers.

But we need to be clear about the basic purpose of industry as we enter the European Single Market, if industry is to prosper as a well-loved, well-respected contributor to a Christian society. This will be the way to clear up some of the popular misconceptions about industry of which industrialists complain. Company law sometimes appears to enshrine the erroneous principle that companies exist to serve their shareholders, and the other stakeholders in an enterprise and in its fundamental purpose may not get a look in. Some people in business talk as if the bottom line in industry is simply the bottom line, and that industry is a Darwinian world ruled by the values of the market. The language of service and stewardship is too often left to clergymen, yet neither service nor stewardship is inimical to wealth creation. They are its allies. But they are not allies of tiny groups of institutional investors who might decide they are unhappy with a company's short-term financial return, and so off-load people's loyalties and talents simply for quick profits. Some of the habits, laws and institutions of industrial life appear designed to nourish misconceptions about industry's fundamental purposes.

The question of who benefits from industrial enterprise remains relevant to its public reputation. Let us cast our minds back to what Jesus suggested God would be looking for when we account for the purposes to which we have put our talents. If prolonged bursts of economic growth, led by the private sector, in advanced industrial countries leave more people than ever in the world hungry, thirsty, naked, ill or in prison, what then? Obviously a question mark would appear over the proposition that industry exists to serve human needs, and it is bound to look as if a minority of people are appropriating a quite disproportionate share of the earth's resources to sustain wasteful patterns of conspicuous consumption.

Within our own society, our collective commitment to industrial enterprise will remain under-powered if the fruits of success appear to be concentrated too heavily in the pockets of shareholders and senior executives. For example, massive individual pay rises during a recession do not encourage public support for wealth-creation. Moreover, when God sorts out the unfortunate goats from the sheep, he tells them: 'The curse is upon you . . . For when I was hungry you gave me nothing to eat, when thirsty nothing to drink; when I was a stranger you gave me no home, when naked you did not clothe me; when I was ill and in prison you did not come to my help.' I doubt if he would have been impressed by the argument that the goats had been waiting for these things to 'trickle down' as a by-product of economic growth!

In addition to the achievements, hopes and purposes of British industry, we must also remember the challenges of the Single European Market. Here too we welcome a further stimulus to use God's gifts creatively to meet people's needs. We must reaffirm this purpose in the light of the gospel and keep it in mind if the Single Market is to be the blessing we all hope it will be. The Single Market, like industry, is there to serve people. The people of Europe are not there to serve the Single Market. 'The sabbath is made for man; not man for the sabbath', said Jesus. Markets, if they are treated as masters, tend to be blind to environmental costs and can consume God's creation and waste our heritage. The glory of Europe is the extraordinary variety of cultures, characters, buildings, landscapes and languages packed into a relatively small corner of the globe: living testimony to the rich diversity of talents invested there over centuries. We must ensure the Single Market is so regulated that this diversity is strengthened. Spread a monochrome Euro-development and we will destroy distinctiveness. The fate of much of the Mediterranean coastline is a sobering warning of where the European Market can take us unless it is made to serve our long-term needs.

We must hope, too, that the Europe of the Single Market will look outwards and serve the rest of the world, not turn in on itself. Some hope is created from aspects of Europe's collective record on world environmental and development issues, but this contribution will have to develop strongly to keep pace with the growing emphasis on keeping economic and environmental refugees out of fortress Europe.

We must resolve that the institutions, laws and practices of European industry are in proper shape to help it fulfil its fundamental purpose of *serving the people*. The new Europe must use God's creation and its own diverse heritage sustainably, so setting an example to the world. And it must not turn its back on its neighbours in other parts of the world.

Let us all pray for God's blessing on industry and industrialists. Let us pray too for God's grace in our lives so that we remember the most important account is the one each of us will render to him of the efforts we have made to use the talents he has given us for his loving purposes.

6

Not to be Served, But to Serve

In the Abbey Church of Westminster greatness is visibly commemorated: greatness in art, science, literature, religion, as well as public service. We may wish to deny that we are great in that sense, but what we cannot deny is that authority and power are central to Parliament and its work. We need to seek God's blessing on our work so that we use our authority and power wisely and well. It is also fitting that we should heed the words of Christ as he sets forth the nature of Christian leadership.

'Whoever would be great among you must be your servant.'

MATTHEW 20:27

Jesus' remark above was uttered as a rebuke to signs of ambition amongst his disciples. Those words set the pattern of Christian authority. It was a duke who once said, 'There are only two kinds of people in the world. Those who are nice to their servants and those who aren't.' But Jesus asks his disciples to look at the world from the perspective of a servant, not that of a duke. That is because it is his perspective – 'The Son of Man came not to be served but to serve, and to give his life as a ransom for many.' (Matthew 20:28)

The temptation of legislators is to adopt the perspectives of the duke, rather than the perspective of our Lord. (As a member of the House of Lords I include myself among the legislators.) We may consider that we are legislating with good intent, that we are being kind to people in our deliberations. But being kind to servants is not in itself service. We are called to see, even experience, life from the servants' vantage point.

Address at the Opening of Parliament, St Margaret's, Westminster, Thursday 14 May 1992.

Jesus reminds us that all power is a gift. The authority we are given is a service to offer to others. I believe that, contrary to the popular view, most people who enter politics recognise this. They seek the improvement of society. They understand that with power comes responsibility; with authority, service.

The Christian gospel proclaims that there are God-given principles about the manner in which we make law and exercise power. Legislators are faced almost daily with moral choices, and we must face them *together*. Morality cannot simply be a matter of individual opinion. There is no such thing as a morally neutral law. Parliament must decide which laws will encourage what it believes to be good, and which will discourage evil. Almost a century ago, Bishop Mandell Creighton, then the Bishop of London, wrote this:

It is quite true that a man cannot be made virtuous by Acts of Parliament, but at least evils can be removed from his path, and it can be made more possible for him to be virtuous than vicious.

Creighton's sentiment still holds true. Acts of Parliament determine how we respond to people who sin against society, who are weak and sick, or who throw themselves on our mercy as refugees. Acts of Parliament influence the distribution of life chances amongst our people, each of whom is equally precious and unique in the sight of God. Acts of Parliament decide the official purposes of education; they regulate the use which people are allowed to make of animals and the natural resources given us by God.

All these and many others are inescapably moral issues. Pragmatism has an honourable contribution to make in political life, but it cannot answer these questions. They can only be answered by consideration of a public morality which, in this country, has long been based upon the Christian faith. That is an important factor in our society's sense of cohesion and direction – and it requires spiritual nourishment. The idea that Christian ethics will retain their potency if divorced from the practice of the Christian religion is, I believe, mistaken. Indeed, one of the difficulties we face in this society we sometimes describe as 'secular' is a sort of spiritual bewilderment which undermines the sense of a shared moral purpose.

Let me illustrate this from the debate which followed the sermon I gave to the CBI (see Chapter 5). I was glad it was so widely discussed. But few were the editorials which found space for a discussion of the theological and scriptural points which were at the heart of that address. It was as if they were too embarrassing or uncomfortable to handle. The inclination was to move the debate on to secular ground, then the challenge to industry to consider its ultimate purpose as creating things of use and value in the service of humankind could be examined without its theological rationale. For the teaching was not mine. It was a direct application of Matthew's Gospel. Confronting the challenge of God's word can be uncomfortable. Jesus always troubles our complacency. A sanitised scripture will have no saving power.

One of the most encouraging signs of our time is that Christians of all traditions are more open about their faith than they once were. I welcome this kind of explicit Christianity. There is no need for us to apologise for our faith or hide it away as if we were ashamed of it. I trust that all of us committed to the Christian faith – which includes a significant proportion of both Houses of Parliament – will not think it bad taste to declare that the examples and teachings of Jesus Christ should be our constant guide as we struggle with the multiple moral challenges of political life today. The vigour of the Parliamentary Christian Fellowship is a sign that many have already taken up this challenge. The existence of a religious service at the beginning of a Parliament, a service with no long history, is another sign that we do not wish to relegate religious faith to a purely private domain.

The danger for legislators is to approach moral issues as if they were merely technocratic or matters for political calculation. I hasten to add that I am not calling for 'conviction politics' insofar as that phrase defines a fondness for simplistic formulas or an intolerant insistence on a single apprehension of the truth. To follow Jesus Christ is not to believe in easy answers. His is the way of service, and as you read the New Testament you discover that he almost always responds to a moral question by asking another, by telling a parable, by forcing his hearers to think for themselves. Nor am I asking politicians to be ostentatious in their religious observance. Jesus let religious show-offs have the sharp edge of his tongue. We need humility as well. Even boasting about the service we give to others will bring us under judgement. Humility, though, is a curious virtue to acquire. A biographer of John Wesley once commented on how difficult it is to be humble, saying 'there is no guarantee that when you have become humble you will not be proud of the fact'. It is rather like the small boy whose headmaster recommended a dose of humility after finding him so cocky and boastful. Things improved for a bit, but then he lapsed back to his old self. When the head asked him what happened to the humility the boy replied, 'I was humble for a fortnight, but no one noticed'.

So whenever I am tempted to say 'in all humility', I resist it. But it is with what I hope is a proper Christian reticence that I ask this. The conviction politics I seek is the unapologetic affirmation of the preponderantly Christian character of our society; I ask for recognition that the sense of shared values, so vital to long-term wellbeing, derives from our Christian heritage; I ask that we should not be ashamed to declare our loyalty to Christ in this nation. If we do so, I believe that we will acknowledge that human life, and hence the ordering of society through Parliamentary Law, has a religious and spiritual dimension which is a source of hope. In the traditional prayer for the High Court of Parliament, we ask God so to direct our deliberations:

That peace and happiness, truth and justice, *religion and piety*, may be established among us for all generations.

I am sure that peace and happiness, truth and justice, will not flourish amongst us if religion and piety are edited out of the script. The societies where that has happened, as we have seen in this century, quickly crumble.

Some may think it strange that I express these hopes in a British society which has a multifaith character. I do not agree. There is no inconsistency between an endorsement of the Christian character of this nation and the warmest possible support for good relationships with different faith communities. The other faith communities in our country do not generally look for the United Kingdom's secularisation as a means of their acceptance. They have no desire to see the Christian religion excluded from public life, for they understand too well that religion is not a private leisure-time activity, but related to all that we are. Indeed, they are a witness to the public character of religious faith.

Those of us entrusted with temporal power and authority pray it may be used to God's honour and glory, and thank God for the privilege of serving others. In this task we can do far worse than to follow that person, Jesus Christ, who calls us his modern followers to a fresh obedience and firmer faith. The Jesus of whom Robert Browning wrote:

> That face, far from vanity, rather grows
> Or decomposes but to recompose
> Becomes my universe that feels and knows.

7

God, Goodness and Justice

Voltaire thought that if his servants ceased to believe in God, they would steal from him. You might say that he was in no doubt that God and goodness were connected. But it wasn't a generous, forgiving God of love that Voltaire wanted his servants to believe in. It was a God who would condemn them to everlasting punishment in the fires of hell if they disobeyed his divine commands. In the gnashing of teeth lay the drive towards good behaviour. The fear of hell was believed to be a powerful incentive towards honesty and truth.

The doctrine of the everlasting punishment of the wicked has been in serious decline for more than a century. This decline would make an interesting study in itself, but it is beyond the scope of what I want to do here. What seems to me undeniable is that contemporary Christians focus much more upon the God of forgiveness and love who is revealed in Jesus Christ, rather than the God of vengeance and judgement, who is no less to be found in the pages of scripture. I, for one, believe that our contemporary concentration upon forgiveness does greater justice to the teaching of Jesus.

The decline in Christian belief in everlasting punishment has, however, coincided with many attempts to separate religion and morality. Ours has been the century in which Bertrand Russell and A J Ayer were amongst those to suggest that morality is based only on 'emotions'. If that seems a flimsy foundation for moral behaviour, then it is an even flimsier basis upon which to do justice. Barbara Wootton, herself no

The Golden Lecture, St Lawrence Jewry in the City of London, Thursday 4 June 1992. Sponsored by the Haberdashers' Company – a trustee of several charities – the Golden Lecture is delivered by a prominent person in a City of London Church each year.

apologist for Christian belief, acknowledged this when she commented upon the impossibility of 'attempting to do justice in an ethical vacuum when nobody knows what justice is'.

In this chapter, I hope to sketch out what I believe to be the continuing links between God, goodness and justice which a society like ours, with a strong Christian heritage, can ill afford to neglect.

I shall take as my starting point the existence of goodness. Although many are willing to dispute the existence of God, few are the people who dispute the existence of goodness. The cynic may mock it, but all of us know there is goodness in the world. Where does it come from? Of what might it be a sign?

Christian theologians have spent so much time addressing the problem of evil that the problem of goodness has too often been neglected. Perhaps Christians can be excused since it is not a problem for them. But it is a problem for a world in which mechanistic interpretations of human behaviour are commonplace.

The problem can be simply stated. Is it rational to be good in ways that go beyond our self-interest unless we believe in a loving God? Nobody needs to be persuaded of the power of self-interest. Goodness which coincides completely with self-interest causes no intellectual problems. But it is goodness which is altruistic, in which no benefits accrue to the person doing the good deed or having the good thought, which presents the real problems in a sceptical age.

Where can we find our examples of such goodness? Mother Teresa is, I suppose, the most frequently cited and most admired example. But the cynic might say that she is responding to a deep need to be needed, and in the course of caring for the poor, she has created a huge missionary order of sisters over which she presides. She has the compensations of fame and authority, and so even the most transparent example of goodness that I know of can be dismissed by the cynic.

More difficult to explain away would be the example of Maximilian Kolbe, the Franciscan friar, who voluntarily took the place of a young Polish serviceman condemned to die in Auschwitz as a punishment because one of his fellow inmates had gone missing. The young Polish serviceman cried for his wife and family. Kolbe asked to take his place since, he said, he had no family of his own. So he was led away to starve to death. Is that goodness or is it foolishness?

Cynics pay a very heavy price for their cynicism. By insisting that moral actions are never quite what they appear to be, they suggest that the moral actors themselves are frauds or dupes. The insistence is that the cynics alone have the correct explanation of moral behaviour. This explanation is, of course, self-interest. We only act in our own interests, whether short-term or long-term, and we delude ourselves if we imagine otherwise.

Put as bluntly as that, such ideas sound like moral nonsense. So they are. But they have a quasi-scientific currency. There seem to be links here with evolutionary theory. It is argued that what is true of our physical development and the world of nature might well be true of our moral actions too. If you read Richard Dawkins' *The Blind Watchmaker*, you will be told that there is no design or purpose in the biological world – just the relentless pressure to survive. It is easy to fall into the trap of seeing everything – not just the biological world, but the social and moral worlds as well – in similar terms. A debate between Richard Dawkins and the Archbishop of York on Science and Religion was fundamentally unsatisfactory because no common language was found. The scientist did not believe that the theologian was talking sense. The theologian – in this instance also a trained scientist – thought the scientist was not allowing for other forms of valid knowledge.

The difficulty of regarding all human actions as a consequence of our biological need to survive is that it fails to account for so many human actions that we admire. Any example of goodness that goes beyond self-interest or does not serve the instinct to survive cannot be understood or must be explained away. But there are some situations where it is difficult to find self-interest on the part of the moral actors. Think, for example, of those who care for and love cantankerous old people. Or think of those who sacrifice so much of their own lives to look after a mentally or physically handicapped member of their family. We need some frame of reference other than self-interest to make sense of such self-giving.

Would the hospice movement have ever got off the ground if self-interest was the only motivating force in human behaviour? And going beyond care for humanity, where do we find the adequate explanation for so much of the art, poetry, literature and music which has exerted not simply an aesthetic influence upon the world, but has had a moral bearing upon many people's lives?

The connection between God and goodness has had its champions, even during this century, when secular accounts of moral behaviour seem to have held centre stage. The moral philosopher A E Taylor, for example, explored the link between religion and morality in his Gifford Lectures at the University of St Andrews in the late 1920s. He gave those lectures the title, *The Faith of the Moralist*. He recognised that morality might exist without religion. He believed that an atheist who had been taught not to steal or lie was equally likely to earn his living honestly, to speak the truth and to live a sober life as a believer in God. But he recognised also that if atheists are in earnest in their view of the world, and believers likewise live out what they believe, then it is the believer and not the atheist who is more likely to go the second mile and do the good deed without any personal reward. When atheists behaved in this way, it was if they had faith. It was an unfashionable view at the time, and it is no more fashionable now. But Taylor saw in the moral life itself a sign of God. He wrote: 'The moral life itself, at its best, points to something which, because it transcends the separation of "ought" from "is", must be called definitely religion and not morality . . .'

Fashionable or not, Taylor believed there were good intellectual reasons for thinking that morality made better sense when seen through the eye of faith, than it did without such faith. He believed that the existence of goodness pointed to a world created by a loving God. That is what he meant by 'something that transcends the separation of "ought" from "is" '. If the world really is created by a loving God, then the goodness, which goes beyond self-interest or survival instinct that we glimpse all around us, may prove to be a pointer to how things 'ought' to be. In the present moment, the time, if you like, of the 'is', we glimpse the promise of the 'ought'. It is in this goodness that human beings can see in each other's actions the intention of the Creator in making them in his image. This simply cannot be the perspective of the atheist. Believers alone – and not only Christian believers – may set morality at this deeper level.

This theme occurs in the thought and writings of other philosophers and social scientists of our century. R H Tawney, Norman Dennis and A H Halsey might be taken as examples of social scientists who have dealt with the problem of goodness within their own discipline, the latter two being themselves disciples of Tawney. Perhaps, however, the most significant study of altruism is to be found in Richard Titmuss' book, *The Gift Relationship*. He simply recognises how frequently ordinary people do things at some cost to themselves which they need not do, and which serve the greater good. One of the examples he takes is blood donation. In giving blood, there is no immediate self-interest on the part of the blood donor. The humour in Tony Hancock's famous sketch, *The Blood Donor*, is partly to be found in his proprietorial regard for the pint of blood he has given. He wanted to know what had happened to it, and needed to be assured that his blood – of the rare AB negative variety – had gone to a good home! Eventually, of course, he receives his own pint of blood back through his own arm, after an accident. But most blood donors receive little or no reward for giving blood, beyond the certificate or badge. In Britain, we have never introduced the selling of blood. We simply give it away. Titmuss saw this as a small, but instructive, act of altruism.

This whole theme is one to which some moral theologians are giving fresh attention today. Significant amongst them is Professor Robin Gill, the first Michael Ramsey Professor of Theology at the University of Kent at Canterbury. His Chair was the result of a joint initiative between the University and the Church of England, the Church raising a substantial proportion of the money required through a public appeal. The Church of England is not interested in hiving off theological discourse from other disciplines. That would only hasten further secularism. In his inaugural lecture, Professor Gill asked the question, 'Why care?' The whole notion of care is linked with goodness and altruism, and I am sure Professor Gill will continue to generate renewed debate about the place of religious faith in shaping patterns of human caring.

Let me summarise. My belief is that goodness presents problems for secularists in much the same way that evil presents problems for believers. I have shown, albeit briefly, that there has always been a tradition of thought which has recognised that altruism is best understood and encouraged through the eye of faith. But in our century, people who have argued thus have done so in a hostile, intellectual environment – one which was self-consciously secular.

That intellectual environment is now changing. The forces of secularism are in retreat. The moral certainties of Marxism now hold little appeal in the wake of the collapse of European Communism. Secular, non-theistic moral philosophers such as Stuart Hampshire and Iris Murdoch now argue for objectivity in morals. They believe there are moral claims upon us which challenge us to act for the 'good'. And, despite the recent debate between Richard Dawkins and the Archbishop of York, there are now relatively few scientists who claim that theirs is the only valid form of knowledge. Most scientists recognise that science itself is never value-free, and that the products of scientific technology can bring harm as well as good to the world. The claims of ethics are recognised. Medical ethics and business ethics have their places in university departments.

But amidst all this, a sort of secular liberalism lives on. It claims there are no moral certainties – everything is changeable and nothing is fixed. Religious ideas are no longer attacked. They are simply ignored as not being powerful enough to consider. Secular morality's strongest imperative is not to judge or harm others.

Christian faith offers a much more challenging perspective on the world. It believes that there is an intimate connection between morality and faith. The way we view the universe has a direct connection with the way we should treat our neighbour. Loving God has everything to do with loving our neighbour, and loving our neighbours as ourselves is, according to the New Testament, the test by which it is known whether we love God.

Much of what I have said about the relationship between morality and religion is not specifically Christian. But no Christian can talk about goodness without also talking about Jesus Christ. For Christianity is not based upon an abstract idea of goodness. It is based upon the goodness of God seen completely and fully in a human being – Jesus of Nazareth.

It is through Jesus Christ that Christian believers find God, goodness and justice linked. It is because of Jesus Christ that Christians find secular theories of justice unsatisfactory. It is in this area that secular liberalism has held great sway. Contemporary theories of justice tend to be based upon a consensus of 'considered convictions' in society. The problem this creates is that in administering justice, a society cannot do anything but reinforce its own prejudices, since there is nothing external to its own behaviour patterns to which it can relate. B A Ackerman, one of the contemporary theorists, explicitly states that nobody has 'privileged insight into the moral universe denied to the rest of us'.

Christians would never claim privileged insights. They simply re-tell the story of a just God dealing with his people. Duncan Forrester, amongst the foremost of our theologians working in this area, once wrote:

Christian theology should have a major contribution to make to the contemporary debate about justice. Insofar as the Church proclaims the good news of the Kingdom of God and his justice, it is bound inescapably to engagement with questions of justice. And as a . . . partial manifestation of the Kingdom, the Church is a community of experiment, of expectation, of moral discourse, and of action relating to God's justice.

Contemporary society needs moral communities to be both critics and contributors to its system of justice. Perhaps the most striking thing about the teaching of Jesus Christ was that so much of it was about justice, yet he did not attempt to impose some new system of justice or morality upon his followers. Rather, his teaching challenged all their moral presuppositions. 'Love your enemies; do good to those who hate you.' (Matthew 5:43–4) 'Judge not, and you shall not be judged; condemn not and you shall not be condemned.' (Luke

6:37–8) 'You have heard that they were told, "An eye for an eye, a tooth for a tooth". What I tell you is this: do not resist those who wrong you.' (Matthew 5:38–9) 'You have heard they were told, "Do not commit adultery". But what I tell you is this: if a man looks at a woman with a lustful eye, he has already committed adultery with her in his heart.' (Matthew 5:27–8)

What Jesus is doing is not producing a new system of justice. Rather, he is proclaiming God's justice, the justice which will exist when his Kingdom is established on earth, as it is in heaven. It is a justice which undercuts self-righteousness, self-satisfaction and self-justification. And Jesus never suggests to his followers that by doing what he says they will receive rewards in this life. Loving enemies is not guaranteed to turn their hearts. They might only increase their persecution. Turning the other cheek is not recommended for its prudence. It is a proclamation of a coming Kingdom, which throws us back always to examine our own motives in the light of the pure goodness of God.

But Jesus not only proclaimed God's justice, he called others to live it. He did this by calling them first to follow him. Unlike Socrates who diverted attention away from himself to the precepts he taught, Jesus Christ set the pattern of his life and death before others as the fundamental way of living in the light of God's justice and goodness. 'Anyone who would come after me, let him deny himself, take up his cross and follow me.' (Mark 8:34) The author of 1 John puts it like this: 'In this is love, not that we loved God but that he loved us and sent his Son to be the expiation for our sins. Beloved, if God so loved us, we ought to love one another.'

The crucial word is 'ought'. There are moral demands upon us because of God's goodness towards us. We are called to imitate God's likeness. He is like Christ – 'in him is no un-Christlikeness at all', as Michael Ramsey used to say. The obedience we owe to Christ makes Christianity far more than an ethical code – it is a way of life. It is a way of living as if the Kingdom of God has already come about. Anthony Harvey, theologian and Canon of Westminster, says that the ethic of Jesus is found in the way he calls us to live *as if* God's rule is sovereign. The hard sayings of Jesus cause us constantly to re-examine our own moral presuppositions. They are imperative – '*Love* your enemies'; '*Turn* the other cheek'. They are God's claim upon us. He still loves us, despite our hostility towards him. He turns the other cheek. His goodness presents a morality with a claim upon us. And his justice is one that promotes goodness and does not simply punish wrongdoing.

The Church, however, is not merely in the business of appealing to people to be good. Its job is to call them to follow. That is the way Christians believe goodness and justice is promoted, and we see it as indivisible from faith. It is telling the story of Jesus and calling people to follow him which is the Church's greatest contribution in the debate about common justice. The goodness of God is linked so closely to his generosity that any system of justice which is mean or narrow or unsympathetic will never encourage goodness to flourish. And even those without faith may appreciate this insight.

George Steiner's *Real Presences*, is subtitled, *Is There Anything in What we Say*? Steiner argues that when the question of God ceases to be debated, and when his existence is forgotten, a whole range of thought and creativity will no longer be attainable. The language of music, poetry, art and literature all depends, so he argues, upon God, and upon talk about him being comprehensible. Without God, human discourse will become poorer, and gradually less intelligible. Without God, I believe our capacity to understand goodness will likewise decay, and our ability to do justice will disintegrate.

8

The Spirit of Charity

As a patron or President of at least 150 charities, I am often involved in work to support many others. Many important charities are Church agencies or founded by them. When I returned to my old home territory of Barking and Dagenham and addressed a large gathering of voluntary sector representatives there, it became clear to me that if all the committed Christians present had left the room, there would have been hardly anyone remaining – and no doubt some of *them* would have been religious people of other faiths.

Indeed, taking responsibility for serving others and caring for God's creation is part and parcel of being a good Christian, not an optional extra. Doing our best to give active expression to God's love in our social relations is as much part of the Christian life as prayer and worship. Small wonder, then, that Christian involvement is integral to so much of the voluntary sector in this country, and that voluntary action is integral to the life of the Christian Churches.

I will go further. It is impossible to encapsulate the Church of England in one label, but in many ways it is itself one of the oldest and largest voluntary organisations of all! Without the voluntary commitment of people who want to worship and serve God, the institution would become an empty shell. Without the moving spirit that motivates people to search for the fundamental purposes of life and reflect them in their own lives, the Church is nothing – and the wider voluntary sector is nothing, too.

So, when I raise questions about the charitable sector in our society, I do not do so as an outsider. We are all in this

---

Address to the Charity Directors' Network, National Liberal Club, London, Tuesday, 9 June 1992

together! I sometimes think that any other voluntary organisation with 30 million sympathisers would have done rather
better than the Church of England has in recruiting members
and financial supporters!

The Charity Directors' Network used to be called the
'Moving Spirit'. I should be interested to know why the name
was changed. Was there a feeling that 'Moving Spirit' was
pretentious? Or embarrassingly spiritual in a secular world? I
do not know, but these questions are of wider relevance.

At Pentecost the Holy Spirit filled and fired the apostles. For
me, the 'Moving Spirit' is something of enormous power and
restlessness. It makes us feel humble, not pretentious, as we
struggle to follow its calling and live up to its inspiration. And
the key questions I should now like to explore with you are
these: Has the charitable sector become *too reticent* about the
'Moving Spirit', about the spiritual purposes of life, about
moral values which are the sector's inspiration and ultimate
justification? Has it compromised too deeply with the wide-
spread secularisation of society and the privatisation of moral
values?

Let me sketch in a few important background factors. The
collapse of Communism removes from our thinking about
ourselves the alibi that at least we are not Communist and
that we should close ranks against the Communist enemy.
The focus can now shift to other problems in a less fearful
atmosphere. These problems include the inadequacies of
materialism and consumerism as the route to contentment or
justice. They include the combination of profound environmental and development issues. They include the spread of
relativism in moral questions, as if morals were simply a matter
of individual opinion and there were no other source of spiritual or moral authority. They include a fragmentation of
spiritual beliefs to the point where a sense of society's shared
values has partly collapsed. It is widely regarded as embarrassing to talk about God, spirituality or even ethical values in
polite society. The purpose of life, in many circles, is a topic
banished to a purely private domain.

These are obviously generalisations, but they may perhaps
ring bells with you. For instance, if you have children at or

approaching school age, I wonder what sort of replies you would get if you asked prospective schools: 'What are the values and ethos of this school?' I suspect that quite a few schools are clear that they are *against* discrimination of various sorts, but are much less clear what they are *for*. And would we not feel uneasy about sending our children to schools which have an uncertain approach to spiritual and moral values; which have a hole rather than an ethos? I use this example to illustrate what I see as a wider malaise in the society of which schools are part. The sense of shared values, and the public recognition of people's spiritual nature, are at a dangerously low ebb. A wishy-washy secular liberalism, with God privatised, is not a promising basis for tackling the world's problems, or pursuing the objectives of our charitable organisations.

I touched on this theme in my previous chapter, where I suggested that a morality based on *not* harming others and *not* judging them is problematical. If we are not called to do positive good, only to avoid causing harm, the heartbeat of charity will stop. Charities rely on something more than conventional morality. They rely on the goodness in which human beings can see the intention of a loving Creator in making them in his image.

The political culture of our country also reflects this spiritual uncertainty. One got the impression at some stages during the last general election campaign that the purpose of life was shopping. I do not disdain people's desire for modern comforts and material advancement, but as an implied description of the purpose of political and social life it is sad and barren. I know there were many exceptions, and I know it would be unfair simply to blame the politicians. I do suggest, however, that the general election campaign, taken as a whole, dramatised our society's weak sense of moral purpose.

As a further piece of evidence, I would add some of the reactions to my sermons. I have addressed the spiritual purposes which should guide social and political, as well as individual activity, and I am happy to say that the reactions in my mailbag have been largely positive. When in one sermon (see Chapter 5), I suggested that the ultimate purpose of industry was to serve human needs, and that making profits was a necessary condition of success in this endeavour, I argued that the market should be the servant of human need, rather than our master. I strongly affirmed the importance of wealth creation, but also quoted from St Matthew's Gospel some of the *ends* to which we are called to put our talents if we are to find favour with God:

'When I was hungry, you gave me food; when thirsty, you gave me drink; when I was a stranger you took me into your home; when I was ill you came to my help, when in prison you visited me.'

I shall leave on one side the exceptionally talented few who are able to pass judgement on a sermon before reading or hearing it. Some of the other first reactions were revealing. Some thought I must be attacking business enterprise and the profit motive. Others thought I must be attacking the Conservative Party. What a muddle! I think the muddle reflects deep confusion in some quarters as to whether the market actually *should* be a servant or master, and whether business enterprise actually *does* have an ultimate purpose beyond making profits for shareholders. Some comments even suggested to me that the quotation from St Matthew's Gospel was seen as a tired cliché from the 1960s. The critics are relatively few, but the underlying confusion is certainly there.

Against this background – and I am conscious how incomplete this sketch is – it seems to me that the spirit of charity, reflected in so many voluntary organisations, is enormously important to a society in a muddle about its collective purpose. I believe that *all* sectors have a role and responsibility in striving for a society worth calling Christian. It is not something to be left to Churches and charities and I am enormously impressed by the serious thinking and strong moral commitment I see in many individual businessmen, politicians, trade unionists and people in all walks of life. No sector, and certainly not the Church, can afford to be morally self-righteous: something which Jesus strongly disliked.

Nevertheless, charities *specifically exist to promote moral purposes*. They aim to find effective expression for the spirit of charity, which has been defined as romantic but unsentimental love for each and every neighbour. They provide a means of encouraging generosity, responsibility and goodness in a society where people feel their individual capacity to decide *how* to benefit their neighbour is limited. Charities come in every shape and size, with a different mix of practical, educational or campaigning work in each case, but if the sector as a whole ceases to be a moral force, it loses its fundamental justification and relevance. That is why charities are so important in a society suffering from shallow materialism and spiritual bewilderment. That is also why I profoundly admire their work.

I would like to share with you some questions about tendencies which could detract from the 'Moving Spirit' of the charitable sector. I do not claim to have the answers, but I think the questions are important. The first is about *managerialism*. I have already said that the Church has plenty to learn from other voluntary organisations about effective management, but at least you will not find on the whole that Church leaders or vicars lose sight of the religious and spiritual nature of their calling. I wonder if some charities, in a thoroughly laudable effort to promote efficient management, are in danger of substituting a managerial ethos for the 'Moving Spirit'?

I remember that William Waldegrave issued an apt warning as Health Minister to managers in the NHS. He told them in effect that the wholesale importation of language from the business world could give the public the impression that the distinctive caring ethos of the Health Service had been abandoned.

As large charities draw – quite properly – on the skills and expertise of the business and government sectors, they may run similar risks. It is no doubt inevitable that in many larger charities the influence of paid staff is much greater in relation to volunteer management committees than it used to be. Of course, effective charities need to pursue value for money. They need to be efficient. They need to review their performance rigorously. They need some people who get their excitement from hitting membership and fund-raising targets. But how difficult it must be to ensure that the management and marketing techniques remain *subordinate* to the spirit of charity: the servants, not the masters! If a charity director is too eager to tell me about the size of the budget, the number of staff under their management, and the scale of the donor list, a warning light starts to flash in my mind!

The second question I have concerns *incorporation*. How many charity directors spend their time saying to a government agency: 'I can carry out *your* agenda for you more efficiently!' I wonder how many government contracts a voluntary organisation can chase, or how dependent it can be on contract funding, while maintaining the primacy of its independent moral purpose. Is it possible that the organisational imperative to expand budgets, posts and the volume of activity begins over time to distort, rather than support, the original moral objectives of the charity? Many charities manage these tensions magnificently, but I must ask: How often do the very deep and close relationships with government or business influence their capacity to be a *moral force in our society*? Is it enhanced, or compromised?

Thirdly, are charities sufficiently *forthright about their values*? Is there a tendency to collude with, rather than challenge, the contemporary reticence about spiritual and moral purposes? If, as I suggested earlier, a somewhat shallow secular liberalism is the order of the day in much of our contemporary culture, should charities adjust their language and image to fit that culture? Many charities are born of religious inspiration: should they shed it? Each charity must make its own decision. But if too many charities opt for reticence and secularisation, the cumulative effect will be, in my view, to reinforce the spiritual malaise of contemporary society.

Fourthly, there is the duty felt by many charities to overcome discrimination against ethnic or religious minorities. I warmly support and share such an objective. But it flows from *affirming our positive values and beliefs*, not from hiding them or watering them down. I think there are problems if ever the determination to be *against* discrimination becomes separated from or even supersedes a determination to be *for* a broader and explicit moral purpose.

Moreover, as Archbishop I do not find that good relationships with people of other faiths can be based on hiding our own distinctive beliefs or finding a lowest common denominator to which we can all safely subscribe. Still less is the solution to settle for a purely secular discourse on the basis that this will not offend religious susceptibilities. The last thing that many people of minority faiths want is secularism! This is what the Chief Rabbi, Lord Jakobovits, had to say in the House of Lords in 1988: 'From schools that had confidence in their Christianity I learned an answering pride in my Jewishness and I discovered that those who best appreciate other faiths are those who treasure their own.'

For me, as for Lord Jakobovits, the lowest common denominator approach is not the way forward and indeed can further contribute to spiritual emptiness.

I have offered here some reflections on our common task in challenging our society to respond generously to the needs of poor and disadvantaged people, care for God's creation and pursue other moral purposes in life. I trust that they will provoke a stimulating discussion from which I hope to learn.

Let me close with a final reflection on the image of the 'Moving Spirit'. In Christian theology the Spirit is that mysterious, other side of God who cannot be pinned down. He is constantly on the move – moving ahead, and often frustrating our instinct to pigeon-hole and compartmentalise. So it is with our work, too: the moment we think we have it sewn up and under control is the time to recognise that the Spirit has gone from it!

9

Trust in the People: Democracy and the Christian Faith

The title of this chapter, *Trust in the People: Democracy and the Christian Faith*, is deliberately double-edged to raise two fundamental points: How do we enable individuals to take hold of and shape their own futures, and what kind of society does that require? In tackling these themes, I need to make it clear that I am approaching the matter as leader of a Church deeply embedded in the life of our nation. We seek to interpret God's purposes in the world around us and, like Barnett, we refuse to turn our backs on it. Accused as I sometimes am of meddling in politics or affairs that do not concern me, I have to reply that a Christianity which is not concerned about the whole of life is not a Christianity I want or the modern world deserves.

As I have already said, there can be no doubt that the modern world desperately needs a clearer sense of purpose. We have seen in our own day the collapse of Communist ideology. The dramatic and swift demise of Communism owes as much to the moral and spiritual emptiness it created in the lives of human beings as to the failure of the economic utopia it promised. The countries emerging from the former Communist bloc are now in search of role models as nationalism, xenophobia and ethnic and religious tensions destabilise Eastern Europe. They need a vision of what a healthy democratic society should and can be.

But are we that kind of society? Admittedly as part of

Barnett Lecture, Toynbee Hall, London, Monday 5 October 1992.
The Revd Canon Samuel Barnett was warden of Toynbee Hall from its foundation until 1906; the annual Barnett Lecture was instituted in his memory.

Western Europe we are enviably rich in material possessions in comparison with many other parts of the world. But is that all we have to offer?

We have to ensure that we do not fulfil the description of the Polish joke which goes: 'Socialism is the exploitation of man by man, whereas capitalism is the opposite.' If such vulnerable, new democracies look to this country for a society whose shared ideals can withstand material austerity and the snares of nationalist hatred – what will they find?

Let us consider for a moment some of our own discontents. Many individuals feel that they have no stake in our society. This is manifestly true of many unemployed people, now officially numbering 2.8 million, and of others afflicted by poverty or discrimination. In less acute form, it is reflected more widely in the relative lack of influence that many feel over the major forces which shape their lives and those of their children. There is unease about the increasing power of faceless people in Whitehall, in the EC, in international business cartels and bureaucracies. It provokes anxiety when our life chances appear to be at the mercy of unstoppable surges of speculative capital which engulf even the Bank of England, let alone the ordinary citizen. There are also fears about the radical weakening of local authorities which have for many generations been a 'buffer' between the individual and central government; despite all the talk of 'subsidiarity' in the European context, I do not myself discern many signs of it within the United Kingdom itself. I believe that the growth of environmental groups in recent years is fuelled partly by fears that technologies appear to be dangerously out of control. I am not concerned here to debate the extent to which such unease has any basis in reality, nor do I want to be drawn on the relative merits of electoral reform, Bills of Rights or the Citizen's Charter. I simply want to note the fact that many people today feel powerless and insignificant. And within that framework, a substantial minority feel they have no real stake at all.

Now, this brings me to the fact that in any body, community or society which balances the interests of the individual and group, of the majority and minorities, democratic decisions can be a form of tyranny unless there are checks and balances. We in the Church have reflected this point in the democratic proceedings which underpin our form of synodical government. I am sure you have all read *ad nauseam* in the papers that the Church is so incorrigibly divided that it cannot make up its mind about anything – with the ordination of women as a topical example. I want to put the other side of the argument. I make the uncontroversial point that Her Majesty's Government rules the country with far-reaching powers having secured 42% of the vote at the General Election. In the Church of England we have made it harder on ourselves by deliberately setting a two-thirds threshold for some kinds of important decision because we are not prepared to railroad an important new departure against the wishes of a substantial minority. Similarly, we are not an authoritarian Church. The Archbishops, bishops or clergy are not allowed by themselves to push through a change, because the Church believes that the laity who make up the majority should have their say too. We listen to each other, argue and pray until we carry a substantial majority of all parts of the Church with us. I claim this as a virtue. To be sure, the resulting decision-making is slow and cumbersome and that can cause pain. Not every feature of our arrangements is necessarily right. But the authoritarian model or the dictatorship of the simple majority can cause even worse tensions and problems in the longer run.

Then I draw your attention to another contemporary problem: the dwindling sense of any shared purpose which all citizens have in common.

Now someone may question if such a shared purpose ever existed. I believe it did. I recall as a young person growing up in the East End that my working-class parents felt a very real affinity with all other citizens in our sense of 'Britishness' and destiny as a nation. Class divisions and the distance between the 'haves' and the 'have nots' were real enough, and admittedly the war helped to pull us together; but growing up after the war I was aware of a strong cohesion in the nation, a sense of shared aspirations held in common across the social divides.

These days I am not so sure. The dissipation of shared

purpose no doubt has many causes. One is that we have become a mobile society, and this has loosened family and community ties. It is now quite rare to find the extended family.

A second major factor is the rise of secularism. The Christian heritage permeates this country more thoroughly than many people realise, but religion is less potent than it used to be as a source of common aspirations, values and symbols.

A third factor is disillusionment with past efforts to build a better society. We have witnessed a powerful ideological attack during the 1980s on the value of public goods, together with strong affirmation of private values and individual choice. There was sustained criticism of a wide range of social institutions. No doubt this has brought benefits at many levels, but it has certainly not encouraged a sense of common purpose shared by all citizens.

To a feeling of powerlessness, and a weak sense of common purpose, I will add to my diagnosis a collapse of confidence in absolute moral standards. Belief in a source of moral authority lying beyond the individual's desires and ambitions has been dangerously weakened, to the point that in some quarters morality has been reduced to a matter of individual opinion. Questions of right and wrong become merely relative to what each person feels, so long as no actual harm is done to anyone else. It is as if it is old-fashioned and illiberal to use words like 'right' and 'wrong' at all. The privatisation of morality threatens to undermine a sense of social cohesion as society itself is broken down into a multiplicity of individual atoms. Each doing his own thing with no commitment to agreed moral goals.

Our society has many strengths, as well as weaknesses; but if I am anywhere near the mark in my brief sketch of some of our underlying difficulties, we badly need to redefine the goals and values we have in common. And to help us do so, I want to examine the thinking of one of my predecessors as Archbishop of Canterbury; the great William Temple, who died in 1944 after an all-too-brief ministry as Archbishop. He made an enormous impact on his generation and his writings still wing their freshness, sharpness and relevance across the years. I want to share some of Temple's insights with you because I believe that our society needs the same sort of renewal of hope which he was able to offer people of his generation.

First, Temple had to reassert the historic right of the Church to be involved in social and political matters at all. He was up against the view summarised in the immortal words: 'ecclesiastical cobblers should stick to their last'. Temple countered this charge vigorously; the Church was bound to 'interfere' he said, because it is 'by *vocation* the agent of God's purpose, outside the scope of which no human interest or activity can fall'. He rejected the facile notion that there were certain areas of life sealed off from Christian concern. Here Temple was at one with John Maynard Keynes who argued that 'there are practically no issues of policy as distinct from technique which do not involve ethical considerations'. Since in Temple's words, 'Christians are the trustees of a revelation who go out into the world calling men to accept and follow it', it was the right and duty of the Church to 'declare its judgement upon social facts . . . and lay down principles which should govern the order of society'.

This may suggest that Temple was a moral idealist, keen to insist upon the character of a society that he believed in, with little understanding of its pluralistic nature. But this would be to overlook his realism. He knew that 'nine-tenths of the work of the Church in the world is done by Christian people fulfilling responsibilities and performing tasks which in themselves are not part of the official system of the Church at all'. Written some 50 years ago that is a remarkable statement. It is commonplace these days to affirm the work of lay people in the world but for a long time the assumption in the Church has prevailed that what matters above all is the official systems of the Church. Here is a refreshing affirmation of a theology which roots the Church in the world. However, he is keen to ensure that the Church's real task is to enunciate principles, not to get embroiled in party politics. He writes: 'We must be careful that we do not give the impression that the Church is an agency for supporting left-wing policies which are often based on presuppositions entirely un-Christian.' His conviction was that Christians were perfectly entitled to disagree about the details of policy but should be at one on broad issues to do with freedom, human dignity and hope. It was, however, the task of the politician to implement the vision. 'The Church may tell the politician what ends the social order should promote; but it must leave to the politician the devising of the precise means to those ends.'

Temple was a pragmatic moralist. He had an all too realistic view of the 'fallenness' of humankind which in his opinion forbade the Church the temptation to offer simplistic solutions to life's problems. No utopian vision would do because we do not live in a perfect or fully ordered world – this applied to the Church as much as to society itself.

It sometimes puzzles people that the Church of England these days shows an astonishing diversity in its political range. I welcome this diversity because it reflects the confusions and diversities of life. It implies that within the Church it is possible to hold contradictory views and still belong. That is why on the bench of bishops in the House of Lords it will be rare to find a unanimous opinion on any matter to do with details of legislation, although there is strong consensus on broad aims. Not every Christian leader has followed Temple's advice. From time to time such people have called the Church to nail its colours officially to one particular policy line or political party. If Church people do not admit that honest and conscientious people can disagree about the best means through which to achieve desirable goals, they deserve to have little influence.

Let me offer a second reflection about promoting ideals in public life without degenerating into naivety. This concerns the place of self-interest in political and social life. No person is completely disinterested. Christ's command was not 'Thou shalt love thy neighbour *instead of* thyself' but 'love thy neighbour as thyself'. As Temple emphasised: 'A statesman who supposes that a mass of citizens can be governed without appeal to their self-interest is living in dream land and is a public menace.' And then come these much quoted words: 'The art of government in fact is the art of so ordering life that self-interest prompts what justice demands.'

Here perhaps we glimpse a constructive new vision of social

purpose which transcends the traditional, crude antithesis between 'capitalism' and 'socialism'. 'Self-interest' encompasses the ambition, initiative and commitment to 'get on' which are intrinsic to progress. But they must not be unbridled: they have to be harnessed to the good of the whole in a moral context.

This is also the right framework in which to order our thoughts about 'wealth creation'. The motivation of self-interest is a good thing if it is harnessed to the good of society and serving our fellow men. Poor nations are not noted for their generosity to their very poor. Distributed wealth can only come from the existence of wealth to distribute. Moreover the nation has to earn its living just as much as any citizen. Nor in my view should the Christian have any inhibitions about striving for excellence through strenuous competition, so long as the winners do not behave improperly or trample on the losers. I do not believe that any vision of society which overlooks these points will be taken very seriously, nor indeed should it. On the other hand, once the pursuit of individual gain becomes *disconnected* from a wider sense of moral purpose – or a substitute for thinking about a shared sense of purpose at all – then we are in deep trouble.

I have argued that the Church has a right and duty to interest itself in social and political matters, that our society is in dire need of a fresh sense of purpose but will not respond to naive appeals to self-sacrifice. There is indeed a careful balance to be struck by the Church and voluntary organisations between 'speaking out' for ideals, visions and goals to which they aspire and recognising the real constraints under which people work in economic and political spheres. This balancing act is very difficult since both elements are crucially important. For example, I am often approached by marginalised groups to 'speak out' for them. Often I am attracted by their arguments and feel their strength. Yet a closer look at what some groups demand reveals a complete unrealism about the constraints under which politicians work. The Church itself will become progressively marginalised if it speaks out too often in this mode. On the other hand, it is equally tempting for any Church, and this is particularly relevant to the

Established Church, to show such a complete understanding of the problems and dilemmas of our political leaders that criticism is stifled and no distinctive Christian vision is articulated for the benefit of the nation.

Temple himself did not get this balance right on every occasion. Although he is now remembered as one of the most influential Archbishops of the twentieth century, he once created a tremendous rumpus by suggesting that banks should create no more credit! No doubt Temple was mistaken to venture that particular opinion, although anyone who sees the human consequences of too much debt will sympathise with his position. But the occasional lapse was a small price to pay for his achievement in breaking through a paralysing tradition that the most essential virtue in a Church of England leader is prudence. Prudence is a fine virtue, of course, but a leader who only watches his back fails to lead others forward.

At this point we come to the crunch question: If we insist on the right and duty of the Church to seek to influence the social order in conformity with what it perceives to be the loving purposes of God, and if we eschew the utopian and political rhetoric so beloved of marginalised groups, what kind of contribution should we strive to make in contemporary society?

First, I suggest we begin with the Christian principle that each and every person is unique and valuable in the eyes of Almighty God. Anything which unnecessarily hampers the development of each human personality, which causes premature death and needless suffering is unacceptable. In some circumstances, this principle has radical and subversive implications for the social order: hence the potent influence of the Churches in the collapse of repressive regimes in much of Eastern Europe and also in the cry for equal rights in South Africa. Hence, too, the turbulent tendencies of priests nearer home in every generation.

From this premise is derived a second principle: that individuals should have the opportunity and be encouraged to rise to their full potential as human beings. This involves a passionate commitment to *both* freedom *and* social concern: not just one or the other. If you thought that William Temple had predictable collectivist opinions, you would be surprised that he wrote this: 'To train citizens in the capacity for freedom and to give them scope for free action is the supreme end of all true politics.' For it is the ability given by God to human beings to exercise free choice which gives them their unique quality and unique responsibility. That is why freedom is the absolute essence of human beings' ability to play their part in God's plan.

Yet Temple combines this fundamental belief with the conviction that 'man is naturally and incurably social'. Temple made a most useful distinction between individuality and personality. True growth enabled each person to develop their personality in fellowship with others and not merely to develop their individuality which, sharpened, divided them from others. Simple freedom from constraints of any kind, without human fellowship, would leave people totally unable to realise their personalities and human potential. It was only through involvement in groups such as the family, the church or synagogue, schools, trade unions and other associations that people could gain their fullness as human beings and exercise freedom effectively and to some coherent end.

The pendulum, having swung towards unrealistic expectations of state action after the War, swung too far towards unbridled individualism in the 1980s. Our commitment to each other and to community, our faith in what we can build *together* as a society, was dangerously weakened. I sense that some of those who promoted the cult of the individual may now be reflecting more carefully on the results when morality itself becomes privatised. Not only is there no escaping the need to take decisions as a society about our collective goods, rights and interests. The doctrine that each person may do whatever they like so long as they do not positively hurt or harm another leads to a society without any sense of shared values. It gives our children and young people no guidance as to what in the view of society as a whole is good, moral behaviour. Individualism then triumphs over community and we are left with a moral void in which everything is relative and nothing is absolutely good. That ultimately leads to the death of society.

The pendulum is now jerking about in a rather confused manner. The vision of what sort of society we want to build together is blurred – and I am not referring to the vision offered by any one political party. Can consumer choice be a satisfactory dominant aim of public policy without undermining social cohesion and moral standards? Do we believe in subsidiarity, and if so, where is it? Can technocratic virtue be combined with a clear sense of moral direction? Is morality simply a matter of individual preference? Can we work for the good of all without denigrating self-interest and enterprise? Is the market our servant or our master? We need fresh thinking, bringing realism and morality together as William Temple did.

In all this, the Church makes its distinctive contribution and suffers like all the rest from ignorance, sin and prejudice. We have as much to learn as to teach. Self-righteous humbug will rightly be ignored. But I dare to offer some vital ingredients which I believe the Church should be injecting into the debate, drawn from our religious faith:

- The idea that there are eternal values, absolute standards of what is good, towards which it is our collective duty to strive, over and above what any particular individual may care to choose.

- A long-term perspective so that the necessarily short-term perspectives of politicians looking towards the next general election can be counter-balanced in a perspective which is related to future generations and to the eternal truths of God.

- Love of each and every neighbour, and hence commitment to freedom exercised in fellowship with other people, and in service to them; hence also a passionate commitment to justice and to the aim that each and every person should feel that they have a dignified place as part of our society.

- Humility and self-discipline – vital if we are to deal effectively with moral, social and environmental problems. Humility before God also teaches us to be tolerant, to regard our strivings for knowledge and truth as provisional, to listen to each other.

- Vigorous participation in the many groups which lie between the individual and central government. The Church and the voluntary sector should indeed remain an independent moral force, enabling people to exercise their freedom, building a healthy civic society, and helping to fashion a sense of common values and vision.

I end with an observation derived from these principles, for the Church must be willing to articulate clear opinions on matters where profound moral issues are involved.

There are reports that the government intends to cut planned spending on overseas aid. I hope these reports are false. Indeed, I suggest, such reports cut across the Prime Minister's words in the debate on economic policy on 24 September 1992 in which he said: 'The voice that is raised to say that we should look after our own interests is the voice of narrow self-interest. Such a voice always has resonance in politics and is almost always wrong. It is a policy more certain to begin with cheers and end in tears than any other policy that has been devised.' If, however, some sharp pruning is about to take place, I want to say that the priorities for cutting and not cutting must necessarily reflect not only political interests but also our sense of values. What sort of society are we? What do we think is most important? I do not underestimate the financial difficulties and political pain which the government faces. But if we think the going is rough here, let us remember the calamities unfolding in other parts of the world struggling with the catastrophe of mass starvation, chronic poverty and disease. The quality of UK overseas aid is good, but its volume falls grossly short of the United Nations aid target – 0.7% of GNP – to which the government is in principle committed. Let us have the moral courage and the moral self-respect to increase it, at least to the extent announced by the Prime Minister after his constructive role at the Rio Earth Summit. To do otherwise would send a sad signal indeed about our sense of values, undermine this country's ability to give a lead in tackling world problems, and give other countries the excuse to go backwards too.

So I return to my title: *Trust in the People: Democracy and the Christian Faith*. I have made it clear that it was Temple's conviction that the Church is rooted in society because it is first rooted in the love and justice of God. Still today, 50 years after Temple lived and worked, the Church continues with that same purpose. Our role is to point to the eternal values and hopes which give humankind its distinctive focus. Morality which is not rooted in a firm religious faith will not endure just as a religious faith which is not strongly social, as well as personal, will be flawed and incomplete. As the Revd Samuel Barnett recognised, 'Trust in the People' and 'Trust in God' go together.

10

Unity and Diversity – On Being European

This is a very significant time for Europe. Members of the European Parliament have worked feverishly to help complete the Single European Act. The Treaty of Maastricht has provoked passionate public debate about our vision of what the European Community should be. Many countries are queuing up to join the different institutions of Europe, but what are they signing up to? What should it mean, to say, 'I am a European'?

In this chapter I would like to explore our sense of identity, and how we define ourselves in relation to other people. I hope you will forgive me if I begin by describing myself rather elaborately in order to make a point. I am the Archbishop of Canterbury, which means that I am both Primate of All England and Bishop to the Diocese of Canterbury. I am a member of the Church of England, and of the worldwide Anglican Communion. I am a Christian. I have so far identified myself in six ways. I am lucky enough to be a husband, father and grandfather, with strong extended family links. I am an East Londoner, a Londoner, a Southerner, English, British and a citizen of the United Kingdom. I am a citizen of the Commonwealth and of the world. All these identities matter to me. I could easily add to the list, but I shall restrict myself to saying that I am also a European.

My point is that our definition of ourselves as we relate to other people has many layers. They need to be held in balance with each other, not regarded as mutually exclusive. Indeed to assert one level of identity at the expense of others is unhealthy and can be downright evil. We narrow our sympathies behind

---

Address to the European Parliament, Strasbourg,
Thursday 11 February 1993.

barriers, we ruin the solidarity between human beings, and we infringe God's commandment to love our neighbour as ourselves. Structures which encourage us to treat other people as beyond the range of our sympathy and concern violate the sacred principle that every single human being is made in God's image and is infinitely valuable.

For me, therefore, being European is precious because it is something additional and inclusive. I do not want to be European *instead of* any of my other identities, but as an extra dimension which brings extra blessings. A jealous Europeanism which seeks to supplant other levels of identity will fail, and will deserve to fail. Moreover, a Europe which sought to erect barriers against the rest of the world would to me be a betrayal, aping the dangerous habits of exclusive nationalism which Europeanism is supposed to overcome.

When President John F Kennedy stood by the Berlin Wall and said: '*Ich bin ein Berliner*', he was breaking barriers down, not setting them up. He was not in any way downplaying his identity as an American, or as a world leader. He was saying, in effect, 'Yes, I am an American and a world leader, and in addition *I identify with you*! I share your values, your aspirations and sorrows, I feel responsible for what happens to you'. It is in that positive, inclusive sense that we can enthusiastically say 'Yes, we are Europeans!'

Let me take another example. The Council of Europe gave birth to the European Convention on Human Rights, and we Europeans are rightly proud of that Convention and associated machinery for its implementation. It is not that European Human Rights are superior to or different from anyone else's human rights! It is not that we seek to deny or frustrate anyone else's rights: indeed, we offer our Convention as a possible model to the wider world. A European Convention represents our attempt in this part of the world to achieve progress together, in a way we could not hope to achieve individually, towards what we believe to be good and right. That is surely what is valuable about being European.

There are many other examples which feature strongly in the work of this great Parliament. I count among them the removal of unnecessary restrictions to the flow of trade and enterprise, so long as these are not mirrored by extra barriers against the rest of the world. I include the co-ordination of policies for trade and aid towards less fortunate parts of the world. I include the growth of sturdy European policies to protect and enhance the environment. In this and other areas it is surely right in principle to seek to negotiate an agreed framework of shared standards, the observance of which by one member will not, therefore, involve a competitive disadvantage as against the others. Here again, through the European dimension – and not least through the deliberations of this Parliament – we can do more to realise our shared values than we could do as competing nation-states alone.

Undergirding all of this is the hope, which Europe should represent above all else, of overcoming the vicious nationalisms, racism and religious bigotries of the past and not only tolerating diversity in peace but cherishing it. That is why the terrible events in the former Yugoslavia have been so traumatic for people in Europe: just as we remembered that this was part of Europe, bloodthirsty nationalistic hatreds burst forth there, as if to mock the growing sense of European identity based precisely on the resurrection of civilisation from such evil atavisms.

The right reaction is surely to redouble our commitment to toleration, love of neighbour, compromise, peace and respect for human rights. Bosnia holds the mirror up to the dark side of Europe's history. It was not so many generations ago that Protestants and Catholics were torturing, burning and murdering each other throughout much of the continent. Moreover, there is nothing new about the collapse of old empires unleashing lethal nationalist and racial conflict, nor the disgusting barbarity of 'ethnic cleansing'. We have seen it all before in Western Europe, and we have also seen that the recovery of hope is possible. There were times when all hope for love, goodness and peace seemed lost, but the suffering of the past gave way to the resurrection of civilised society. The new Europe represents above all the triumph of peace, forgiveness, compromise, co-operation, toleration and human rights over the horrors of nationalism, xenophobia and tribalised religion. That is why the hundreds of thousands of people demonstrating against racism in Germany have been asserting the values of the new Europe as well as the new Germany. We all stand by them and identify with them. We all recognise the responsibility to stand up to the same evil forces at work in our own countries.

Let me make a distinction. I believe that *national identity* is for most people an important and proper part of how they understand themselves and their place in the world. It is part of the feeling of belonging which need not supplant other levels of identity and obligation. Its natural corollary is a similar respect for the national identity of others. *Nationalism*, on the other hand, is inherently dangerous, because it links national identity to the belief that the nation is entitled to a territorially defined state through which to express its collective will to the exclusion of others. There are brief periods, for instance in 1848 or in the last few years, where nationalist movements pitted against corrupt empires can appear to be the vehicle for noble democratic aspirations; but the logic of nationalism proves otherwise. The logic leads to the repression or removal of those who do not share the national identity and to wars with rival nationalisms with designs on the same territory. Nationalism offers only endless suffering and conflict in Ireland, Israel and Palestine, the former Yugoslavia and throughout the world. It thrives on blinkered refusal to extend sympathy and understanding to fellow human beings and stirring up hatred against the alien Other – hence the frequent usefulness to nationalists of racialist stereotyping. We see examples of this trend all over Europe. Nationalism will not tolerate a multi-layered sense of identity and seeks to take the other layers over or eliminate them.

For example, nationalism will try to suborn people's religion to its own identity. Religious institutions, alas, have too often succumbed. As the Revd Samuel Hosain has said: 'When monotheism assumes a national, ethnic or territorial character, God is tribalised and injustice, confusion and strife follow in its trail.'

But the universal character of true religion is always a problem for nationalists and racists. It refuses nationalism's monopolistic demands on our sense of identity and loyalty. One of the most dramatic and moving insights recorded in the Bible is the dawning realisation in the New Testament that the 'people of God' are no longer to be understood as a chosen tribe, but as – everybody! The scales fall from the early Christians' eyes as they realise with wonder and joy that God loves every single person equally, that his perfect goodness and salvation is for all people. The writings of St Paul constitute an irreversible triumph of Christian theology over the boundaries of race and nationhood.

Human institutions can so easily run counter to this sacred insight. A mature Europe will remain self-critical. We have recently witnessed the downfall of the political and ideological centralism based on a subjugated population and inflexible economy. What has replaced it is a European diversity of cultures and interdependent economies which brings both hope and dangers against a background of spiritual confusion. I have already considered the dangers of nationalism and racism. There are also dangers in the triumph of free market capitalism, unless structured so as to serve moral ends. Indeed, the German theologian Jürgen Moltmann asks the question: 'Is democracy in capitalism possible?' His answer is hesitant. He is rightly concerned that, while the 'free market' requires and encourages individual initiative and liberty, the market itself does not concern itself with those who are unable to succeed and who bear the cost of failure. Moltmann is right to raise the question and draws our attention to the need for social justice which should be the mark of any civilised society, within nations and internationally.

In much of Europe, the Churches have surely helped to model and nurture the values of the new Europe, drawing on our own understanding of suffering and resurrection, of sin and forgiveness, of universal love which transcends all human boundaries, of humility before God. Murderous enmity and intolerance between Churches have given way to much dialogue, ever-closer understanding, constant practical collaboration and joyful acceptance of our diversity. I pay tribute to the way in which an increasing number of ecumenical Church bodies are systematically making available their theological insights, their pastoral experience and their knowledge of fellowship and harmony in diversity, to the various institutions of Europe, including this Parliament. The ability of the Churches to bear common witness on social ethics is already highly developed.

Nevertheless, the Churches have more work to do with each other before they can fully realise their potential contribution to the new Europe. We have not yet done enough to deal with our own historical divisions. There is indeed an urgent obligation laid upon all Churches to seek the unity which is the will of God. Our common mission and service is vitiated by our disunity and our unwillingness to acknowledge one another's Churches as full and equal.

Hence, there are two-way benefits from the relationship between European institutions and the Churches. The diversity of Europe meets and welcomes the diversity of the Churches. Diversity need not be another word for disunity but rather a recognition that we all have something to give and share. The diversity which may well be Europe's gift to us all will encourage us to a new spirit of generosity as Churches. Generosity in the sense of recognising the spirit of God working among us and generosity in a willingness to admit failure, faults and weakness. No Church possesses all the truth about God and a simple admission of this fact may well provide a starting point for fresh ecumenical initiatives. In this way, I believe that the Churches need Europe, as much as Europe needs the spiritual vision and energy that Christians can bring.

This brings me to my final point. We shall not strengthen and develop the new Europe on the basis of a spiritual void. Vaclav Havel has complained of 'the omnipresent dictatorship of consumption, production, advertising, commerce, consumer culture' in the Western world, and of a system which 'drives each man into a foxhole of purely material existence', undermining the will and capacity to build a good society together. That kind of civic and spiritual impoverishment is a recruiting ground for the false gods of fundamentalist religion, nationalism and racism. Hence, the appropriate response to the hatreds of the past is not to banish belief to a private domain, leaving no shared values to give direction and purpose to the life we live together as a society. Jacques Delors was right to tell

Church representatives that 'the game will be up' for the new Europe if it fails to develop a sense of shared values with a spiritual dimension as an aspect of European identity. Here again is a reason for intensifying dialogue between the Churches and other institutions of Europe.

I hope this chapter will prove that I am an enthusiastic European, but that this is additional to my enthusiasm for the many other identities with which I began. For me, to be European means to be the opposite of exclusive. It is to embody the values of co-operation, tolerance, forgiveness and peace. It is part of the search for progress in building good, just societies of a kind which could not be achieved by each one acting separately. It is to nurture values and rights, as well as prosperity, which are shared with the wider world. It is to commit oneself to resisting nationalism, xenophobia and racism, and to encouraging a healthy, balanced, multi-layered identity for every citizen. It is to express national, religious and racial identity in peaceful co-existence and respect for others, not in aggression and bloodshed. It is to see each institution and level of identity, from the family and the local town through the nation and the international bodies of Europe and the world, as a means to an end – never as ends in themselves, but each with the potential to contribute towards goodness and justice, in obedience to the loving purposes of God.

I shall pray that the millions of innocent martyrs claimed by religious bigotry, nationalism and racism over the years will be remembered, and that a tolerant, peaceful, open Europe will be built as a fitting memorial to them.

11

Human Rights in Europe

A long queue of new democracies is waiting to join the Council of Europe: it looks as if its new building, which has the capacity for 45 members, will fill up rapidly. The Council has the challenge, it has been aptly said, of helping to anchor them in the logic of democracy. Meanwhile, the passionate debate about the Maastricht Treaty has raised many questions about what vision we should have for Europe. Perhaps the very intractability of some of the issues facing the European Commission leaves the Council of Europe moving nearer to the centre of the stage with its work on the culture of democracy and human rights.

President Jacques Delors recently told Church leaders:

If in the next ten years we haven't managed to give a soul to Europe, to give it spirituality and meaning, the game will be up. This is why I want to revive the intellectual and spiritual debate on Europe.

At a historical turning-point for Europe, full of possibilities for good or evil, it is surely the task of the Council of Europe to represent and articulate a vision and a conviction that the *whole* of Europe matters, not just a part of it.

Certainly, the hopes and values vested in the Council, its conventions and instruments, are part of the soul of Europe and a significant factor in Europe's intellectual and spiritual development.

Not that pluralist democracy and human rights are irrelevant to economic prosperity, either. Surely one of the fascinating and conclusive lessons in recent years from experience around the globe is that long-term, stable, economic prosperity depends to a very large extent on open, democratic structures,

---

Address to the Council of Europe, Strasbourg, Friday 12 February 1993.

effective and impartial administration of justice and a civic culture nurturing liberty, honesty, morality and respect for human rights. One-eyed preoccupation with economic requirements is not only morally flawed, it doesn't work.

On a recent visit to Strasbourg, Her Majesty Queen Elizabeth called the European Convention on Human Rights the Council's 'greatest single achievement'. Indeed, it is widely regarded as the world's most successful human rights instrument. I can hardly exaggerate the importance I attach as a religious leader to this achievement, or my admiration for those who work so tirelessly to administer and develop it.

But it matters how human rights are understood. A notice seen in a Parisian hotel, attempting to be user-friendly to English speakers, said: 'Please leave your values at the desk!' We do not want human rights to be understood like that. Because they ultimately depend on specific and positive beliefs about what is good, it is not enough to regard them as somehow 'self-evident'. They cannot be sustained by utilitarian calculation of what brings the greatest happiness (however defined) to the greatest number. On that basis, why bother about the individual rights of a prisoner? Seen merely as individual entitlements, moreover, rights could encourage an unhealthy concern with self. We need to bring rights and responsibilities together, because both are part of pursuing what we believe to be good. Indeed, a person's rights cannot be effective unless others accept a parallel duty to respect and enforce them.

There is particular danger, it seems to me, if our approach to human rights – or indeed the law generally – becomes too legalistic. If human rights are perceived as essentially a matter for legal experts, the active sympathy of the mass of citizens is switched off, and human rights can begin to seem like a refined minority interest. Only slightly less worrying is another perception that human rights are essentially about the protection of vulnerable minorities, and hence they are the concern of legal experts and liberal pressure groups. That is still much too narrow a constituency, and the Churches have a responsibility to help represent a much wider cross-section of society. For human rights are not only about the rights of minorities, they are above all *an expression of the values of society as a whole*, and testify to how we view human nature.

Indeed, in my view human rights will only be secured for all people if they represent the active moral commitment of the broad mass of citizens. They require the passionate apprehension and advocacy of each successive generation. They need constant nourishment from our fundamental beliefs about human nature – its dignity and abiding significance.

Therefore, as a European and as a Christian, I wish to point up without apology the essential and continuing contribution of Christianity to fertilising our collective commitment to human rights.

First, it is well known that the bedrock of the Judaeo–Christian approach to human nature resides in the value we believe that God gives to human nature, irrespective of class, colour or creed. This starting point leads to a rejection of all opinions that divide people into first, second or third class citizens. Any kind of 'ethnic cleansing' which insists on an ethnically homogeneous nation state is a terrifying form of disobedience to God's will. Civil rights within a society cannot be independent of universal human rights which are the birthright of every person everywhere. These universal and civil human rights require that national identity – of which we may be proud – is relativised in the light of this prior ethic.

Second, Christianity regards humankind from the perspective of *sub specie aeternitatis*. We reject the notion that we are simply finite beings doomed to die and perish without hope. All of us are made in the image and likeness of God and carry within us a divine spark that is precious and unique. This belief in the dignity and infinite value of individual human life is a crucial part of the legacy of European Christianity. I think, for example, of the many Protestant religious–social movements which have resisted tyranny and injustice. I think further of the codifying of Christian social theory in the Papal Encyclical *Rerum Novarum* of 1891 and *Laborem exercens* of 1981 and *Centesimus Annus* of 1991. In these three documents the Christian affirmation of human beings is presented with classical clarity.

Hence, I affirm most gladly the alliances between the

Council of Europe and many other bodies, but particularly the Churches because of their fundamental commitment to human rights as shaped by what we believe about God. When it comes to human rights and morality, there is a never-ending task of education and mission to complement the work of lawyers and judges. Indeed, we must all admit that human rights machinery severed from moral commitment achieves relatively little.

Take some of the precious achievements of the Human Rights Court in Strasbourg. It is good to force certain improvements in the rights of prisoners, but this does not constitute a positive penal policy. Preventing the beating of boys at school is not the same as providing a good education. And limiting the ability of governments to stifle press enquiry does not, alas, of itself produce good newspapers. I make these points, not in any way to belittle the role of human rights machinery in preventing abuses of power, but to emphasise that human rights are the expression of belief about goodness and justice which, by the same token, must be applied in *all* dimensions of our personal and social behaviour.

This is no academic point. As I have pointed out already, in much of Europe we are faced with the privatisation of belief. Pluralism is developed to the point where the aspiration to define shared values is lost. The idea of what is good becomes a matter of individual opinion. Absolute values are abolished, since no authority is accepted beyond the individual conscience. Human rights can be seen by some as an expression of this extreme individualism and privatisation of morality. But, in that case, we have no basis for good prisons, good education, good newspapers or good anything in our social life together. Moreover, if human rights are *not* the expression of shared values, are *not* seen as the embodiment of absolute goodness, but merely a lowest common denominator of individual subjective views with no absolute validity, our collective commitment to human rights will be fatally weakened. This presents a huge challenge to the Christian Churches to represent the values of Christianity in such a way that it may once again become the inspiration of individual and social lifestyles.

However, it is one thing to have a wholesome, positive

commitment to human rights as an expression of shared values, it is another to enforce them effectively in practice. I am extremely concerned about the major backlog of cases which has built up at Strasbourg. I understand that an individual petition lodged today may face five or six years' delay before adjudication. Justice delayed may be justice denied. Sensible lawyers will often advise their clients not to bother. Governments and state agencies have much less to respect or fear. Moreover, five to six years is a very long time in the life of a new fledgling democracy. Will not the new members of the Council from Eastern Europe feel bitterly disappointed, even cheated, if the long-awaited catalyst of justiciable human rights is postponed *sine die* by administrative constipation? Precisely because the European Convention on Human Rights is such a precious embodiment of our aspirations and values at a critical time of change, reforms to ease the log jam are to me of the highest priority, and I am delighted to note that the Presidency has committed itself to pursuing this matter with great urgency. For unless something is done, the arrival of new members to the Council will make matters worse and worse. I know that there are different proposals on the table, and endless scope for prevarication. The political will to find a way forward must, however, be summoned rapidly if one of the most substantial collective achievements of Europe is not to degenerate into frustration and ineffectiveness.

It might well be said that my country is part of the problem. I understand that more cases have been brought to the European Court of Human Rights from the United Kingdom than from most other members. Part of the explanation is that the United Kingdom is one of the few members of the Council which has no written constitution and which has not incorporated the European Convention on Human Rights into our own domestic law. British judges cannot enforce the European Convention in British Courts, so that many cases have to be taken to Strasbourg where the individual can face up to six years' delay. I wonder if this is a tenable position. Where is the famous principle of subsidiarity when it comes to the adjudication of such human rights? I confess to a feeling of unease that we in the UK have to rely on a Court in Strasbourg to blow the whistle on certain human rights abuses in our own country. There is arguably an element of irresponsibility in leaving our citizens to seek their rights through the lengthy procedures of a Strasbourg Court which is struggling with ever-growing responsibilities after the fall of Communism. I hear an argument about parliamentary sovereignty; but if cases are brought to Strasbourg judges anyway, parliamentary sovereignty has already been limited. If we can put our trust in judges in Strasbourg from all over Europe, I cannot myself see why we should not trust our own as well. I dare say there are weighty constitutional considerations which lie beyond the area of an Archbishop's expertise and authority. I respect the dilemmas of the policy-makers. But with more and more countries ready to sign up to the European Convention on Human Rights, putting greater pressure on Strasbourg, the arguments for incorporation of the Convention into British law grow more pressing.

The debate must go on and not be left to lawyers and parliamentarians alone. For the Convention on Human Rights, as I have argued, represents *the aspirations and values of the majority,* not merely the entitlements of individuals and minorities. For European Christians, it represents a significant aspect of obedience to God's commandments and a collective effort to reflect his perfect goodness and love for every human being.

MISSION
IN A QUESTIONING
WORLD

12

Church Planting – A Tool for Mission

I believe that church planting is of immense importance to our Church and all Christian groups. I do not want to give church planting a kind of Anglican 'imprimatur' – that is, a completely clean bill of health. Nor do I wish to give it an episcopal 'health warning' – it's all right as far as it goes, but 'too much of it might damage your church!'

No; I seek only to encourage. An Archbishop should never speak without encouraging his people and there is much to encourage in church planting. But encouragement does not always mean that people will agree with what they hear! So I am making no predictions that you will agree with me and the particular emphases I place on the mission of the Church today. I recently visited a primary school in Lambeth and one of my colleagues carried my robe case into the school. He was rather taken aback when a little girl asked innocently: 'Has God arrived then, Sir?' I am not sure what answer he gave but I am not the Almighty and I therefore make no claims for infallibility on this subject.

What is church planting? The term seems to suggest a building but that is not the case. In most cases 'church planting' is not the founding of a building but the planting of Christians in an area where the Christian presence is weak. It is the transfer of part of a congregation in an area of need with the evangelistic expectation that new people will find faith and the renewal of their spiritual lives. They could be planted in another church building but it is just as likely to be in a secular building – a pub, a community centre, a doctor's surgery or a home with a large lounge.

Address to Church Planting Conference, Holy Trinity Church, Brompton Road, London, Wednesday 22 May 1991.

But why all the fuss about church planting? After all, there have been examples of this throughout Christian history and no one thought twice about it – suddenly someone gives it a grand name and it becomes another cult word! I recall, for example, that Ian Bunting was doing something like this in Durham in the 1970s and no one got over-excited about it then. Many are the parishes which have started congregations on new estates within their boundaries, meeting first in schools (I even heard of one that met in a garage), before putting up a church building. By such means a lot of daughter churches began, some of which are now parish churches. The congregation was created first, often a plant from the parish congregation itself. The bricks and mortar came later. I will return to this dynamic of Church growth later.

One reason for the interest in the subject is most likely that the conditions which now prevail make it a relevant and helpful model of discipline. Let me offer some brush strokes to paint a picture. First, the mood in the Church suggests that we are ready for new initiatives. You may not expect too much from bishops when they gather together but, surely, the Lambeth Conference of 1988 must go down as recording this new mood as the bishops, in an unprecedented way, demanded a massive shift in mission orientation throughout the Communion. The Resolutions did not ignore social concern or pastoral care, but emphasised the priority of evangelism as underscoring other aspects of mission. However the Lambeth Conference should be seen as an expression of a remarkable ecumenical convergence that the final decade of this second millennium should be expressed in proclaiming faith in our risen Lord. To be sure, there are different agendas and different understandings at work. For some it is plain unadulterated preaching of the gospel which is required; for others it is celebration which will draw others in by the sheer attractiveness of a faith expressed in worship and witness; for others still it is evangelising the already evangelised (but who don't look it); and then there is the recovery of the lapsed – one of the targets of the Roman Catholic Decade of Evangelisation and perhaps the most difficult task of all.

Another brush stroke is the plain fact that the church on

the corner with its traditional patterns of ecclesiastical life does not seem to pull in the customers. Whereas the church plants of the 1950s on new estates were mirror images of the life of the nearby parish church, now the plants seem to allow a new freedom. That is part of their very attractiveness, and so we must not be surprised when they run into conflict with the Church of England's structures.

A third brush stroke is the fact of sweeping changes in society resulting in different kinds of communities from the ones which shaped our towns and villages so that we are more mobile, more urban, more individualistic and more critical. We are less likely to be influenced by what our parents and grandparents believed and thought than previous generations. So religion, as I have already noted, is less likely to be a matter of culture, more of choice. But the impact of peer group pressure is as enormous in religion as in anything else. Young people like to think of themselves as not conforming to earlier generations of 'blinkered tradition'; yet not to conform to the expectation of your peers is very testing indeed. That is why it is so difficult for many people outside the Christian community to break into it for they are often moving from one sort of peer group to another. It is also the reason why so many Evangelicals who often talk about outreach actually spend most of their time with other Evangelicals.

But having said all that, there is no evidence that modern people need God less; there is still wistfulness for a genuine spirituality. Many would agree with Sir Neville Mott who wrote an article in *The Times* which ended with the words: 'I believe it better and more interesting and fulfilling to build a personal faith in our historic, religious tradition than to throw it all away and start again in the arid plains of atheism.'

So to the question: Why church planting? The answer could be as simple as the answer of Willy Sutton the American gangster. When asked why he robbed banks, he replied: 'Because that is where the money is!' And the church planter could reply: 'Because that is where people are; away from historical forms of Christianity – in their homes and clubs and there we must go.'

Let us now dig a little deeper and apply some theological insights to church planting.

First, the Anglican understanding of the Church is rooted in episcopal leadership and parochial structure. I am sure that in stating this I do not have to justify episcopacy. We are not talking about authoritarian oversight but leadership of God's mission to take the love of Christ into the world and to build up his Church. Historically, episcopacy is arguably the most ancient of Church orders. It is clearly evidenced in the foundation of our Church. Gregory the Great sent Augustine to evangelise Britain and after planting the Church Augustine returned to the Continent to be consecrated Bishop of the English by St Virgilius. The parochial structure of our country followed soon after the foundation of the Church. Theodore of Tarsus, an Archbishop from Asia, must surely be one of the most remarkable Archbishops of all time. It was he who structured the parish base of our Church, rooting its missionary concern in pastoral care and regular worship. It was he who saw that by dividing the country up into districts or parishes, the form of the Church could be given local expression. He thus gave utterance to an incarnational view of the Church, that is to say, wherever a person might be in our land, there he or she can receive the benefits of the Church and gain hope and challenge; there in the local worshipping church, we can receive the grace of the sacraments; there in the preaching of the word, we can be built up in faith.

The physical building was also more, far more than a mere building, it stood as a visible sign of God's presence. As Michael Nazir–Ali writes in his book, *From Everywhere to Everywhere*: 'The parochial system has been instrumental in creating a meaningful Christian presence in an effective way and made the church approachable and familiar.'

But the question we face is whether this familiar presence is, or can be made to be, an effective tool of proclaiming faith in God in a modern world.

The deficiencies are all too obvious. What might have been possible for one clergyman and a congregation in maintaining an effective Christian presence in a small rural parish is hardly possible in an urban one of 10,000 souls – and there are many,

many far larger units than that. The thin surpliced line of readers and clergy is stretched to breaking point in all our dioceses, deaneries and parishes.

Church planting, therefore, is seen by many to offer attractive possibilities because it does suggest a way by which more successful churches with energetic lay people can help a neighbouring parish which has fallen on hard times. However, the planting of congregations in someone else's parish, deanery or even diocese raises important theological questions which need to be addressed, and many of them are raised in their sharpest form in David Pytches' recent book, *New Wine in New Wine Skins*. What theological criteria should control our response?

First, I applaud the genuine motive in church planting to be a tool at the service of the Kingdom of God. Parish boundaries are not meant to be separate kingdoms, yet too often there can be an unhealthy competitiveness between parishes. A parish church which, for whatever reason, falls on hard times in its congregational life may find some of the vigorous Christians living within its boundaries worshipping at nearby lively churches. Our mobility has made us more eclectic and, to use a topical word, we can 'opt out' when the going gets tough. And there is an understandable attractiveness in belonging to a large and lively Christian community.

What I hope though is that the dynamic of church planting might lead to greater co-operation across parish boundaries and that people might move back to worship in their immediate locality, not in ones and twos, but as a body. Christian witness in a local community is not aided when our worshipping lives are conducted miles away from where we live. I was told the other day by someone who had preached at a church in central London that he met a family there who come each week from Brighton. That is an extreme example. I confess I don't really understand it, nor do I approve of it!

There are a number of things which stand in the way of the co-operation I am hinting at. One of them is the abuse of the parson's freehold, whereby a priest remains in full possession of his benefice unless he vacates it by death or voluntarily. It does seem from one point of view an iniquitous misuse of privilege if the parson's freehold prevents outreach into the community. While the majority of our clergy are hardworking, conscientious men and women there are sometimes to be found people who have lost their way and who may resist the help of other Christian groups. That is one of the reasons why I hope that we might see the end of freehold or at the very least some reform of it, because its very independence paralyses the mission of the Church – freezing episcopal leadership and cutting off lay participation. In reality, in some situations instead of an episcopal form of Church government there is to be found a despotic form of congregationalism. Such cases, I must repeat, are few – but they do happen. But as things stand at the present moment it is wrong – legally wrong as well as blameworthy – if another Anglican church quite unilaterally decides to muscle in on another parish. While the motive may be honourable, the very action of setting up shop in another person's parish does nothing to build up a sense of co-operation and working together. Rather the reverse, it may even weaken good work being done in the name of Christ and undermine the ministry of a fellow minister and congregation. Let us be truly sensitive to all these personal factors.

Second, we must bear in mind the need to 'inculturate' the gospel. The temptation is to assume that what God has blessed and is blessing in one place he will do next door. But it does not work out that way. At the human level, worship is a curious amalgam of personality, gifts, class structure, relationships and experience; to say nothing of the slow building up of congregational life which may take generations. To believe that we can perpetuate instantly the same kind of experience which launched the church planting vision is a mistake. I believe this needs to be heeded carefully because many of the groups involved in church planting have been heavily influenced by charismatic renewal and there may be the innocent idea that all that is required is faithfulness to the vision and all will be well. The biblical pattern of ministry is that of dying: 'Except a grain of wheat falls into the ground and dies, it abides alone but if it dies it bears much fruit.' There is a cost involved in any real identification with the people we seek to minister to. The moment you plant a congregation of 15, 20, 40, 60 in an area you are committed to that area; to its problems of lostness, to the soullessness of modern life, to the silent cries of the unemployed and the muted screams of the helpless. We dare not go with our own ideas of what they want but listen to what they are asking of us. If the Church is to root itself in the real community then it must reflect that community. This will not be easy.

Now church planting seems to be ideally positioned to reflect that concern. We live in a society which appears to have turned its back on the sacralisation of life. Go to any cathedral and see the hundreds milling around; I have often wondered how many of them really have any concept of sacred space; that here in this place made valid by prayer they are standing on sacred ground. The glorious sounds of choir and organ may ring around them but it is not merely remote and cerebral. Sometimes their expressions and attitudes suggest that it is. So the home, the centre of the community where the informal group can meet for coffee, for some singing to the music group, seems somehow more immediate and accessible.

Yes, we can all understand that and it is one of the reasons behind the growth of the house church movement. But hold on. First, we can assume all too quickly that the sacralisation of space is dead and gone and then we can compound our mistake by assuming that the two approaches are rivals and not allies. For example, do two million people visit Canterbury Cathedral every year just because it is an ancient building? I would guess they go because it is that – and much more besides. I have personal evidence from my experience of Wells Cathedral of people who in Karl Rahner's marvellous words were 'unmusical in religion' finding there and in them a refrain which has led them to the living God – through the tranquillity of a holy place. Second, in a society such as ours when it is so easy for a person to feel overwhelmed by the pressure of life with the consequent feeling that nobody cares, the local church – open, attractive, accessible – still embodies Theodore's principle that the Church proclaims, 'We are here for you'. So Church and plant are not rivals but allies.

But this leads to a third area which poses a question: What are the tangible symbols of Anglicanism in a church planting context? I have a few worries to share with you. For example, how do we distinguish an Anglican church plant from, say, a Nonconformist one? My first worry is that there is a tendency to cut corners on Anglican ways of worship with little or no liturgy and few robes. The service may thus be free and easy, with few frills and no pomp. All well and good we might think. But are we really serving our Church if we obscure important marks of identification? In such a mobile society as ours, the people we bring to faith and who move away should be grafted into Church life elsewhere – have we helped them to feel part of a wider group than our intimate circle? Will they feel part of a national Church, and indeed a worldwide Anglican family? And returning to the very immediacy which is so attractive about simple, unaffected worship, it is certainly the case that when people meet with God they enter upon a journey which takes them more and more into this mystery. Worship erupts and results from encounter. The emerging love relationship can and often does lead to a dissatisfaction with 'wordy' kerygmatic Christianity. History demonstrates how many evangelicals have moved 'up the candle' to embrace a wider catholicism. So there is a real issue here to be addressed: What place has the numinous – quietness, beauty and waiting – in a church plant situation? Just to sharpen this point: I can fully understand the anxiety not to be fettered by tradition, but as history demonstrates profusely, any group quickly creates traditions of its own. We can never be free of tradition and if, as all church planting literature suggests, there is a desire to be biblically based, then precedence, history and Anglican practice must be taken seriously.

Let me attempt to pull this together by flagging up some of these concerns:

1 *Strategy*

I suggest the time will shortly come when bishops will have to develop a strategy for church planting. Initiatives which advance beyond parish boundaries should not be left for DIY enthusiasts. Such a strategy will obviously start from a partnership between the local church and the wider Church represented by the bishop. So, on the one hand, a large church might wish to say to its bishop, 'We are here to be a resource, how can we be used by the wider Church?' There are obviously geographical limitations on the response, but the willingness to be used would be welcomed enormously by bishops. On the other hand, this vision should include the bishop's vision for his diocese: Where are the areas where the Church is demonstrably weak or under-represented? What churches might make a contribution to the life of that place? The Church we are in today offers positive models of such a spirit of co-operation between an active local church and the needs of the wider fellowship.

ii *Authority*

The authority of a bishop is there not to quench the Spirit but to recognise what God is doing and to allow for the exercise of ministry in the wider Church. The bishop has to ensure that the ministry of the local church is properly trained and thoroughly Anglican in its approach. This is not, I repeat, to argue for a rigid conformity; certainly not, for variety of traditions has always been a mark of our comprehensiveness. But the issue of where authority is located is a real issue, especially if the reality is that the authority that really matters has very little to do with the bishop but everything to do with the parent church.

iii *Church Planting as Extension*

Church planting is a tool of mission not the be-all and end-all of mission. As I have already made clear, I do not see it as a replacement for the parish church but as an extension of its life. That is why I strongly urge all parishes of moderate size to consider church planting in its own area. It must be done carefully and prayerfully. But it can be done by a committed group of people who believe they have something to share in an area of the parish. For example, I notice that fewer and fewer churches have evening services; I regret the drift to becoming 'oncers' very much indeed. But if there is no great enthusiasm for Evensong, let us seek ways of growing Sunday evening congregations – by Agape meals, by groups of Christians covenanting to start little house churches on housing estates, etc.

IV *Every Member Ministry*

I welcome church planting because it takes seriously evangelism by the whole church working together and particularly by lay people. We must not underestimate the enormous amount of commitment that will be required by any group which covenants to leave the security of a larger fellowship for a ministry which for months and even years may not be particularly fruitful – the costs can be very great. But I believe that the rewards can also be very great.

V *Ecumenical Consultation*

No attempt should be made at church planting without considering the ecumenical implications of what we are doing. Anglicans cannot afford the luxury of thinking that what we do in our patch is our affair. It is not; any new venture will affect other Christians – Baptists, Methodists, or whoever is working in that area. Let us consult and draw others into our planning so that even though they may not agree with the vision, they can understand why we feel it is right to press on.

Let me close by repeating something I said in my Enthronement Address. There I gave expression to my commitment to growth. I want the Church of England to grow stronger. As a Church inextricably linked with the constitution of our land it is in an unrivalled position of trust and influence. There is a new confidence abroad in our Church; the sap is rising and new life is flowing through the body. Church planting, along with other initiatives in our Church, has great potential as an exciting and positive resource for the Church.

13

The Challenge of Renewal

There is a verse in Romans 12:1-2 in which Paul asks his readers for total commitment: '. . . present your bodies as a living sacrifice . . . transformed by the renewal of your minds.' It is that word *renewal* that I want to discuss here within the context of the Decade of Evangelism.

We live at a very important time for the Christian Church in our land. It has never been easy to be a Christian at any time, but today is particularly hazardous because of the pressures, the problems and the difficulties we face. The kinds of things I have in mind are these. At one time the Church was the centre of activity – now it has to compete with burgeoning leisure industries. From a religion of Christianity as culture we now have Christianity as choice. People can even 'pick and mix' their choice. Then there is the problem of maintaining ancient and expensive buildings, which can result in congregations becoming preoccupied with survival and burdened with fund raising. The problem of an increasing secularism implicitly hostile to any meaningful faith and sometimes explicitly hostile whenever the Church is strong in witness and faith, is another problem. In addition to these things, from time to time we encounter opposition from some people within the Church who do not want to face up to change but want Anglicanism on their own terms. Listen to what Dr A D Gilbert says about Anglicanism in our country: 'Anglicanism is a religion which demands minimum commitment and requiring neither deviation from the generally accepted ethical and social requirements of the wider society nor burdensome donations of time, money or energy.' Paul Avis commenting

Address to Chester Diocese on its 450th anniversary,
Sunday 30 June 1991.

on this agrees that being an Anglican, at least in England, is not too arduous – the conditions for membership are minimal, the requirements for membership of the church electoral roll being merely baptism, and for full communicating membership, confirmation and communion three times a year, of which one occasion shall be Easter Day. Bishop Stephen Neill states: 'To be a bad Anglican is the easiest thing in the world; the amount of effort required . . . is so infinitesimal that it is hardly to be measured. But to be a good Anglican is an exceedingly exacting business.' My point is that there are those who want the easiest possible profession and they will resist any change that might suggest a greater commitment to the tasks facing us.

So there are great challenges facing us, and I could give you many, many more – such as the serious task of reaching the many young people who are alienated through their fault or ours from the Christian Churches. The fact is that an increasing number of people are unaware of the basic story of the Christian faith and Christian morality is no longer the common cement of our national life.

We could so easily give up, but, instead, I offer you a fourfold challenge: the renewal of faith; the renewal of Church life; the renewal of our structures; and the renewal of service.

Let us first consider the *renewal of faith*. I make no apology for starting here, because what people need to hear is that we are thoroughly committed, heart and soul, to the Christian faith which has irrigated and refreshed the hearts and minds of our people since Christianity first came to this land. We do that faith a grave disservice if we undermine it with doubts and questions. That faith is earthed in the fact that Jesus came preaching the gospel of the Kingdom: he died a criminal's death; his followers fled, but within a few days were proclaiming boldly that he was alive; the Christian Church emerged from that amazing maelstrom of death and resurrection. A Church that has any doubts about this deserves to die. From those events the Church of Jesus Christ emerged with vigour, hope and expectancy and has given hope and life to the world.

This is not a cry for fundamentalism – of course not. I am all for sensible, intelligent exploration of the faith; I do not mind real, heart-searching questions. Indeed, that goes on in my life every day. What I am calling for is a confident, bold and uncompromising stand on the faith of the Church. If you know Bristol at all you will know the glorious Clifton Suspension Bridge designed by Isambard Kingdom Brunel. Let me fantasise. Let us suppose he went along to the committee and showed them his marvellous drawings and they 'oohed' and 'aahed' over them. Then he said, 'The only problem is that I have some uncertainty about the bridge on this side as to whether the foundation will be solid enough and I have grave doubts about securing it at the other end!' And the committee will say coolly: 'Well, do your work Mr Brunel and come back to us when you are sure your bridge is solid and secure for people to cross safely over.' I speak with the full knowledge that no architect would ever work in that way, but that is sometimes the way Christians seem to speak. And other people have every right to ask us: 'Do you really believe it yourself? Has it made a difference to the way you live and your lifestyle?'

But in fact you and I have no scriptural authority to talk with diffidence about the faith we hold and we are not encouraged to be timid about the gospel we preach. What gave Paul confidence in Romans 12 was his experience of God's amazing grace which lies behind the first eleven chapters and his assurance that the gospel has the power to change the lives of men and women. And this is still the basis for our faith today. Now this does not mean, as I have said, that we preach it six feet above contradiction. We are all aware of the complexities of modern life; we all know that arrogant and simplistic teaching will only alienate people further. What I call for is a full-blooded commitment to a faith which in Anglican terms is both catholic and reformed.

This leads in to a second renewal – the *renewal of our church life*. Now, in spite of the problems I spoke about at the beginning, we have much to encourage us. I have witnessed a revolution in the life of our Church since the 1970s. Churches are much more open, vibrant and expectant than they used to be. We still complain, but the churches weather on, the work gets done. Some churches explode with people, while others plod on patiently and quietly. I am not among those who almost seem to assume that we have to expect decline as an inevitable fact of English church life. But a renewal is clearly called for. Let me suggest some of the things for you to consider.

First, the revolution of our times is the fact of pluralism. We have moved from religion as culture to religion as choice. This introduces a wholly new element into our thinking; people will not naturally think of your church as a church they might or must join. It means that we have to work for disciples. If the Church is to make disciples it has to go to others; it has to have doors wide enough to let others in. And there are deep challenges for us all whether we are evangelical, catholic or whatever. Let me discuss some of them.

Our worship will change. In spite of what has been written about me, my call is not for modern worship. My call is for accessible worship that meets people's needs. I believe wholeheartedly in the comprehensiveness of our Church and an implication of that is that I want all traditions to grow and for their worship to enrich us all. My challenge to those who are crying out for Prayer Book worship is exactly the same challenge as to others – grow. I ask them, and you all: Where are your ordinands? Where are your young people? What are you offering the wider community? What is your missionary giving like? Let me see what difference your worship is making to your witness, your mission and your outreach programmes. The Church is not a society for the protection of the Prayer Book or the ASB or anything else; it is a society for the propagation of faith in Jesus Christ and there are many different ways of going about that.

I would like to share with you an amazing experience I had when I celebrated at the Festival of St Paul's, Deptford. It is an exceedingly high church in a very poor area with lots of different ethnic groups. The rector at that time was David Diamond, a highly dedicated Anglo-Catholic priest.* The event was called a Pontifical Mass. First I was taken to a leisure centre which had cost the community £7 million; then

*David Diamond died in 1992.

to the church where Romford Drum Band played as we approached the church steps. We entered to find a packed church with 100 or so children crowding the sanctuary. They sang 'Make yourself at home . . .'. We had ethnic dances, followed by a very high mass. The songs and hymns varied from 'Our God reigns' to 'Jerusalem the golden', to the 'And did those feet' to 'John Brown's body'. And would you believe, just after the communion, before the blessing, the band came back in playing 'Jesus Christ, superstar!' There then followed a disco with ethnic foods and a firework display which ended late at night. It was an amazing experience and one I shall never forget. Of course, I found myself uncomfortable theologically at various points, but I rejoiced to see a priest and people reaching out in a deprived area with such vision and relevance.

And this leads into another element; be very careful that in these days when there is such indifference and when disciples are very hard to make that you and I do not erect hurdles that people find difficult to meet. I know the integrity of the gospel makes us want to make sure that people know what they are doing when they bring little children to baptism; I am aware that we do not want the Church to be used for the convenience of others. But we can do incalculable damage when we make demands that do not take into account where people are at. I recall talking with a conscientious vicar in my last diocese who was insisting on a discipline that would mean people coming to church for six months and instruction classes before he would even consider baptising their child. I remarked that I was grateful to God that when I was a baby my parents, who did not go to church, were not rejected by their priest, because I would not be a practising Christian today. Remember the Old Testament picture of Christ in Isaiah 42: 'A dimly burning wick he does not quench.' That is to say, be very gentle with people. Well, we might respond, we don't want God to be used. But who are we to say that? Did God say it? And isn't he used to being used? I speak with reverence but do you never think he must get fed up with being treated by us all as a kind of 'lifeboat God'? But that is the nature of the gospel and woe betide our Church when we start to erect barriers around it. We might think to do so is to protect the purity of faith, but we may find that it is seen as keeping people out. I know there are often worthy and honourable motives at work – but the nature of the Anglican Church is to keep the doors open as wide as possible.

The third renewal is the *renewal of structures*. Paul in Romans envisages the gospel irrigating every aspect of Christian life – social as well as personal. Have you noticed how we tend to apply two standards to the Christian life? We call upon the individual to live a life of faith but when it comes to the Church as a body we seem to apply a different standard which almost comes from the world. Let me explain what I mean. I remember when I was an incumbent in Durham, the PCC got very worried when I and a number of other people tried to apply the lesson of faith to church life. We looked at our missionary giving, which was less than 5%. As I dug deeper I found that the PCC's attitude was that our needs had to be met first; then we paid the diocese very unwillingly and any other demands even more unwillingly. So I made the suggestion that we put ourselves last; we considered our missionary giving and started with 10% of our gross income; then paid the diocesan share on time; and then with what we had left we dealt with the needs of the church. The treasurer was aghast and resigned! We struggled on; a new treasurer was appointed who was prepared to live with the risk and then remarkable things started to happen. Of course we had problems and had to turn to prayer; we had to challenge one another with the demands of realistic giving, but the donations went up and faithfulness was rewarded with vision, with commitment and with new church members.

In Australia there is an awful weed, the seed of which is carried by birds and falls into the branches of trees. The seed puts down a runner in the soil below the tree which steadily grows around the tree and over a period of time strangles it to death. The thing that gives the weed life, is finally killed off by the structure which grows around it. It is an inexact analogy, but it is a warning. Our structures – be they PCCs, deanery structures, ecumenical structures, diocesan bureaucracy, sector ministries, general synods – can create their own life, rest in the branches and steadily take life from the body. Constantly we have to watch this and maintain the servant ministry of such organisations. Constantly we have to ask, whether our structures are serving the purpose for which they were appointed. Are they resourcing the Church generally and lending vigour, imagination and spiritual direction? For many years I resisted requests to put my name forward for General Synod because I felt it was a waste of time. I used to quote Basil of Caesarea who in the fourth century said, 'Synods I salute from afar!' He happened to believe that the harm they did outweighed any good that came from them. Well, it is easy to get cynical. But isn't it time that we did something about it by attempting to make prayer central to such life, by making positive contributions that direct others to a God who wants synods to show faith, hope and love. I hope that in every diocese its synods, its bureaucracy, and its structures may be anchored in a deep spirituality and expressed in a humble confidence in a God who calls us to a radical discipleship.

Finally, there is a *renewal of our service in and to the community.* Paul speaks of the renewal of our minds and sees a place for the renewed Christian community in society, witnessing to its faith and demonstrating by its actions and life that its faith is real and radical. I have already spoken of the church being 'open' and I want to develop that idea. Perhaps one of the greatest developments in the 1980s was *Faith in the City.* In that report of which the Church Urban Fund is but a part, there was a recognition that the Church must never become a ghetto, removed from the pain and suffering of the world. I believe as a result a new confidence in the mission of the Church developed. *Faith in the Countryside* followed and heightened our awareness of the challenges facing the Church there too. But essential to both is the conviction that the gospel is incorrigibly social in its outworking. There are those who want us to preach a spiritual gospel only but it cannot be done. The Christian has something to say about our environment; he has something to say about unemployment; she has something to say about human dignity; he has something to say about matters of war and peace and about moral values and about caring for the homeless and elderly and young, because it flows from gospel values.

This too is part of our mission. Not of course to speak constantly about politics, but to allow the faith we practice to overflow into our social lives. This has exciting possibilities for mission today. Because the genius of Anglicanism is that of the parish structure, we are naturally grafted into the fabric of English society, and our roots are there in our communities. This is a positive element to build on. I can take you to a number of churches in my old diocese where growth has taken place because of churches' commitment to their community. Take the little church in a village near Wells. A number of the lay people were concerned that so few young people came to church. They did a survey and found that there were very few amenities for young people, so they started a youth club based at the church. Gradually that fellowship became a popular feature and young people were grafted into the fellowship of the church. Or take the church near Weston-super-Mare. They did a survey too and discovered the presence of a large number of single parents. At first they recoiled from the problem; they did not know how to handle it. Then they recovered, realised the needs of a number of the young women – unemployed, poor, frightened and helpless – and they started to help. The girls eventually discovered that this church cared for them and they started to care for the things the church cared for. Never despise the context in which you find yourself. Too many people are looking to God to work miracles when the potential for such miracles is there in the soil all around them.

But, of course, it requires more than just one person to set to work. The vision has to be caught by one, then spread to two and three and then a group into the body. We all know the loneliness of ministry. I have great sympathy with the story told of the vicar in the North East who every day went along to the local railway station and as the London express shot through used to cheer at the top of his voice. When asked why he did this, he replied that the train was the only thing that moved in his parish that he didn't have to kick, push or shove!

Renewal. Yes, how we long for it. Renewal of our faith;

renewal of our structures; renewal of church life and community. And all of it is possible. How do I know? Because I have seen it happen time and again and in very ordinary situations too. Relax about results; that is God's affair. Your job and mine is to do our part wholeheartedly. God wants living sacrifices. An American friend of mine put it well when he commented wryly, 'Yes, living sacrifices – the only problem is that we keep wriggling off the altar!'

I mentioned earlier that remarkable service in Deptford, where we sang the modern hymn 'Our God reigns'. What I did not mention was that they made a mistake in printing the chorus which made it read, 'Our Gold reigns'! It made everybody smile because there is not much gold in that part of London. But I am aware that in another church some time back a printer put an 's' in the word 'reign' making it read, 'Our God resigns'. But he never does. It is his work we are doing – so we can be relaxed about it; it is his mission – so we can rejoice; it is in his power that we work – so we can celebrate. Because he reigns – we rejoice.

14

Evangelism – The Glory of God

I have every reason to be personally grateful for the impact of charismatic renewal in my life and for enriching my theology and experience of the Holy Spirit.

We live at a very important time for the Christian Church. I have repeatedly said that for Britain this decade will be a 'make or break' time. Will it result, I have wondered, in churches more committed to evangelism, more open to each other and more open to God himself? Will it result, I have gone on to question, in a greater willingness to enter into the sacrifice of Christ? I hope and trust it will. If the Decade of Evangelism is of God, he will bless it. This decade gives us all a chance to put our house in order, to return to fundamentals, and to ask the Living God to renew us in a new unity of love that 'the world may believe'.

The wonderful chapter of John 17 has been called 'Jesus' high priestly prayer', but that is a description I often question. The title is not so much mistaken as inadequate – it is not high enough. It is not a high priest who is praying but a son who intercedes for his people. This is the theme I wish to explore: the Glory of God, expressed in the glory of a Father's gift and lived out in the glory of Christ's Church.

Glory is the key word of John 17. First we have the 'glory' – *doxa* – of a father's love. The first and last verses of John 17 set the scene. 'Father', says Jesus, 'glorify thy son that the son may glorify thee.' And in verse 26, 'that the love with which you have loved me may be in them'. The glory of God is never abstract and never unrelated – it is always expressed

---

Bible Study teaching at the ICCOWE (International Charismatic Consultation on World Evangelisation) Conference, Brighton, Tuesday 9 July 1991.

in action. And we look for his glory not primarily in images of splendour, wonder and beauty, but in his action in creation and salvation. That glory is expressed in John 3:16: 'For God so loved the world, that he gave his only Son.' We must never separate the Father from other persons of the Godhead – the Father's love is the origin of his gift of Christ and every gift of the Spirit he bestows on his people.

It is in the context of the glory of the Father that we speak of Christ's deity and humanity. Scholars identify two main types of Christology. The first is 'Christology from above'. Christ comes from God: is the divine Son, sent from heaven to earth. The other is 'Christology from below'. In this Christology Jesus is seen primarily as a human being, distinct from us only by reason of his exceptional gifts and spiritual understanding of God. The first Christology sees the distinction of Jesus from us as a distinction of 'kind', the second only of 'degree'.

We need to hold these two Christologies together. I have no doubt that the Church must affirm the glory of God's love in the sending of his Son. That is to say, we should uphold unambiguously the clear New Testament teaching that God sent his son into the world to save humankind. He did not send a prophet, a teacher, a supernumerary, an ambassador – he sent his only Son. And the umbilical cord of mission is cut when the deity of Christ is ignored, challenged or compromised. The great mission-theologian, Max Warren, wrote: 'Mission is not primarily a geographical expression at all. It signifies God sending his Son to share our human condition. Nowhere man is found is outside the range of mission.'

We have to admit that sometimes in charismatic circles the spotlight falls on Christ the Lord to such a degree that a kind of 'Jesuology' emerges. This is not truly biblical. Here Jesus the Son stands before his Father and it is the Father's glory he seeks because he sees mission and service flowing from that source. 'Father, glorify thy son.' But why? Why should Christ be concerned about glory? Verse 3 gives us the answer: 'That they may know thee and Jesus Christ whom thou hast sent.' That is what it is all about – that the world may believe and be brought into the Father's presence.

The glory revealed in Jesus is the glory of self-giving love. This was a constant theme in the teaching of my predecessor, Michael Ramsey. Sometimes it seemed as if every sermon he preached was about 'Glory'. But, he would say, so it should be; that is what the scriptures tell us Jesus reveals. 'Glory', though, is a dangerous word. We bring so many worldly assumptions to it. According to Michael Ramsey:

There is a sharp contrast between divine glory as Jesus discloses it, and human glory as man understands it . . . in ancient secular Greek the word *doxa* meant a man's personal status . . . whereas in biblical Greek it meant the divine power and splendour – now identified in the fourth Gospel with divine self-giving love.

That moves me on to my second point – the glory of a Father's gift. How is the glory of the Father expressed? As Michael Ramsey pointed out, glory in human terms is usually expressed in terms of status, riches, honour and splendour. It is the kind of thing brought to mind by the glamour in glossy American television series. In State and Church life we usually mark it by such things as 'coronations' and 'enthronements' – even of Archbishops of Canterbury. I have to say that I personally did not like that term 'enthronement', even though the term is not serenading an individual but a significant office in the Church of God. The alternative term, 'installation', is no better. That sounds like the sort of thing you do with the central heating or a dishwasher. But I caught sight of a fresh understanding of my enthronement when one of my children came home and said, 'Guess what, today I heard someone talking about the "entombment" of the Archbishop of Canterbury.' My immediate reaction was one of delight because that is exactly what ministry in any form is about – being entombed, going down into death. And that is the way of Christ's glory – it is the obedient and painful entering into the sin, pain and distress of God's creation. John 17:4 says, 'I glorified you on earth'. How? The verse continues, '. . . having accomplished the work you gave me to do'. You can see from this how radical Christianity is in its emphasis on God in his Son taking human form and entering our human life. Here is the scandal of Christianity to all generations – here is the wisdom or the folly of God. You may know of the discovery of the fourth-century mural on the Palatine in Rome of a little page boy, Alexamenos. The mural shows him kneeling before a person on a cross but the figure on the cross has an ass's head. The mocking words below are *Alexamenos sebetai Theon* – Alexamenos worships God! Alexamenos was a brave lad, but in that mural we see expressed the sting and offence of the cross. Let us never forget it. It mocks human wisdom. But there is its glory. The impact of one who stooped so low to raise us so high is revealed. Of course this is very much the emphasis of the Greek Fathers who saw this as a way to interpret what Christ had done: 'He took our nature that we might take his.' This theology known as 'deification' is a very beautiful idea, that God by coming to us has entered into every aspect of human living – our youth, our adulthood, our dying, our sorrows, pains and joys – and he raised it to the very heights of heaven.

I would like to consider some of the implications of all of this for us as I turn to my third point, the glory of Christ in the Church. I know that some will immediately recognise this as very Pauline – Ephesians 3:21, 'To him be glory in the Church and in Christ Jesus'. But the same idea is in John 17. Look at verse 22: 'The glory which you have given to me I have given to them, that the world may believe that you have sent me.'

The glory of the Father's love and the glory of his gift in Christ will always be abstract and irrelevant ideas unless they are earthed and lived out in the life of the Church. That is the burden of Christ's prayer in this chapter. Let us examine some of his points.

First, that we express the glory of Christ when we carry on Christ's mission of manifesting God's name. Here it is expressed in 'keeping the words given to us'. I have no doubt that this means faithfulness to the gospel entrusted to us as a Church. I am sure that this is among the reasons why Charismatic renewal has grown so rapidly and strongly – its commitment to the gospel of Christ and belief that he still confronts people today with the word of life.

Secondly, note the emphasis of Christ's prayer. Of course,

this is one of the reasons why the passage is called the 'high priestly prayer' because Christ intercedes for all people. He stands before God and lifts up his Church and people. And we are reminded by his great example of the importance of prayer for any form of ministry and renewal. We are doing that every time we share in Christ's victory over sin and death and lift up our hearts for our churches in their ministry, mission and life. Some of our churches are facing great times of trial, persecution and social disorder; all are facing complex moral issues; some face the stagnation which is one of the consequences of the great apathy which surrounds the Western Church. And all we can do is to enter into Christ's prayer for his people and the Spirit of God 'who intercedes for us with sighs too deep for words'. Out of a praying people, the glory of God often comes.

I note also the emphasis in verse 15 on entering into the world with Christ. 'I do not pray that you should take them out of the world but that you should keep them.' No, true evangelism is never imposed – it is lived, then believed. Here is an insight we must all heed; the way of Christ is to live *among* us and from that living true sharing of faith will *grow*. I strongly believe that the incarnation gives us the most genuine biblical insight into evangelism. Of course, we need our special evangelists and I think we should be praying for God to raise up a fresh generation of them, but along with such gifted people we need the Church to allow its life to be genuinely evangelistic as we live with others and as our lives testify to the presence of God. This reveals the difference, I believe, between proselytism and evangelism – proselytism is the imposition of my faith on you, not taking into account your culture, your needs and your history. Evangelism is the genuine love for another person which takes on board your culture, your present understanding and allows you room to grow. The Russian philosopher Lec once said memorably: 'God never leaves identical fingerprints.' That is to say, he always allows us our individuality and no two journeys into God will ever be the same. There needs to be a recognition of the preciousness of human nature. A similar thought was sown in my mind by Christopher Lamb, the missiologist, at Selly Oak

College who remarked one day: 'If evangelism is a form of midwifery [Galatians 4:19], we have to be very careful with the forceps.' How true – we need to adopt the art of gentle, loving, patient waiting in and for the Holy Spirit.

Finally, there is our unity in which the glory of Christ is seen. The divisions between the denominations are a terrible wound affecting our evangelism. I believe our gospel is vitiated by the fractured body of Christ. I do not mean that people cannot hear the word of God because of our divisions; I do mean that our witness is deeply hindered by the obvious contradiction that we who preach reconciliation are separated from one another. If we read Acts 15 where we have the account of the first Christian council and compare it with our separate Eucharists as Protestants and Catholics and then try to imagine groups of those early Christians breaking bread separately, it is inconceivable. But that, alas, is the reality now. We are so divided, so flawed. But God is doing new work among us. The old barriers are being torn down. And God's spirit is moving among us – through the reforms begun by the Second Vatican Council; through theological schemes and dialogue; through charismatic renewal where a significant bridge has been erected. And it is my hope that in the Decade of Evangelism we shall grow together, not by denying or ignoring our Church rules, but by patient affirmation of one another's Christianity. The time will surely come when we shall say in unison: 'This is madness; we have no reason to stay apart.' For the last 30 years the search for unity has taken the form of theological dialogue; I believe the form that search will now take is in common witness to the world that in Christ God has revealed himself as our Lord and our God.

Glory – the glory of the Father's love; the glory of a Father's gift; and the glory of Father, Son and Holy Spirit in his Church – in you and me. In the whole Christ, God and man, we have the entire substance we need for the preaching of the good news. And in the Holy Spirit, we have all the resources we need.

15

Hope for the Homeless

In a passage from Luke's Gospel, Jesus is heard reading the scriptures. He takes a portion from the Book of the Prophet Isaiah and proclaims:

'The Spirit of the Lord is upon me, because he has anointed me to preach good news to the poor. He has sent me to proclaim release to the captives and recovery of sight to the blind, to set at liberty those who are oppressed, to proclaim the acceptable year of the Lord.' LUKE 4:18–19

Then Jesus preaches one of the shortest, but among the most stunning sermons on record. He simply says to the congregation, 'Today this Scripture has been fulfilled in your very hearing.'

The history of Christianity is, in part, the out-working of that very claim. Those who follow Jesus are called to share his concern for the poor, his compassion for prisoners and captives, his desire to heal the sick, his longing for freedom for the oppressed. All these are inescapable obligations of loyalty to Jesus Christ and faith in him.

I preached in Southwark Cathedral at a service organised by Shaftesbury Housing to celebrate its twenty-first birthday. In itself it was a sign of the greatly increased Christian activity in this area of housing the homeless over the past decade or more. The involvement of the churches in the homelessness problem in London is impressive. One list I saw recently showed 72 Church-related organisations currently active in this field. Some, like the Church Army or the Salvation Army, have a long history of this form of social involvement. But

---

Address to a Vigil for the Homeless, St John's, Waterloo, Monday 4 November 1991.

what I found striking, as I looked at that list, was how many of these bodies had been established in the 1980s. The Church is often unfairly labelled as being ineffective and irrelevant, yet it continues to respond imaginatively to some of the most pressing demands of our time. That is what discipleship involves.

But it is uncomfortable work, and it teaches the Church itself not to be complacent. It reminds us that there are still many people who drop through the net, who are reduced to a level at which they can scarcely begin to help themselves. These are the people for whom Jesus desires liberty, upon whom he wants to bring the gifts and benefits of the Lord's favour. While everyone knows that a lot of people – a thousand or more – sleep rough in London every night, the problem we are addressing today is much more serious than it appears on the surface. Indeed, over the past century, we have never managed to find an adequate answer to the housing problem.

In 1884 a report was published by the Royal Commission on the Housing of the Working Classes. The very title has a message from a different age. But it reminds us that the problem we are addressing in 1991 is not new. The difficulty then was that the working classes could not pay for the sort of housing that they needed and deserved. Without a subsidy there has never been sufficient financial incentive for the private landlord to provide for the poorest people, without overcrowding them. That Royal Commission more than a century ago discovered appalling conditions, a prime cause of which was poverty, or what they called 'the relationship borne by the wages people receive to the rents they have to pay'. Too little money. Too high rents. Consequence – poverty and homelessness.

The conditions in which *most* people live today are vastly improved on a century ago, but the availability of rented accommodation has been reduced enormously. And this adds greatly to the difficulty single people and low income families have in securing a home. Rarely do I find statistics impress me, but when I learned that over the past decade over 350,000 units of rented accommodation have been lost in London alone, I began to understand the magnitude of the problem.

Too often we see homelessness simply as the problem of those who are sleeping rough. Theirs is the most tragic manifestation of this phenomenon, but it is not the only one. The thousand or two thousand people who sleep outside each night in London are part of a small army of squatters, people in night shelters and hostels, people in temporary accommodation, people living in overcrowded conditions, often as unwilling guests of an acquaintance. There are simply too many people, especially single people, who have some sort of shelter but don't know what it is to have a home.

Why should an Archbishop be bothered about this? It is clear that some of the people who write to me wish that I did not concern myself with social issues. But I look back to that text from Luke. It is the oppressed, the captives, the poor, whom the Lord Jesus Christ wants to be free. I believe we need to take his words literally. Jesus Christ wants people to have life, and to have it in abundance. Homelessness can lead so easily to utter hopelessness, and above all else, Jesus comes to bring us hope.

There are two dangers for the Church in exercising a ministry to the homeless and seeking to help them. One is strategic and the other spiritual. The strategic danger is to ignore the providers of the resources which can most effectively deal with this problem. Recent government initiatives to help the homeless have begun to reverse some of the worst trends of recent years. The task facing all Church agencies is to work in partnership and co-operation with the statutory bodies in this field. In a recent speech at a Church Urban Fund seminar I chided those who seek to pit Church and State against each other. We will sometimes be coming at the same problem from different angles, but that only makes it more important to find ways of working together.

The second, more insidious, danger is a spiritual one. There is nothing worse than the Christian who ministers to the needs of others without recognising that their own needs might be as great or greater. The poor, the oppressed, the captives, include *us* as well. No matter how secure our homes, how regular our incomes, how stable our family lives, each of us needs to know the freedom that Jesus Christ can bring.

The 1991 World Council of Churches Assembly was held in Canberra. It was at its best in its worship. Even those more traditional in their preferences could not fail to be moved by the imaginative but restrained use of dance and drama. 'Come, Holy Spirit, Renew the Whole Creation' was the theme of the Assembly. This longing for renewal and freedom, for dignity and identity, for security and acceptance was illustrated one day by a group of young people bound in chains around the altar. They were gradually released from their chains as the gospel was read, the gospel being those same verses from Luke. As the words were read, the young people removed their chains, and laid them on the altar. It was a sign that their chains had not disappeared or become immaterial, but were taken up by God himself in Jesus Christ. For the gospel is not only about a liberation from the horrors of slavery or captivity or wretchedness. It is about a stronger freedom, a liberation from the power of death itself. That is what Jesus, the truly free human being, offers us.

We pray that all homeless people may know the security of a home, the stability in relationships it can bring, the identity which having a place of your own creates. But we pray for something deeper too – the freedom for which we all long, and which is offered to us in the life and work of Jesus Christ. We have our chains from which we need to be liberated by the grace and power of Christ. And when our world glimpses that, then truly we can pray his will be done, and his Kingdom come on earth as it is in heaven.

16

The Church's Priorities

One of the most intriguing road signs simply declares 'Changed priorities ahead'. It is rather unnerving. You are not sure what you might encounter. So you scan the horizon to see what lies ahead.

What are the priorities for the Church over the next five years? Although we live in a rapidly changing world our priorities remain those our Lord gave his first disciples. These days, companies issue their own mission statements, but the Church does not need to do so. From the beginning we have been charged to be a people of praise and worship; to call people to the living God and spread the message of God's redeeming love in Christ; to build up the body of Christ in the world.

To these goals all of us willingly say 'Amen'. They are enshrined in our Ordinal, Homilies and Prayer Books. But each generation must ask: How should *we* interpret the gospel message for our society? What are *our* particular priorities?

There are three essential priorities I want to commend:

1. to build *confidence* in the message and work of the Church;
2. to grapple with the challenge of *evangelism*;
3. to deepen our *internal* unity.

First, with regard to having *confidence in the message we proclaim*, the Church finds itself on the defensive in the face of an increasingly secular society. As material prosperity grows, so people focus increasingly on that prosperity as the sole measure of human wellbeing.

Presidential Address to the General Synod, Church House, London, Thursday 14 November 1991.

My personal commitment to the pastoral ministry makes me feel especially sympathetic to the despondency experienced by some parochial clergy. As I have said earlier, they face enormous competition from the leisure industry, and the burdens of trying to maintain expensive church buildings. They also worry that they have insufficient lay leadership to keep existing organisations going. I remember the despondent voice of a young clergyman in my last diocese. When I was addressing his deanery on 'Bringing a congregation to life', he responded, 'A cough in my congregation is the only evidence of life!' If we add to all this the constant refrain from the media that the Church is in decline, in confusion and always squabbling, there is good reason for confidence to fade in any congregation.

What is the antidote? First of all, we must recognise that there are plenty of good things going on to encourage us and give us confidence. I expect we all know of growing churches of every tradition. People are coming to faith in Christ in a myriad of different ways. We might point to the 1.5 million children who are in touch with the Church each week. We might think of the enormous impact that the Church Urban Fund has made on many communities. And so I could go on. We are not good at blowing our own trumpet, which means we may fail to observe the ways in which God is blessing his Church.

Of course our confidence is misplaced if it is merely in ourselves and our own successes. Our confidence must be in the living God, who continues to bring life from death and hope from the darkest places. Our gospel is always honed in opposition to sin and death so we should never be surprised to find ourselves constantly challenged. My meeting last week with Patriarch Alexii of Moscow made me thankful that our Church did not have to face the 70 years of oppression, persecution and hatred that his people had faced. But an indifferent secularism is no kinder than hostile atheism. It still offers us a challenge. In the place of the individual imprisoned by power and material values we assert her or his unique worth in the eyes of God. Instead of greed, we preach sacrifice.

Instead of conflict, we urge peace. This gospel message is timeless.

As well as showing confidence in the message and its power to change people and structures, we need greater confidence in the work of the Church. Synodical government is central to this. Reservations about synodical government are expressed from time to time in the media, and more worryingly in the parishes. Some criticisms are based on ignorance; others, however, are less easily dismissed and the challenge must be addressed. Even synods can lose their way and get out of touch with the needs of the people they represent. Honest evaluation is essential if we are to do our work well and for the glory of God. For these reasons, a committee has been formed by the General Synod and will consider how best to set up the major review of synodical government which we hope to complete before the end of this quinquennium. It is appropriate that twenty years after its inauguration, the foundations of synodical government should be examined in the light of experience.

In the meantime, I hope we shall take what steps we can to improve our synodical procedures where these are manifestly unsatisfactory without necessarily waiting for the outcome of the proposed review. I shall be encouraging the Standing Committee in that direction, whenever sensible suggestions for reform can be agreed. Finally, a heavy onus rests on the Synod of keeping before it the vision of itself as a *holy gathering*. That its members worship together is an integral and important part of its meetings.

Secondly, I turn to *encouraging evangelism*. The task our Lord entrusted to his Church was to preach the gospel to all people, to baptise them and to make disciples.

Some people question the need for a Decade of Evangelism. Have we not, they ask, been proclaiming the gospel before 1991 and shall we not go on doing it long after the Decade has gone? Of course we have and of course we shall. But none of that diminishes the value of the Decade as a means of focusing our gaze, renewing our commitment, and ensuring that we are better equipped to make new disciples.

A new and prominent role has been given to two

experienced teachers and evangelists for the work of the Decade. Bishop Michael Marshall and Canon Michael Green accepted an invitation I issued, with the full co-operation of the Archbishop of York, to work with us. This is a personal initiative which will, I hope, raise the profile of evangelism in our Church, and release more resources for it. We will hear more of Springboard, as it is called, as the Decade progresses.

Anglican evangelism, however, has always been multi-faceted. There is a place for the gifted evangelist, but evangelism is also made possible through pastoral care, through bringing children to baptism, through the nurture of those who are confirmed and through the regular teaching of the faith in Sunday schools and Sunday sermons. Churches which are not giving priority to work with the young are not building for the future. Clearly Synod's role in all this is limited. Its task is to ensure that dioceses and parishes are adequately serviced and resourced to do their work effectively.

Evangelism, however, is not just about individual conversion. It is also about witnessing to Christ in the world. The Church cannot confine itself to matters of individual morality. Inevitably it will be called upon to apply Christian values to society. As we have already said, misunderstandings make this difficult there too. Church leaders are called on to condemn wrong doing, but are also obliged to draw attention to the circumstances in which wrongdoing flourishes. We are called upon to attack sexual licence, but we cannot do so with integrity without also pointing to the responsibility of the media and advertising in fostering such licence. Preaching the gospel always takes us into the public arena – where people live, work, make love and die. That is where the Church is called to be.

Thirdly, there is an *urgent need to deal with our internal unity*. On that curious ecclesiological map which is Church life each of us has both a starting place and a present home. The wonderful breadth of Anglicanism gives its members the reassurance that they have a right to belong. Anglican comprehensiveness is something to be cherished. But there are times when it is brought to breaking point. When facing potentially divisive issues, such as the ordination of women to the priesthood, we must always remember that deep concerns, passionate commitment, fierce integrity and distress about the unity of the Church, are not the prerogatives of one side only. We are all committed, all concerned, but all of us are fallible stumbling creatures. Throughout the noise of debate we need to keep three important considerations in mind.

Firstly, the need for sensitivity towards each other. We must listen courteously to our opponents and respect the integrity with which they hold their views, however much we disagree.

Secondly, the unity of the Church is a sacred trust. We must be mindful of the effect which our words and actions will have on that unity. I remind myself that applies to Archbishops as much as to anyone else. So we must not make reckless prophecies about what might be the effect on the Church if any piece of legislation is either rejected or accepted. We simply do not know.

Thirdly, we must at all times be open to the workings of the Holy Spirit. I recall the decision of the Apostles recorded in Acts 15 on the circumcision of the Gentiles which opened up a new ministry for the Church. For balance and fairness I remind you of the Holy Spirit's operation in Acts 16 where a door the apostle wanted to open was refused. God had other ideas.

But enhancing our unity is not enough. Our task is to build up the wider unity of the Church of God, a unity which is bigger than Anglicanism itself. We stand at a moment of great opportunity. While the obstacles to unity are considerable, the prospects for real progress are encouraging. In Great Britain the newly-established ecumenical bodies are beginning to mature. Future relationships appear very strong. In Europe too the Churches face great opportunities with some apprehension. Anglicanism has much to offer as a catalyst for unity between the great traditions which continue to prosper in Europe.

These then are the three main priorities for the Church which both the Archbishop of York and I wish to endorse most strongly. The need to build up confidence; to encourage evangelism; to deepen our unity.

But how are they to be achieved?

I believe three factors are essential to our success. The first is *resources*. We are about to be faced with one of the most difficult financial challenges the Church has ever encountered. The Church experienced a decade of financial prosperity in the 1980s because of the wise investment policy of the Church Commissioners. However the recession is having and will have a marked impact on the income of the Commissioners which can only be passed on to the dioceses and parishes. As well as recognising the difficulties, we must also see the opportunity that this presents. We have been cushioned from harsh financial realities through the generosity of the past. We are now being challenged to improve our stewardship and increase our giving.

That we can do it, I have no doubt. People are ready to give generously. But they will not do so unless they are convinced of the gospel, the vision which impels their giving. And they must have confidence in the Church, a confidence that it is a lively witness to the gospel in its debates and decisions.

The second factor is *improved communications*. We must make our message plain. At Church House, the Communications Department has already been greatly improved, and individual synod members have a major role to play. They must respect one another, by their commitment to the mission of the Church and by communicating effectively with those they represent in the deaneries and dioceses.

The third factor required to achieve our goals is *deep spiritual roots* for evangelism and mission. People will not be drawn to a work-dominated, activity-driven Church. Instead they will be drawn to a Church in which prayer and the spiritual journey are both the hallmarks and guiding vision.

I began with one road sign. Let me end with another. As I travel along the A2 towards Canterbury each week I am often amused by the large, glossy sign put up by the London Borough of Southwark. It reads: 'Regenerating the Old Kent Road'! Well, if you are familiar with the Old Kent Road you will know only too well that it needs regenerating! The paradox is that the regeneration means that travel is even slower now than before and the bottlenecks are even more frequent and more wearing.

There is a parable there. Regenerating the Church will mean

that for a time there is disorder, chaos and bottlenecks. The same holds true in our individual lives. The Church must always live with the provisional in its own life and that of its members. But if God is the architect of our future, the bottlenecks and the disturbance to our journey as pilgrims along the Christian way will ultimately be worthwhile.

17

Who Do You Say I Am?

One of the real pleasures my wife and I have had since taking this demanding post has been meeting many of our country's political leaders and I am glad to say that strong friendships are forming. I have always been an admirer of the commitment and ability of many politicians, and I for one do not subscribe to that cruel definition of a politician as 'a person who approaches every question with an open mouth'. But, of course, we clergy have our eccentrics too. I read about an elderly clergyman who lived into his nineties. He claimed that the sole reason for his longevity was the fact that instead of sprinkling sugar on his cornflakes he sprinkled gunpowder. He died when he was 95. He left a widow and three sons and a very large crater where the crematorium used to stand!

If you have ever been to Israel, you will probably have visited Caesarea Philippi in the very north of the country. In the New Testament it is associated with one of the most important episodes in the life of Jesus. There was in Jesus' time a shrine there to the god Pan, god of all living things. It was at this place that Jesus asked his disciples, 'Who do people say I am?' They speculated. Peter replied, 'Some say that you are a prophet; some even say you are Elijah returned to earth.' Then Jesus, very casually I believe, said, 'But you – who do you say I am?' And there came Peter's tremendous confession of faith: 'You are the Christ, Son of the Living God.' Jesus then called his disciples to take up their cross and follow him.

This is one of my favourite passages because it goes straight to the heart of what it is about. I still struggle with its implications and it still beckons me onward in my journey.

Address to the Parliamentary Christian Fellowship, Westminster,
Wednesday 4 December 1991.

The passage speaks of the *greatest question we could ever be asked*: Who do you say I am? We live in a very questioning age, where we rarely stop for answers. I find it interesting that both Houses of Parliament have a 'Question Time'. It is not called 'Answer Time', I suppose because if you are in opposition it is considered axiomatic that the replies are never answers. They do not satisfy the opposition. But normally questions drive us on in search of new knowledge; of finding better solutions; of finding answers.

But sometimes there *are* no answers, yet the questions are still important. Modern people have to live with the provisional – sometimes the issues we face are so intractable that we have to put them in our pending tray and hope that one day the answer will come.

I have little doubt that the question Jesus asked his disciples – 'Who is Jesus Christ?' – is among the most important we could ever be asked. Logic will tell us that if he were truly who he claimed to be then it is the most thrilling, awesome and wonderful discovery we could ever make. I believe that the mission of the Church – my Church and your Church – is to draw attention to Christ in our day, without apology, without shame or embarrassment, and to make him known – not as an ancient historical figure but as a Living Lord and friend.

Why is this important? The temptation for any Church is to retreat into moralism; to talk about being good citizens, about right conduct, about Christian behaviour and so on. And all that is good and proper for Christians to talk about. I notice, for example, that when I talk about social things – or anything which appears to be the sphere of the politician – the media swarm around me like maniacal bees! Yet I, too, am a legislator. When I speak about faith, about relationship with God, my views are not reported. While we must never renege on our commitment to the social implications of the gospel, I and my Church must never wander away from our primary task – to present Jesus Christ in such a way that people are drawn to his life and discover him to be very much our contemporary.

And make no mistake – he is our contemporary. I still get excited about the New Testament as I read it. I am quite certain that few serious readers of the New Testament can avoid what J B Phillips called 'the ring of truth' – that quiet conviction that as you study the resurrection, for example, you find yourself caught up in the sheer excitement that, yes, it really did happen because all the other hypotheses are out of the question.

'Who do you say I am?' really *is* the most important question you and I could ever be asked. From the tiny beginnings of Christianity we have a worldwide Church of something like 1,800 million followers. Yes, we are so divided; so weak; so pig-headed and lazy – but the show still goes on and disciples are being made day by day. I received a letter the other day from a lawyer who after years away from the Christian faith made a slow journey back into the Church. What was the key factor for him? It was discovering that Jesus Christ was real – and that he was alive today.

The second thing that leaps from that story for me is the impressive person, Jesus himself, and I have discovered over the years that he is the greatest person who ever lived, and I want to base my life on him. I know that there have been many, many great historical figures – Socrates, Paul, Thomas Aquinas – so very many. But Jesus Christ somehow eclipses them. Is Jesus significant because of his teaching? He would, by now, be a forgotten hero if he had relied on his ethical code being remembered. Isn't his pre-eminence in history caused because his suffering and death and resurrection were all of a piece with his life? His teaching took on a new significance because the eye of faith saw who he really was. Isn't that why he's more than a passing hero?

We live in a society which thrives on heroes, but many of them come and go. You may recall that not all that long ago Kevin Keegan was the hero of the Kop at Anfield. There used to be a banner that they waved: 'Some say "God" we say "Keegan".' Well, a few years ago I tried an experiment. I asked a few boys of about twelve, 'Who is Kevin Keegan?' and no one knew his name! How quickly our heroes come and go!

Let me share with you another concern of mine. We live in a society profoundly influenced and shaped by Christianity. Its ethics, theology and ideas are impregnated in our culture, customs and life. It has been the genius of Christ who has stamped us. But we are in danger of losing it for a 'mess of potage'. From my vantage point I see the Christian faith being pushed out little by little. It is constantly being marginalised and distanced – in education, in the media, in the professions, in our laws, in our cultural life. Whatever view we might have about Sunday trading, the fact remains that the idea of Sunday being special because it is part of a covenant relationship with God is only held by a very few. People are more likely to be convinced by the view that people have a right to choose, and if they want to spend their Sunday shopping then good luck to them. It is a reasonable point of view if all days are alike and if secularism reigns. But today the Church is given freedom to practise its religion and it is up to us to create a prevailing Christian ethos in which Christian morality may once again be the norm, and to ensure that young people do know the story of Christ and have the basics to make up their mind about him.

In a recent sermon I quoted these words by Ernst Bloch, the famous Marxist philosopher. Commenting on Western civilis-ation, he said that modern society is suffering from a disease called 'death by bread alone'. He writes: 'It is like a vast supermarket in which absentmindedly, yet intent on what we are doing, we push our shopping trolleys up one aisle and down the other, while death and alienation have the run of the place.' This 'death by bread alone', he argued, means that Western people have lost sight of spiritual and eternal values and now only perceive material and temporal aims to be the ones that matter. It is ironic that it was a Marxist who wrote those words, but perhaps not very surprising, because it is from the secularism of an atheistic communism that Alexander Solzhenitzyn wrote some years ago, 'Man needs spiritual revival for physical survival'. In recent years we have seen millions abandoning communism and returning to their churches again. Hungry certainly for bread, but not bread alone. And we must seriously consider that if Christianity declines in this country secularism will not reign for long – other spiritual faiths will come in to take its place.

This leads me to my third point – the question, the person

and the call to follow. One of the most moving things I have ever heard happened when I was at Trinity College, Bristol. I had a Ugandan student named John Waromoyi. We were drinking coffee together one day. On the spur of the moment I asked him to tell me when he decided to be a Christian. I knew he came from a Christian tribe in the north of the country. He then told me a horrific tale.

I was nineteen at the time. I was with a group of friends talking together when two army trucks rolled through the village. We did not pay them much attention because the army was often around chasing terrorists. But on this occasion they stopped and about twenty of us were rounded up and lined up against a wall. We were accused of being terrorists and a machine gun was set up in front of us. Suddenly I realised that this was real and I was going to die: I felt unprepared and ashamed that although I was from a Christian village, my faith was skin deep. I started to pray within. People were screaming and crying. Suddenly I was ordered to one side and kicked into a ditch. Then they opened up and machine-gunned the other nineteen – among them two cousins and the rest of all my friends. I don't know why I was released – but that was the time when I decided to take up my cross and follow Christ.

Well, I nearly choked on my coffee because our Christianity seems so easy in comparison. But is it? Perhaps not; it is difficult to swim against the tide. Young people find it hard these days to stand out as Christian followers and we older people find it no easier. I honestly believe that what our society needs is more explicit Christianity; more people prepared to stand up and be counted. That is why I was so delighted to see so many at the National Prayer Breakfast – people who were prepared to be seen at such a thing. But our society needs more people who are prepared not only to live quietly as Christians but to be seen to be supporting the Church, people prepared when the time is right to say: 'Well, you know, I am a Christian – perhaps not a very good one and not always a good example – but one who is struggling to follow.'

There are different ways of living the Christian life, and following God's call. Some people are vocal in their evangelism; others seek a quiet life of prayer. Both can be effective. For example, at the end of the war Brother Roger Schutz settled in Taizé in the Burgundian countryside and founded an ecumenical religious community dedicated to peace and reconciliation. He had no plans to evangelise young people. His plan was simply to pray with his brothers and leave the rest to God. Thousands of young people have, for years, come from all parts of Europe and further afield and found renewal in faith and hope at Taizé. They see there the call to discipleship in worship and service – and they are drawn to the focus of it all – Jesus Christ.

There are different ways of ministering in response to the gospel. I am glad the Church of England can embrace such different styles. I want to belong to a Church which includes the charismatic, the conservative evangelical, the liberal, the traditional catholic. From each strand of our tradition I have benefited personally. Last August I visited Papua New Guinea where the Anglican Church, now one hundred years old, is firmly in the Catholic tradition. I felt entirely at home. The worship was deeply reverent, full of local culture in dress, dance and songs, and the Church knew how to make disciples and had learned that its martyrs were indeed the seed of its growth. Then, at Westminster, I find myself in surroundings so different to some of the makeshift arrangements we knew in Papua New Guinea, and I give thanks that Christian ministry lies at the heart of Parliament. Twenty-six Lords Spiritual sit in the Upper House, and the office of Speaker's Chaplain is not some minor ceremonial task. He reminds all MPs by his reading of prayers each day that it is upon God that we depend for wisdom, guidance and grace. His ministry is not simply a personal one to the Speaker, much though he or she may need spiritual counsel after taking a battering in the Chair. The Speaker's Chaplain has a ministry to the whole House. What I want you to cherish is both variety of Christian witness and the sheer availability of Christian ministry. We are immensely privileged.

Let me return to that original question, 'Who do you say I am?' What does all this add up to? The question 'Who do you say I am?' is one that haunts us all. Peter answered softly: 'You are the Christ, the son of the living God.' That is the kind of answer I gave long ago. I hope you have too or are at least struggling to reach it. It doesn't mean of course, that from the moment we say that all our questions are resolved. Indeed not; we aren't insulated from life's problems and questions. But I will say this, when we have been able to say: 'Yes, Lord, I believe you are the one I have been struggling to find', then we shall discover that all our remaining questions find their centre in him and he helps us to work out the answers. In following Jesus we find that forgiveness and tolerance are central to what it is all about. He becomes the centre of life itself and the inspiring focus of our ambitions and future.

Jesus' calling is to 'take up your cross and follow me'. In other words – work it out. There is no exact blueprint; no magical formula – just take it up and work it out following me. I do not know what it means in your life. I am still trying to discover what it means for me because Archbishops do not have it any easier than anyone else – religion can get in the way. But one thing I am convinced about is that out there there is a world which desperately needs what I have been talking about. We have to find ways to reach them. We have all been given a marvellous opportunity to be bridges of hope.

18

Healing in a Broken World

How is it possible for intelligent, modern people to believe that a caring God created this world and still cares for it? What sort of minds do we need to understand it? Is there a wisdom that can help us cope with it all?

The title of this piece assumes that the world is broken. It suggests an answer through healing, an image taken from medicine. Let us stay with medicine for a moment. Think of a serious road accident at which we arrive unexpectedly on the scene. We see it and are horrified by the cries and groans, the smashed limbs and blood everywhere. We are overcome by a sense of helplessness. We are paralysed by the chaos and do not know what to do. But quickly the emergency services arrive – ambulances, doctors, police and fire brigade. They too see the chaos, but in addition they see other things. They note what they have to do and what their priorities are.

What is the difference between us in reacting to the situation? Through many years of study and experience the specialists at the scene have had their minds trained to make sense of some of the innumerable things that can go wrong with the human body. Disaster does not disable them. They know how to respond appropriately.

Faced with the brokenness of our world we may only see the horror. At the very least, we are perplexed. We may even recoil in disgust from it. Perhaps we are so overcome by this that we reject any purpose for the world. We cannot believe in the providence of God.

But it may also be possible to attempt diagnosis and even acknowledge the possibility and reality of healing. We can

---

Opening address, Oxford University Mission 1992, University Church, Oxford, Monday 10 February 1992.

learn from those who have grappled with that reality at some of its darkest points, who have been involved body, mind and spirit in responding to it. What wisdom do they have to share? What sort of mind-set do you need?

St Paul tells the Romans: 'Do not be conformed to this world but be transformed by the renewal of your mind'. That is a verse of scripture to which I shall return, for I want to suggest that we need to face up to three challenges to the way our minds are formed by our culture and education.

A few years ago the American philosopher Nicholas Wolterstorff lost his 24-year-old son in a mountain-climbing accident. Out of that tragedy, he wrote a remarkable book, *Lament for a Son*. He described with great tenderness his journey into faith through that loss. It was not a journey into a comfortable, insulated faith. He went through great pain, great heart-searching, and much doubt and disbelief. There is one striking passage in which he writes: 'It is said of God that no one can behold his face and live. I always thought that this meant that no one could see his splendour and live. A friend said perhaps it meant that no one could see his sorrow and live.' That is quite a thought, isn't it? That if we were to see God for ourselves we would not behold a serene God, distant from the world and untouched by its life. We would see a God in whose face would be reflected all the pain and suffering of the world. What Wolterstorff is getting at is that we could not look at all the unspeakable suffering of the world and survive. It would be too much for us to cope with.

All of us have our own ways of avoiding such intensity of evil and tragedy. I don't know about you but I find it almost intolerable when I see those searing pictures on television of young children starving in the Sudan or the victims of civil war in Somalia. There are we, in our comfortable homes gazing upon all too familiar pictures of people dying next door in our global village. It is intolerable, not simply because of their suffering, but because we feel so helpless. My pain and your pain are caused because we feel unable to respond adequately. A credit card donation does not assuage it. The pictures do not bridge the chasm; they only widen it. But we don't have to go to Africa to feel this shock. Wherever you are you will be able to go to places where the brokenness of the world is unmistakable: you find people who have nowhere to go and are sleeping rough; people who have to cope with dreadful handicaps, both mental and physical; indeed the whole range of human weakness and suffering.

Where is God in all this?

For Wolterstorff the book of Job is a powerful paradigm of finding God in human tragedy. Job is stripped of everything – his wife and family, his wealth and good name and finally his own health. The religious tradition at the time believed that sinfulness and suffering were linked. Job's unspeakable suffering must be due, people thought, to unspeakable evils that the so-called good Job had committed. The good name of Job is called into question. His friends crowd round to help him. Like some zealous Christians today they ply him with prayers, texts from the Bible and tracts from their times. The one thing they cannot entertain is the possibility that Job is actually and genuinely an innocent sufferer and that his brokenness is not a punishment from God. Job holds on to both his innocence and his belief in a just God, without cursing and blaming. In the end he is mysteriously vindicated. The book offers no explanation of *why* Job was vindicated or *why* God could allow such evil to fall on a good man. What is clear is that the story of Job re-interprets the entire religious tradition of his day.

And it is this transformed Wisdom tradition that Wolterstorff draws upon in order to face up to his own grief. He comes to believe that in Christ God takes upon himself the suffering, sin and death of the entire world and so redeems it. He writes: 'God is love. That is why he suffers. To love our suffering sinful world is to suffer. God so suffered for the world that he gave his only Son to suffering. The one who does not see God's suffering does not see his love. God is suffering love.'

This accords with the experience of many. A friend of mine, Sir Norman Anderson, was Professor of Arabic Law and Literature in the University of London. He is now retired and living in Cambridge. By the world's standards he is a successful man. But he and his wife share a terrible sadness.

Their three children died within eighteen months of each other. Hugh was President of the Cambridge Union; Janet a successful psychiatrist; her sister, unknown to me, was also very clever. Hugh died of cancer; Janet in mysterious circumstances in Kenya and the other daughter committed suicide. I asked Norman didn't he wonder why God allowed this to happen. Norman replied gently: 'I have learned over the years not to ask "why?" but "how" – how can I use my suffering for God's glory and for the good of others.' Well, we might say, it takes either a very mature and committed Christian to overcome anger and despair like this or, some would say, a person who won't revise their beliefs in the light of experience. I know which I believe it to be.

Perhaps all of us must face up to the possibility that our understanding of the world has to be revised? Like Job's friends our mind-set may be circumscribed too narrowly and too uncritically by assumptions that need to be challenged. No one is hearing these words of mine with empty minds, no matter how open minded. You have been shaped and formed by all sorts of influences, good, bad and ambiguous. In this broken world we are victims of falsehoods and distortions. We are also shaped by our deliberate oversights and self-centred interpretations of ourselves and the world. Realising how deeply we may be wrong is part of growing in wisdom. We could just be disastrously wrong about the most fundamental matters. Our world seems to have a yearning for great certainties and absolutes, for the security of systems and cut and dried world-views. Sometimes there needs to be a healthy opening up of minds. Last week I met the Minister–President of Brandenburg. He praised the role of the Churches in East Germany before and during the overthrow of the communist regime. The Church, he said, was 'the one place in which you think alternative thoughts – and express them'. That is, I believe, part of the vocation of the Church if it is to help us to be free.

I do not want to be understood as suggesting that the Western intellectual tradition leads to closing of minds. Far from it! This leads into my second point – the integration of mind and heart. Close attention to the various branches of knowledge is not only a way of honouring the truth of our amazing world; it is also a training of the mind for many aspects of life that are not met in university disciplines.

All this is a call for humility – to be willing to have our ideas confounded, the boundaries of our minds extended, even to have our minds converted. I find this idea excitingly assisted by a thought which comes from the masters of prayer in the Eastern Orthodox tradition who spoke of *'bringing the mind into the heart'*. There is a strong tendency in our culture to separate head and heart. It is all too common in our churches. This is a form of brokenness which is destructive of health and wholeness. Bringing the mind into the heart lets our thinking relate fully to our feeling, desiring, willing and anticipating. It leads to the possibility of healing as mind and heart engage, and integrate one with another.

I would like to suggest it leads to the possibility that hypotheses about the rich, mysterious universe of which we are insignificant parts cannot be merely intellectual. They must also be imaginative and include the possibility of thoughtful faith, of constructive belief, of imaginative insight. 'Imagine the impossible', wrote Nils Bohr, the great physicist, 'it may be true.' Certainly the universe is a more profound place than we ever imagined, as thinkers like Stephen Hawking, James Gleick, Danah Zohar and others inform us. Why is this so? Because of our experience of being highly self-aware, of being conscious of our unique capabilities even though we may feel lost in the vastness of the universe.

And thinking, feeling people have to be open to the possibility that here in the brokenness of all things God is, and heals. In spite of attempts to get rid of the 'God idea' the notion is remarkably persistent. Yes, there have been many things done in the name of God that have to be rejected and they have contributed to the brokenness of all things. But it doesn't follow that God himself is to be dismissed.

I would like to offer a couple of points of intellectual imagination which I put as questions:

What if the divine permeates all things? It is all too easy to think, with our expert knowledge of one tiny corner of human knowledge – biology, physics, botany, mathematics, history and so on – that we have a handle on human knowledge that holds together the rest. But what if all our knowledge is itself permeated by God himself who holds all things in being? What if the brokenness of the world, which is used as an argument to reject a God of order, is itself the medium through which he makes himself known? What if the broken people in the world are actually vehicles of God's revelation?

And then another question: *What if the divine is specific?* There is a tendency today to talk about 'religion'. But there really is no such thing. There are religions and there are believers. In the end you have to be specific, otherwise you have not grasped what you are accepting or rejecting. Intellectual and emotional honesty demands this. Christians claim that this specific is Jesus Christ; that he is, *par excellence*, the form God's revelation took and through his brokenness we are healed.

We have considered the brokenness of creation and have considered the brokenness within each one of us. We have also entertained the fact that in our Western culture we assumed too easily the self-sufficiency of human intelligence to understand without bringing the mind into the heart. Let us ask a third question: *How can our minds be renewed?*

Part of the answer is suggested by Paul's cryptic and astonishing idea in 1 Corinthians, where at the end of an argument rejecting human wisdom he says: 'But we have the mind of Christ.' How is it possible to have the mind of Christ? Paul's argument is that the crucified Jesus is the 'wisdom of God'. Through the foolishness of crucifixion God's perfect wisdom is found. It is a way of seeing; a way of finding; a way of belonging. There is something extraordinary here, a wisdom that we can only learn by receiving this mind, this Spirit. It can hardly be called a 'solution' to the 'problem' of brokenness. But what I suggest happens is that our minds are renewed by a twofold encounter – with a healing God on the one hand and the reality of a broken world on the other.

It is the temptation of all missioners to make global claims for God and Christianity and demand absolute commitments which many find impossible to make. This has been a tendency of the tradition from which I come. Its strength is in the presentation of the radical demand of the gospel upon our lives. But there is a weakness. It fails to meet the response of the many people who simply cannot make absolute commitments or accept conscientiously a world-view that clashes with their present, rather provisional, perception of life. God, however, is able to make something even of the provisional faith we offer. He can meet the person who comes with half belief – 'Lord, I believe; help thou my unbelief'. There is hope for people who are aware of such brokenness within them that healing seems to be impossible. Or the person wistfully aware of the need for a renewed mind but who cannot understand what he or she needs to do to be open to new possibilities.

It is my hope and prayer that our perception of what God is doing in this broken world and what needs to be put right in ourselves may be deepened. It is my hope that God will make us recognise our utter inadequacy in the face of the immense problems of life, and will draw us into a love that cannot be broken: a love which Wolterstorff found to be the answer to his quest – the answer of God's suffering love. That was Paul's testimony. He could speak about the renewal of his mind because in Christ he had found a way of interpreting reality. Will you trust it and give yourself to it?

19

Decoding the Decade

It was H L Mencken, the American humorist, who once said: 'For every difficult and complicated question there is an answer which is simple, easily understood – and wrong.' That statement flashed through my mind as I set myself the task of decoding the Decade of Evangelism.

In 1988, the Lambeth bishops called upon the Anglican Communion to declare the 1990s a Decade of Evangelism. I admit to being a little perturbed at the time that there was hardly any discussion and no controversy; I wondered whether such a unanimous response might mask unresolved issues or suggest a lack of passion. Since then, however, the Decade has certainly caught on. The Churches recognise that as the end of the second millennium approaches, we need to bear witness to the Christian faith with confidence and vigour. We know that we are faced with a challenge to live the gospel of love, bring it boldly to more people and make our churches places of joy where God is known. But we need to keep working hard at defining *how* we are to do this today, and to keep on questioning what the Decade of Evangelism is and is not.

I want to emphasise at the outset that I am totally committed to this Decade. I rejoice at the Church's determination to look outwards and engage with millions of people in the wider society. But the Decade of Evangelism is *not* one of Mencken's 'simple answers', and we must dispel the oversimplification to which the phrase can sometimes give rise.

My starting point is that the God of the scriptures is an evangelising, loving God. It has been traditional to make evangelism an adjunct of mission – so that mission represents the

Presidential Address to the Canterbury Diocesan Synod, Saturday 21 March 1992.

broad sweep of God's purposes in history and evangelism the narrow call to follow. I question that approach and I want to turn it on its head. Evangelism for me is what mission is all about. Because God loves, he reveals himself as a saving God, and calls people to follow and obey him. Because God loves, he reveals himself as a caring God, and calls us to care for others.

Against this background, the Decade of Evangelism reflects two fundamental convictions. First, *the Church must look outwards*. For too long we have been preoccupied with internal Church arguments. This obstructs God's purposes because it alienates people who are longing to find God. Worship, liturgy and prayer are central elements of our faith, but they are not enough if they are not linked to Christian proclamation and action in today's society. One of my top priorities as Archbishop is to help counter any tendency for the Church of England to degenerate into a sect. I know that some sects today are growing! But, as Hugh Montefiore has written: 'The characteristic of a sect is to look inwards to itself rather than outwards to the society of which it forms part, and this tends to make people outside its membership disregard it.' The Decade of Evangelism sets the Church's face against that vicious circle.

Secondly, the Decade signals *profound confidence in the relevance of the Christian faith*, to the needs of humankind in the late twentieth century and far beyond. It challenges the tendency in some quarters to talk ourselves into gloom and defeatism by ignoring all that is good in the Church today. We reject any arrogant belief in our superiority as people; indeed, I want to come back to the point that we must always remain humble servants. But we are glad to express our boundless confidence in God and in the redeeming power of his love in our contemporary world.

This then, is the core of the Decade of Evangelism: we look outwards in love for God's world, reflecting and proclaiming our total confidence in him. This attitude can bring rich blessings for the Church and our society. It presents a tremendously exciting challenge to all of us.

In Britain, we are very conscious of crossing frontiers as

the Channel Tunnel nears completion. It seems to me that the Christian Churches can give a lead to our society, during the Decade, in crossing several great frontiers. I think of Brother Bernard's prayer: 'Set us free, O God, to cross barriers for you, as you crossed barriers for us.'

As I have said elsewhere, one barrier we must confront is materialism. I spoke to an elderly clergyman the other day who has had 40 rich years in the ministry. He compared the beginning and the end of his time and freely admitted that it is far harder these days for the Church than it was in the early 1950s. He said: 'It is not that people are rejecting the Christian faith because they have thought about it, but they are rejecting it because the alternatives seem so much more attractive; materialism has grabbed the hearts of our people.' Now that may be a sweeping judgement but there is some truth in it. At the same time, I am convinced that most people in our country fear the emptiness and bewilderment of a secular, consumerist society. Materialism results from people's inability to find a satisfying meaning in their lives, or to understand their own spiritual nature.

In the Decade we are presenting a challenge to the tendency of materialism to sweep the spiritual out of the lives of our people. How is this challenge to be conducted? The task is twofold. The first is an unapologetic proclamation of the truths of the Christian faith based on the love of God for all. Because God *is*, we *are*. Because God loves, we are of inestimable value to him. The Christian faith asserts the unique value of each human being, that each one of us is irreplaceable. The principle and truth is reinforced by the incarnation. The message of Jesus Christ is that we are children of God and called to a relationship which is eternal and precious. Materialism will all too quickly drift into meaninglessness without a personal God because without God everything is finally futile. The message of a God who calls people into a relationship of love is central to giving meaning to mankind.

This leads on to the second task. We must acknowledge the fact that in our society there are many who are well aware of the importance of the spiritual yet they are honestly not com-pelled by traditional Christianity to accept it. They do not perceive that the Church can satisfy their spiritual longings. A Decade that looks outwards must also therefore be a time of reflection on the language and images we use, the relevance as well as quality of our theology, prayer and worship, so that we connect with the hearts and minds of our diverse society.

Another frontier we need to cross will lead to the full understanding that *this world is God's and not ours*. In my frequent visits to schools of all types one thing that is of nagging concern is the assumption that this planet is without ownership. What appears to be communicated too frequently to our children is that the world around us is a marvellous quarry for our science, technology and art; it is our playground for us to revel in; it is our capital to exploit. I miss the language of awe, wonder and contemplation. These arrogant attitudes, and what they lead to, constitute a threat to our planet. The voracious consumerist aspirations of Western society cannot be replicated by developing countries without ecological disaster, and yet it is hard to see why they should accept environmental restraints unless we show more self-discipline ourselves. The Church can help encourage self-restraint, humility, reverence for God's creation, the love of neighbours and commitment to a fairer world order. From the Jewish–Christian tradition of the land we assert the gift of creation for all to enjoy. This is one example of how much the Decade of Evangelism should mean to our society, not just to the Church as an organisation.

A further frontier is that of *helping people to meet and discover the living God*. Evangelism used to be seen as personal and individual. I grew up as a young Christian feeling burdened by this – that I had to share my faith with others. I felt a sense of guilt when I didn't and a sense of frustration that when I did, my efforts seemed to be false and sometimes irrelevant. We are beginning to discover that although individuals *are* expected to share their faith and show an example of Christian goodness to others, the base camp for evangelism is the local church to which we belong. There we find our place, not as individuals crushed by a sense of responsibility for a task which is too huge, but as members of a fellowship who are called to witness to a God who is here with his people. Hence, individuals in their calling to evangelism find support and encouragement within the local church; and not only those local churches which are considered 'evangelical'. Indeed not one tradition but the whole Church, and therefore *every* local church, is called to be a centre of evangelism.

'The Church exists for mission', Brunner said, 'as a fire exists by burning.' I see signs that many local churches are beginning to realise that they are meant to be far more than privileged centres of belief, protecting a set of values. They are rediscovering their vocation to proclaim the gospel by both their word and their lives. In this Decade I hope our Church will realise that evangelism is not something very different from pastoral care, but is rooted in pastoral care and love. Anglicans have always blended the two, but sometimes even our clergy forget this. I well recall in my last diocese, meeting one of my clergy – a fine man who had spent fifteen years in his parish and had done an excellent job. To his town one week came a team of young people from Y-WAM (Youth with a Mission). At the end of the week the team told the vicar that 25 young people had been 'converted'. The vicar confessed to me that although he was so pleased with the way the team had reached those young people and helped to graft them into the church, he felt marginalised. 'I have to say, Bishop', he said, 'that in my fifteen years I can't say I have led one person to our Lord.' I saw that a chasm had opened up between two types of evangelism. Gently, I said, 'Come off it! During your fifteen years how many youngsters and adults have you baptised? How many confirmees have you prepared? How many youngsters have you taught in your Sunday Schools? How many people have you prepared for their dying? How many homes have you visited to show you care? How many bereaved people have you visited? And look at your congregation – you have maintained a steady witness – the church is there proclaiming its faith with conviction and hope.' His face brightened – because I had reminded him of truths he well knew when he was beginning to think that he lacked something of importance. In fact his quiet painstaking ministry was, and is, deeply evangelistic.

Let me give another example. As I remarked earlier, when I

returned to Barking and Dagenham and met representatives of its flourishing voluntary organisations, it became clear to me that if you were to take away all the committed Christian people from those organisations, there would be hardly anyone left. Those people would not think of themselves as evangelists – but they are a fundamental manifestation of a flourishing, outward-looking Church in the Decade of Evangelism.

Hence, the Decade is not something *separate* from the Church's pastoral mission and commitment to Christian action: they are part of the Decade, and the Decade must nourish them. This is the basis for Anglican evangelism – that we are here to minister to people as well as to draw them to the living God. Thus the special contribution of Bishop Michael Marshall and Canon Michael Green, who will be exercising their distinctive evangelistic and teaching gifts in our Church, will be part of the wider vision. Our desire is for a Church which lives the gospel as well as talks about it.

I have tried to define the core of the Decade and illustrate some of the dimensions of what it should mean. Let me also say what it does *not* mean. Because we remain humble servants of God, it does not mean talking down to other people as if we are 'holier than thou'. Jesus disliked self-righteousness and so should we. Secondly, it does not mean that we can lecture people without listening; on the contrary, in looking outwards and engaging with the wider society, we have much to learn as well as teach.

In relation to other faiths this means that we should respect their integrity while proclaiming and acting out our own firm belief in Jesus Christ as our Lord. Deliberate confrontation with other faiths would be counterproductive and divisive. A predominantly Christian society nurtures tolerance and constructive relationships with minority faiths; and the Christian Churches need to work with people of other faiths in combating the shallow materialism of much contemporary life. We must never *hide* our beliefs; nor would other faiths respect us if we did. But our mission is to society as a whole, to all who have ears to hear, and especially to those who are half-hearted in their Christian commitment or have lost their faith altogether. Friction with minority faiths is an unproductive distraction from the enormous, positive agenda of the Decade.

Moreover, the Decade is not a number-counting exercise, treating fellow human beings as prey for the Church. That would not reflect Christian love for our neighbours. Nor is it principally an exercise in skilful oratory, though this can have a part to play. If proclamation in words is not linked to setting an example in our own lives, to Christian action to help our neighbour and save God's creation, to deep prayer and self-discipline, to excellence and richness in our worship, then people will soon see through it. If we commit ourselves to all these things while facing outwards, our Church will be more open, more vital and more responsive to God and that is why our congregations will grow, as I passionately believe they should.

Finally, the Decade is not our alternative to self-questioning and reflection. It starts with appraisal and self-renewal. What are the strengths and weaknesses of the Church? What ministry has it to the young? What is its role in the community? How is it making disciples? What financial need has it got? How is it going to meet those needs? In what ways does it need to change in order to grow? But this questioning is not of the anxious, introverted kind. It stems from our confident determination to reach out in faith to millions of our fellow citizens. It will not be easy; it will cost us everything. But we shall do it with joy.

Spring is the time of year when green shoots of life appear on bare branches and in the empty earth. God's creatures leave their winter hideouts or return from migrations. People turn outwards from their winter hearths and rejoice in the warmth, freshness, bustle and renewal of Spring. That is what the Decade of Evangelism should be like. And Spring brings Easter-time, the season of the resurrection. Evangelism is rooted in the resurrection. The Decade of Evangelism is about a resurrection faith, ever springing forth in new life. Let us carry it forward with joy and hope.

20

A Charter for the Church

It was my distinguished predecessor who sometimes said that 'the centre of the Church lies in its circumference!' That may not be good geometry but it is excellent theology because quite simply the Church is the clergy and people in the many ordinary parishes up and down this land.

In this piece, I would like to reflect on the nature of the Church today and its mission. I have called it *A Charter for the Church*, but I do not mean by that a list of rights, as in the Citizen's Charter. I use the word, as in the United Nations Charter, in the sense of a foundation document incorporating a mission statement. In a deeper sense, of course, the founding document for all Christians is the gospel itself, but the Church of England also needs to be clear about its mission as an organisation. It is about a *vision* of God's Kingdom; it is about a *pilgrimage* towards the heavenly Jerusalem; it is about being *bearers* of God's good news to our generation.

So what is our charter? I bring to you five points:

1. To be a Church rooted in historic Christianity

Bishop Charles Gore once said to his friend Lord Lathbury: 'The Church of England is an ingeniously devised instrument for defeating the objects which it is supposed to promote.' And so it might seem when with monotonous regularity at high points of the year a few clergy and laity appear to deny the central tenets of our faith. No wonder Bishop Mervyn Stockwood once described the 'C of E' as a 'comedy of errors'. At Easter 1992, Lambeth Palace received a hundred or so

Address to the clergy and laity at two gatherings in the Diocese of Derby: Chesterfield Parish Church, Friday 8 May 1992; Derby Cathedral, Saturday 9 May 1992.

letters from distressed lay people protesting at a *Heart of the Matter* programme on BBC TV and asking me to intervene. In the programme, a number of clergymen from the Diocese of Leicester expressed doubts about the basic Christian tenets. I can understand viewers' distress, and my response to them has been to point out the unswerving commitment of our Church to historic Christianity.

We are a credal Church and in our services we recite the creeds possibly more than any other Christian body. We are rooted in scripture and the faith of the Church; let no one be in any doubt about that. And at the heart of that has been and is an unwavering commitment to the resurrection of Christ. Without that there can be no Christian faith worth speaking of. We are not in the business of 'keeping the rumour of God alive' as some have put it. I am not interested in rumours. I am interested in reality and the Church affirms the reality of God in Christ and in his people. We need to reassure people that those who are sceptical of any resurrection are but a tiny minority of the many, many clergy and readers who Easter Day by Easter Day proclaim the resurrection with conviction and zeal. Unfortunately, as with most divisive elements, it is the tiny minority who often attract attention. There was a very good letter in the *Radio Times* which said: 'Unbelieving clergy are neither new nor numerous. On Easter Day millions of Christians celebrated the fact that, 2,000 years ago, Jesus Christ rose from the dead. To suggest that the Church in this country is in crisis because a few clergy have doubts is ridiculous.'

None of this suggests that we close our minds to questions. The closed mind will eventually lead to the closed Church. And I want our Church to remain a Church which allows people to ask questions. Take the resurrection as an example of this. The New Testament declares most firmly that the tomb was empty and the body of Christ was raised to life; that is its clear testimony. But the *mode* of the resurrection is tantalisingly unclear: Christ's body appeared to have properties which transcended the earthly body of Jesus; he appears and he disappears. Throughout Christian history the nature of Christ's resurrected body has been a puzzle to scholars and a holy mystery to believers. People do ask questions of that kind and within the limits of Bible, tradition and reason that is a very proper thing to do. The other day I was reading in Bell's life of Randall Davidson about an event in 1914 when the House of Bishops was being asked to speak out condemning liberalism. The then Bishop of Ely wrote some wise words to the Bishop of Oxford in which he spoke up for a tolerant Church which offered space for people to grow. He wrote: 'There are an infinite number of stages between belief and disbelief and apparent disbelief at the moment is very often temporary and passes away. Some of us – certainly myself – have in past days gone through experiences of this kind when we have been overdone or disappointed or out of health bodily or spiritual. Then the light of God's countenance has again been manifested and the difficulty has passed away.'

So, the first point in my charter calls for the kind of Church which stands firm for the faith first delivered to the saints but which is an open, tolerating Church that allows others to grow in understanding and grace.

2. *To be a Church open to the world and society in which we live*

We are a national Church. This gives us immense privileges as well as responsibilities. The strength of being such a Church is that there is a recognisable parochial network throughout the land. People have a right to call on us and seek the sacramental ministries of our Church. It is a privilege that we treasure; it is indeed a reflection of the grace of God which is unconditional. That is at the heart of our charter. God the giver ever gives. We forego the benefits of a sect with tight boundaries because we do not wish to impose on others a rigid framework of belief and behaviour. There are some who like that sort of security – they will probably find too many blurred edges. Well, I want to suggest to you that we have to live with that kind of tension and even rejoice in it; on the one hand we *are* a Church with a recognisable doctrinal framework, but we are also a body which is not too keen to draw the boundaries too tightly. And the results show in the splendid ministry going on in our many parishes throughout the country. Through the sharing of Christian life that flows from congregations, some of them very tiny, into the wider community. Through our Church schools; through charitable organisations; through individuals who care. In many rural communities the Church is often the only surviving focus of community – the post office may have closed, the bus may no longer come and even the pub may have been taken over. But the Church remains as a welcoming signpost of God's declaration that this is God's world.

In these days when we are all feeling the financial strain of keeping ancient churches open and sometimes despairing of that load, maintenance of such places of worship should be seen not as a barrier to mission but at the very heart of it. There are many Christian bodies around the world – some within the Anglican Communion – which would love to have our rich heritage of buildings to aid their missions, buildings which lift people's hearts and minds to God, which have been places of prayer for centuries. I have seen so many times in my ministry that when clergy and lay people have shown determination to grow, things have happened, vision has returned, imagination has been fired and communities united in a common cause.

All that is to do with the life of the local congregation, but we also must remain unrepentantly committed to the world and our society. Long gone are the days when the Church was only interested in its own life – indeed, I am not at all sure if that ever was the case. The Christian gospel is incorrigibly social and if it stops at the individual it stops! It never ceases to disappoint and surprise me that whenever I make a comment which passes into the political and social arena some people suggest I am interfering in matters which should not concern me. How shortsighted this is and how wrong people are to believe that this is confrontational. It is only insecurity which speaks in that way. The Christian faith is committed to a just, free and ordered society, not because this is a political statement, but because this is God's will for all people. Because we are all made in the image and likeness of God the Church is in the business of caring for everyone and this is something it must honour today.

So the second element of our charter calls us to be a Church which is open to our society and serving it with joy and integrity. More than that, we care about God's wider creation: we have to help our society to understand that God wants human beings to be responsible stewards, not blind destroyers, of his creation. We must help each other be humble, disciplined and reverent in our stewardship of God's world.

3. To be a worshipping Church

The splendid definition of humanity's chief end in the Westminster Confession is that we are to 'glorify God and enjoy him for ever'. This is not simply the task of the Church but of all humankind. It may seem desperately sad to us that so many go through life without realising that the true destiny of all people is to be worshippers – not of ourselves, but of God. Well did the Psalmist say: 'Thou hast set eternity in man's heart', and the wistful longing of hearts for beauty, for joy, for permanence, for happiness, for fulfilment – find their expression in worship. Indeed, it is a mistake to say, as some do, that the first task of the Church is to evangelise. Important though that is, our primary task is to reflect the eternal worship of heaven in daily and weekly acts of praise and adoration and thanksgiving.

I offer you four reflections regarding our charter. First, it belongs to our tradition to emphasise *common prayer*. I am well aware that some argue that since we have introduced the Alternative Service Book our worship is never common. But this is a mistaken notion. The ASB has enriched the variety of our common worship, as an alternative to the Prayer Book. Most of our churches value it. But it has not meant that our worship these days is un-common. I have travelled up and down this country and abroad and there is something distinctive about Anglican worship whether the accents are American, Australian, African, Welsh, Geordie or Derbyshire! What we must retain is liturgical worship, balanced, ordered, dignified, joyful and relevant. Long live the Prayer Book but let us not put a freeze on liturgical experiment.

Secondly, our worship must be accessible. I cannot forget that once I was an Anglican non-attender! Christian worship can sometimes be a terrifying experience for people who occasionally encounter it. They feel ill at ease because they are not used to the strangeness of what others regard as familiar. We must ensure that worship is not only dignified and reverent but inclusive; not only worshipful but welcoming. There is something inherently mysterious about worship. It must reflect the mystery of God. But it should not be obscure and alienating to those who really desire to pray.

Thirdly, let us affirm the richness of our traditions in worship. I value the comprehensiveness of our Church – it is a mark of the coming great Church. I once worshipped at a wonderful black church in the heart of Harlem, New York. The church was called The Church of Intercession, and the congregation was 95% black. It was a bi-lingual Mass, English and Spanish. It was a high Mass with smells and bells, chasubles and choirs, gestures and genuflections. No one could say it was immediately understandable. But it was alive and welcoming. It was inspiring, not only because of the dignity of it but the way it was done. Such joy, such energy, such devotion. And preaching which would make any evangelical envy the directness and passion. I came away thankful that I could say that that was my church too. I come from an evangelical background, as many know, but I value the contribution of other traditions and we must all try to learn from one another.

Fourthly, let us cherish the refreshment and inner peace which we find individually and together in prayer. I believe that people in our society need the space for quietness, for making contact with their spiritual selves, more desperately than ever.

Point three of my charter calls us to offer accessible, open, joyful liturgical worship and prayer, and worship is directly linked with my next point.

4. *To be a witnessing, growing Church*

We have designated this decade as a Decade of Evangelism and in so doing we join with our sister Churches throughout the world in a commitment to share good news with others. From one point of view it is doing what we have been doing better. It is essentially a reminder of the fact that the Church's task is to *point to* God and *lead people* to him. It is not an easy task and we fail again and again to be effective signs of God's presence in his world. But let us demystify this word 'evangelism': Isn't it essentially all about the Church telling its story about God's love and living in the light of that fact?

So the fourth point of the charter is to set out targets for growth; to identify with God's love and care for all people.

5. *To be a Church committed to unity*

This is the final element in the charter. Inevitably we have to consider our internal unity. Sadly, polarisation and fragmentation is rife in our society and, I fear, in our Church. So often we think the worst of others instead of the best. We all too easily attribute insincere motives to others. But unity is vital to our mission. If our message is reconciliation, people will not be convinced if we are riddled with disunity. And this year our internal unity will receive its toughest test yet as we face the debate on the ordination of women to the priesthood. One thing is clear: there must be no triumphalism. In a sense, whatever side we are on, we will all be losers because every Christian will sorrow if other Christians are wounded. Are we capable of staying together even when we disagree so sharply? Can opponents stay within if the legislation is passed and can the majority remain if the legislation is defeated? I believe we have the resources to stay together if we refrain from adversarial campaigning, if we refrain from antagonistic language, if our fellowship is steeped in prayer and earthed in mutual affection.

There is another unity which matters too. The reunion of all Christian people. Let no one be in doubt there is a long hard road still to travel before the Anglican and Roman Catholic Churches can be united. We shall not reach that desired goal in my time. But the aim is clear. In the meantime we should do all in our power to share a common witness, to meet whenever we can for prayer, Bible study and mutual support. The fifth point of the charter calls us to be a Church determined to *treasure differences, but at all costs stay together.*

A fivefold charter for the Church. It is not original because its points are all things we know so well, but it stems from our responsibilities to God and the world around us. What really matters is God and his Kingdom. The marvel is that even the most imperfect Christian and the most imperfect Church can be used by our Lord. I treasure the words of Bishop Geoffrey Paul, the late Bishop of Bradford, who said in his Enthronement address: 'There is no way of belonging to Jesus Christ except by belonging gladly and irrevocably to the glorious ragbag of saints and fatheads who make up the Only, Holy and Catholic Church.' Fellow saints and fatheads – we have a big job to do.

21

The Gospel as Public Truth:
The Challenge to the Church

In St John's Gospel, Christ declares of the Holy Spirit, 'He shall guide you into all truth and the truth shall make you free'. It is not so much the word 'truth' that grips my mind in this verse, but 'all truth'. That is to say truth is many-sided and multi-faceted. There is breadth and depth to it which lies beyond present experience and present knowledge. This is the verse of scripture found as the inscription on the Compasrose, the symbol of the Anglican Communion. You will find the Compasrose on the floor of Canterbury Cathedral, dedicated at the end of the 1988 Lambeth Conference. I dedicated another at the Cathedral of St John the Divine in New York in 1992. That scripture speaks of the truth of the gospel found in the enormously diverse multi-cultural life of the Anglican Communion.

The truth of which it speaks defies simplistic reductionism or distorting over-simplification. If I have one abiding fear of the Decade of Evangelism, it is that the Church could so easily settle for easy answers which will satisfy only those already convinced that Christ is the Truth. Quick generalisations about secularism, about spiritual needs and about the claim of faith, can rob us of seeing the full story. 'Arouse people from their stupor', some cry to Archbishops. 'Declare this to be a Decade of Evangelism. Issue a clarion call, a call to arms, bring in the evangelists, alert our congregations, do things better and get things better done – and the country will be evangelised.' So we are doing many of those things, and I am personally

Address to the Consultation at Swanwick, Tuesday 14 July 1992.
The Consultation was the central object of the Gospel and Our Culture *Programme, which exists to promote Christian mission.*

involved in a number of these initiatives. But these things, in themselves, are not enough. Without an analysis of the discontents of modern human condition and of the structure of Western society and culture, and without awareness of the gulf between Church and society, such prescriptions for the Church's mission will fail as they have failed in the past. Clarion calls will only wake those for whom the Church is already a relevant factor in their condition. What about those who have *already* assumed that developments in the sciences make it intellectually suspect to hold religious beliefs, who have *already* assumed that the application of science in technology is much more effective in advancing human dignity than religious faith, and those who have *already* assumed that whatever the truth is and where it may lie, it is certainly not to be found in mainstream Christianity. Indeed, a call to 'repent and believe' is hardly likely to reach those who have already tacitly acceded to the pervasive assumption that there are no absolute values and that everything is relative. A Decade which ignores these issues is doomed to failure. The Church must therefore think seriously about the encounter of gospel and culture.

What is 'culture'? I have a few misgivings about the term itself, even though I do not reach for my revolver, as Goering is reported to have said. It is all too easy to speak of 'culture' as though we already know clearly what it is we are defining. The dictionary definition describes culture as, 'The intellectual side of civilisation, the training and refinement of mind, tastes and manners'. Whilst accepting that broad definition we should recognise that there has never been one single British culture but many. When we talk about 'multi-cultural' Britain, we are generally referring to the presence of the variety of ethnic groups now living in these islands. Yet, this has long been a land of many cultures. I was brought up in a working-class culture, vastly different from the one I now inhabit. British working-class culture has traditionally been regarded as peculiarly difficult for religion to penetrate. It presented a separate world to the world of faith. Yet it would be an over-simplification to speak as if Christianity is over against that or any other culture. Indeed, if we keep faith with the truth of the incarnation, it is not over against but wedded to, and inseparable from, the living communities and tastes and fashions which thrive culturally. We must avoid treating culture, as Gregory the Great is reported to have done, as comparable to the effect of the knives of the Israelites who went to the Philistines to get them sharpened! On this Gregorian view culture is a weapon we have to use in order to beat the enemy at their own game. But fresh, invigorated Christianity which is allowed free rein to breathe life into the structures of society, and into its literature and thoughtforms, can create a culture in which human life can flower abundantly. It has no interest in cutting away culture as an end in itself. Unlike Gregory the Great, C S Lewis believed that culture may be an ally of the gospel. He wrote:

My general case may be stated in Ricardian terms – that culture is a storehouse of the best (sub-Christian) values. The values (in themselves) will save no one. They resemble the regenerate life only as affection resembles charity, or honour resembles virtue or the moon the sun. But though 'like is not the same' it is better than unlike. Imitation may pass into initiation. For some it is a good beginning. For others it is not; culture is not everyone's road into Jerusalem and for some it is a road out.

There is another way in which it may predispose to conversion. The difficulty of converting an uneducated man nowadays lies in his complacency. Popularised science, the conventions or unconventions of his immediate circle, party programmes, etc. enclose him in a tiny windowless universe which he mistakes for the only possible universe. There are no distant horizons, no mysteries. He thinks that everything has been settled. A cultured person on the other hand is almost compelled to be aware that reality is very odd and that the ultimate truth, whatever it may be, must have the characteristics of strangeness . . . thus some obstacles to faith have been removed already.

Well, I am sure that Lewis was overly sanguine about the predisposition of intellectual culture towards faith, but we cannot deny the stress Lewis placed upon the importance of culture itself in shaping all our lives. We need to rise to its challenges.

There is one factor which I must acknowledge as making this challenge difficult to see clearly. Western European culture has been shaped by the Christian tradition. The echoes of faith are heard even in the most secular of minds, tastes and manners. The task of re-evangelising is not a very familiar one. The New Testament naturally offers us little guidance in this area. And the Churches of Western Europe have their own culture, which in their different ways, reflect the culture of the people they serve.

This leads me on to the culture of the Church of Jesus Christ. A church culture ought by its very nature to be life-giving, open and free. We know the reality. So in what ways does the 'Gospel as Public Truth' challenge the Church?

I want to point to three major areas.

First, it calls for an *open, generous Church*. Two weeks ago I was ordaining deacons and priests in Canterbury Cathedral. From where I was sitting, as I laid hands on the candidates, I could see the great West door of the cathedral. The glass doors were firmly closed. But scores of people approached and pushed their faces close to the glass to watch intently this strange ceremony inside. After a while, they would walk away, whether puzzled, amazed, intrigued or curious to know more about the gospel, who can say? As I saw this my mind flashed back to my visit to Papua New Guinea. We visited Popondetta where I preached in the cathedral of the resurrection. What was unforgettable about this cathedral was that it had no doors and no walls. People were able to come in, or stay on the edges, listen for a while if they wished and then walk away. Or sometimes they listened and drew gradually nearer, eventually sitting down with us. I know I would not get much support from the Archbishops' Commission on Cathedrals if I proposed the removal of cathedral walls. The climate of Canterbury is very different from Popondetta. My point is a parable. I want an open Church which is not afraid to be *in the world*. There is no such thing as the 'Gospel' which exists in some sealed independence separated from Church or world. After Pentecost the gospel is incarnate in the Church. There can be no complete identification, of course. But the principle of incarnation speaks of God's truth being rooted in human experience, taken up in human confession and then lived out in the world. That is the gospel. It has to be *embodied* as it was first enfleshed in the incarnation of Christ.

For the Church today it must mean an encounter with the world of ideas. An open Church must be rooted in historic Christianity, but unless it is unafraid to open its faith to examination and challenge, it will remain on the fringes of human life. Hugh Montefiore touched on this when he talked of the dangers of sectarianism when groups look inward to themselves rather than outwards to the society of which they form a part. My fear for this Decade of Evangelism is that it may encourage the forces in our Church which actually wish to erect fences of doctrine and discipline leading to a sectarian fellowship of believers. I resist that, because I believe with all my heart that the Church of Jesus Christ should be a Church of blurred edges and, to return to my analogy, a Church of no walls where people can ask their hardest questions without condemnation and share their deepest fears without reproach.

My second point is that *the Church needs to recover its story of resurrection.* I want to put a gloss on Eric Ives' splendid chapter in *The Gospel and Contemporary Culture*. Whilst the 'empty tomb' is at the heart of the resurrection story, there is much more to it than that. Along with the event there has to be the experience – 'I met the Lord'. Testimony throbs through the pages of the New Testament. The Apostles know not only the mystery of the resurrection but encounter the equally mysterious act of the appearance. He appeared to them. Similarly in our experience and that of the Church. Event and experience has to go hand in hand; mind and heart have to be in tune; belief and behaviour must harmonise.

So I ask: What is the Church's testimony to the risen Lord today? We can think at once of all the counter-testimonies – to the bickering, the divisions, the failure to agree on fundamental matters of faith and our proneness to domesticate Christianity and make it comfortable and easy. We are all too aware of the often repeated charge by young people that our worship is 'boring' – and yet we do very little about it. We have the most amazing good news for people and yet we manage somehow to make it seem so unattractive.

And that side of the testimony can detract from and hide

the very things that actually speak of the resurrection story in contemporary society. I think of the Church of all traditions with vibrant teaching and preaching. I think of the Church's response to the needs of our inner cities. I think of the Church's considerable work among the socially deprived, the sick, prisoners, in schools and youth organisations, with the deaf, amongst the homeless, with the housebound – the range of activities is enormous. And the genius of the Church has been to encourage its voluntary organisations to extend the frontiers of its work. We are not good at telling this side of the story. It is ignored by those of us who are within the Church, let alone by those we are trying to reach to show that the Church and its message is relevant.

What, of course, I am pointing to in stressing this challenge is the simple fact that our task is not simply an intellectual one. Christianity is only fully known when it is lived. Living the gospel is in itself part of the way – a big part – of the way it becomes public truth.

My third point is that *the Church needs to recover confidence in the proclamation of faith*. Here I express a personal worry. I was brought to a lasting faith, not least because I was taught that Christianity, though a revealed religion, was also a rational faith. That is to say, reason was not in any way opposed to the journey of trust and obedience. My church, in a solidly working-class culture, took apologetic preaching seriously. There were times when my fierce Calvinistic vicar took on the entirety of Roman Catholicism and tried to show the biblical superiority of the Protestant way. The reasoning was not always accurate or fair, but at least there was a clear epistemology; although I would not want to identify with that today. There were, I am glad to say, many more times when he and his much cleverer curates thoughtfully and articulately showed the reasonableness of the faith, even though the centrality of revelation and experience was never lost. But somehow we have strayed from this emphasis. Too often we hear moralistic or experiential sermons which have no epistemological basis. I raise the question: Will the gospel ever be public truth if our preachers are not grappling with the challenge of scientism from their pulpits, or drawing on literature, art, science and theology to show that the Christian world-view is meaningful and relevant today? We have played down the significance of preaching for far too long. The consequence of our neglect in this and related areas is that our understanding of the Christian story itself becomes a jumble. Irrationality takes over. Recently I came across an essay purported to be written by a Sunday School student with a poor attendance record. It summed up the problem!

There was a good Samaritan going down from Jerusalem to Jericho and he fall among thorns and they sprang up and they choked him and left him half dead.

He said, 'I will arise', and he arose and came to a tree and he got hung on the limb and he hung there for 40 days and 40 nights, and the ravens fed him.

Delilah came along with a pair of shears and cut off his hair and he fell on rocky ground.

He said, 'I will arise' and he came to a wall and Jezebel was sitting on the wall and he said, 'Throw her down', and they threw her down. And great was the fall thereof, and of the fragments that remained they gathered twelve baskets full. And whose wife will she be in the resurrection?

High upon our agenda should be not just clear biblical teaching but the need to develop a fresh Christian apologetic. In the eyes of the media and popular understanding, Christianity and other religions too are no longer regarded as communicating the truth about the nature and character of the world in which we live. This is not to say that everything to do with religion is therefore treated as valueless. There are many people – atheists and agnostics amongst them – who are prepared to concede that religions can, and often do, make major contributions to society. But the unspoken assumption is that religious faith and a scientific world-view are implacably opposed. One deals in values and the other in facts.

But we have given way too readily. There was no need to give so much ground and today there are new opportunities for religious and Christian apologetics which we should explore. What are these areas of new opportunity?

I think of *cosmology*. Stephen Hawking's enormously successful, but little-read book, *A Brief History of Time*, is perhaps the most striking sign of the interest in this area. But John Barrow's *A World within the World*, Paul Davies' *The Mind of God*, and Stephen Clark's *The Mystery of Religion*, are likewise reopening questions that we once considered shut. Our intention is not to smuggle back an argument based on 'God of the gaps' but to explore theologically those questions which scientists themselves are beginning to address. Derek Parfitt's recent article in the TLS, 'The puzzle of reality', is an excellent commentary on this new mood. The God idea is not so implausible after all. In the words of Fred Hoyle: 'The universe looks like a put-up job.' But we must not jump to a too-ready acceptance of the God to be found in contemporary philosophy of science. There is a big gap between the God of the physicist and the God of Abraham – between reason and revelation – but the questions are again being raised. Talk of God is no longer described as meaningless.

A second area is *aesthetics*. Here, some of the groundwork has already been done by George Steiner in his *Real Presences*, which I have mentioned before. Taking on the 'deconstructionalism' of Derrida, Steiner says that questions like 'What is poetry, music, art? How do they act upon us and how do we interpret their action?' are, ultimately, theological questions.

A third area is that of *values and morality*. This is an area I have been exploring myself, first in a lecture at the University of Kent last year, entitled *Do we Need God to be Good?*, (see Chapter 3) and more recently in an address in London on *God, Goodness and Justice* (see Chapter 7).

The connection between morality and religion is no longer self-evident to many people. So much so that an exploration of the connection between goodness and godliness is likely to be misunderstood. Not for a moment would I suggest that atheists cannot be good or that Christians have a monopoly on goodness. Rather, we may ask why it is that so many human beings – atheists, agnostics and believers alike – go beyond self-interest in their behaviour. Is our capacity to be good in ways that go beyond our self-interest a sign of God's presence in the world? Since Christians believe that all humankind is made in God's image, we have no difficulty in recognising that image of God's goodness in the life of atheists as well as believers. Atheists can hardly be expected to agree, but can certainly not ask Christians to restrict our world-view so as to exclude them. We may see even in the behaviour of non-believers a testimony to faith.

Mechanistic interpretations of human behaviour have been commonplace in this century. Human beings, we have often been told, act instinctively in their own self-interest. Indeed, we frequently hear 'enlightened self-interest' (whatever that may be) applauded as the highest form of moral basis we can expect for a life in business or commerce.

Yet, look at the evidence around us. As I have already pointed out, we can think of many examples where people do good without any benefits accruing to them. It is this form of altruism which presents the real intellectual problem in a sceptical age. We need some frame of reference other than self-interest for such self-giving.

We possess the resources to develop a confident apologetic for our times. We live at a time when the intellectual environment is changing. It is often said we now live in post-socialist, post-capitalist, post-modern, post-ideological societies. No one, however, seems to argue we live in a post-religious society, no matter how much people might wish to imagine that Western culture is now post-Christian. The prevalence of faith suggests there is something in us which reaches out to God and will not be satisfied with anything less.

Professor Oliver O'Donovan once remarked that 'no earthly good can be worth dying for unless there is a heavenly good worth living for'. Part of our task in proclaiming the gospel as public truth is to reconcile those two 'goods' – the earthly and the heavenly. And in that task we have the assurance of those words in John's Gospel about the Holy Spirit: 'He shall guide you into all truth, and the truth shall make you free.' While we believe that we have met God's truth in Jesus, we must never minimise the nature of truth and the mysteries still to be revealed in him. That is why the future never worries the mature Christian but calls him and her into discovering more and more about God's work in the world, in revelation and in nature. John Donne's lines sum it up so well:

On a huge hill,
Craggy and steep, Truth stands and he that will
Reach her, about must, and about must go.

In your own life, work and ministry, may you be encouraged to take the themes of these days further in what you think and do. And may you be blessed in doing so.

CHALLENGES
FACING A CHANGING
CHURCH

22

Affirming Catholicism

As Archbishop, I delight to affirm the Catholic tradition within Anglicanism. Although my own faith was nurtured in Evangelical Anglicanism, I have nevertheless grown in my appreciation of the Catholic tradition: its vigour, its understanding of ministry, its colourful history, but perhaps above all, its spirituality. As a result I have become personally comfortable with the tradition without denying the Evangelical faith which first drew me into the Christian family. But I believe the importance of the Catholic tradition is not limited simply to the history of the Church, but is also vital to its future. I have no doubt that the integrity of Catholicism is vital for the wellbeing and future of Anglicanism. (I believe the same about the Evangelical tradition, too, of course.) The decline of Anglican Catholicism – and there *has* been a decline even though some Catholics dislike acknowledging it – hurts us all. Its demise in the Church of England would be a tragedy.

And yet the gloomiest prophets see this as a real possibility. The reasons are manifold, and three years ago I charted some of them in an article in *Theology* entitled 'Parties in the Church of England'. Although not exclusively about the Catholic tradition, it was Catholics who responded most warmly to what I had to say. I remarked that the success of Catholicism in the Church of England is directly related to its decline as a movement. We are all aware of the remarkable revolution that the rediscovery of our place in Catholic Christendom has wrought in our Church. A mere hundred years separate us from the bitter disputes of the Victorian era about regular Eucharists, the mixed chalice, vestments, auricular confession

Address to the Affirming Catholicism Conference, York, Tuesday 2 July 1991.

and so much else which is taken for granted by Anglicans today. I noted that partly due to its own success Anglican Catholicism seems to have lost its sense of direction these days. And indeed, its obsession with the single issue of the ordination of women seemed almost to indicate a death wish – a desire to waste away. The very existence of the Affirming Catholicism movement is a pertinent reminder to the Church that Catholicism stands for much more than a particular attitude to the ordination of women to the priesthood.

If there is one thing I regret about my *Theology* article, it is its title – 'Parties in the Church of England'. Catholicism is always weakened by party spirit. Anything which restricts its vision or narrows its sympathies detracts from Catholicism's witness to the wholeness of the Church. Its contribution to Anglicanism has been a reminder that our Church forms part of a universal body of believers. Our communion with those outside Anglicanism may be imperfect but with them we share the Catholic creeds, the same scriptures, the apostolic ministry and that quality of the entire Church which is predicated by the term 'Catholic'. All that I want to say about Anglican Catholicism needs to be seen in the context of this wider vision. If the Affirming Catholicism movement gets bogged down by simply creating another party in the Church of England, its mission will have failed.

Yet there is more to be said about the definition of Catholicism than I have done so far without narrowing its horizons. We need to hold on to the original meaning of the word 'Catholic' in the epistles of Ignatius of Antioch, where it is an adjective qualifying the word 'church' and means a 'worldwide' body of believers. Later 'catholic' came to mean 'orthodox' in distinction from those who deviated from the faith of the Church. Today it is a widely used term with as many meanings as those who claim it as their possession. But it is worth pointing out that contrary to what many people believe, the opposite of 'Catholic' is not 'Protestant', but 'heterodox' or 'sectarian'. In its proper historical context the opposite of Protestant is not 'Catholic' but 'Papist'. The claim of our Church to be 'Catholic and reformed' was and is no empty formula because our Reformers did not reject Catholic faith;

they wished for a restoration of Catholic faith and practice. This is not, of course, to open up old wounds or assert old shibboleths. Roman Catholic, Anglican and Protestant theologians are now agreed in abhorring the bitterness that led to that split, whilst respecting the motives that led to all sides taking up passionate positions.

Yet whatever meaning people bring to Catholicism, it does represent a multi-layered theological, ecclesiastical and social mosaic which is of great importance to the Church. Catholicism in all its richness is vital for the progress of the faith in our land. I would like to explore just some of the patterns of the Catholic mosaic.

Catholicism embraces a faith that is truly *incarnational.* This may appear to be an unexceptional observation, but it is not to one brought up to view the Christian faith and life as stemming mainly from a theology centred on the death of Christ. Such a view sometimes leads to an other-worldly attitude to spirituality and to a didactic faith devoid of symbolism and beauty. Protestantism may lead, as we know well, to a dreary and dull attitude to life because the Christian hope is almost entirely projected into the future. In contrast to this, Hilaire Belloc gave exuberant expression to the world-affirming qualities of Catholicism in his verse:

> Where'er the Catholic sun doth shine,
> There's music and laughter and good red wine.
> At least I've always found it so –
> Benedicamus Domino!

Belloc spoke, of course, for Roman Catholicism, but the vista painted is of a Catholic view of life, stemming from the incarnation of the Lord within the world, redeeming it by his life, death and resurrection, and thereby making it our home. The implication of this for ministry is obvious. A Catholic view of ministry has seen the incarnational spirit as being pivotal for the exercise of a genuine priesthood, in contrast to other theologies. Thus the notion of surrendering oneself to a ministry in a given place – to its suffering and gloom and death, as well as its joys and hopes – is rooted in a Catholic incarnational theology.

I was born in the East End of London. Although I am too young to know the great Anglo-Catholic Fathers of the East End – Bethnal Green, Poplar, Stoke Newington, Bow – my parents regaled me with stories of their commitment, life and love. And since my parents were not regular churchgoers, this shows the impact of these sacrificial ministries. I recall hearing about Brother Andrew who worked among the tramps and sang 'Count your blessings, name them, one by one', while innocently plucking fleas from his cassock, fully aware of the irony of the words! Of course, it is not only Catholic priests who live and work and die among their people, but Catholic incarnational theology sees the action of God in and through the Son, who comes to be among his people, and is prepared to sacrifice everything for their sake.

Within the Catholic mosaic there is a second element which is very closely connected with the incarnational – the sacramental principle. Sacraments speak of God, operative and present through the visible, the tangible and the historical, indeed through the entire created order. Richard McBrien puts it in this way: 'The great sacramental encounter with God is Christ, and the Church, in turn, is the sacrament of encounter with Christ, and the sacraments in turn are the signs and instruments by which that ecclesial encounter with Christ is expressed, celebrated and made effective for all.' The implication is that no thing and no person is ever outside Christ's presence and love. The infinite capacity of Son to redeem, renew and restore is taken up by the Church's ministry and mission to declare the triumph of grace. I caught a glimpse of this at the Deptford Festival, which I talked about in Chapter 13.

I was greeted with 'consider yourself at home' as I entered the Church; Chinese children danced; there was more exuberant singing around the baroque altar. The local culture was being brought into church, celebrated and baptised. This was not an encounter with the Church on the Church's terms. It was clear that the local community helped set the agenda too.

However, the sacramental approach itself is not without its dangers. These principally arise from the very openness which is its deep attraction. Hans Küng notes that if Protestantism might be accused of being too little or too narrow, then 'Catholicism cannot escape the accusation of being too much, a syncretistic collection of heterogeneous, misguided and even unchristian elements'. He continues: 'There is a sin of *peccatum per excessum*, a sin of excess, as well as *peccatum per defectum*.' The question then arises: What controls a tradition? On what basis do we say that a development is legitimate or illegitimate? Newman's ingenious attempt to justify development as a natural element of Catholic doctrine is not without its problems, as Chadwick's *From Bossuet to Newman* shows so admirably. Principally it is that a so-called development may be so far from the original deposit of faith that it appears to be a new revelation.

This directs us to a third element within Catholicism – namely its anchor in, and commitment to, the original deposit of faith. Newman's doctrine of development, whatever its problems, is a testimony in itself to this. Even the earliest definitions of Catholicism against the heterodox views of Gnostics and others viewed the identity of the Church essentially in terms of its faithfulness to the *kerygma*, to the deposit of faith. The classical expression of it is found in the famous Vincentian Canon: '*Semper, ubique et ab omnibus*', i.e. 'What has been held everywhere, always and by all'. The inclusiveness of this statement, taking in time and space, is very questionable, as Newman and others saw. It appeared to rule out the development of doctrine and dogma.

Whatever the difficulties over the development of doctrine, Catholicism is rooted in the historic faith of the Church. Its claim to be so is questioned only when it departs from the *regula fidei*, the Church's rule of faith. Our Reformers were quite clear that the Reformation had not made a new Church, but had merely restored catholicity to the Church by returning scripture to its rightful place at the heart of the Church and by making tradition and reason as subservient to God's word.

However, where do we stand today when it seems that Catholic doctrine is in danger of being overthrown by new developments? This question is brought sharply into focus by the issue of the ordination of women to the priesthood. Anglican Catholics – some of them anyway – have felt that unity with Rome was becoming a real possibility, but that the ordination of women will mean such progress as we have made will be lost. This is not the place to say whether their optimism was justified, but I do want to stress that those who appeal to the unity of the Church in the debate are not drawing our attention to anything we did not know.

On what basis then dare we as a Church take such a momentous step of ordaining women? Some would say that we dare not and cannot do such a thing without damaging our claim to be part of the universal Catholic Church. But that argument has to be examined. Is it really the case that such a change must be submitted to the scrutiny of Churches with whom we are not yet in communion? This is a novel argument even though those who propound it begin with an appeal to antiquity. Orthodoxy does not submit developments in its life to Rome before ratifying change. It is unlikely that the reforms of the Second Vatican Council would have taken place – certainly not as quickly – if Rome had waited for the approval of the Orthodox. Our Reformers would have regarded the idea that major changes in the Church's life should await some General Council with complete amazement. It would have ruled out the Reformation itself. However regrettable you might think the Reformation, it is difficult to be an Anglican without recognising its positive contribution to our understanding of Catholicism. William Wake, Archbishop of Canterbury (1717–37) said that: 'The Church of England as a national Church has all the power within herself over her own members, which is necessary to enable her to settle her doctrines, government and discipline.' To Dr du Pin in Paris he wrote: 'In short the Church of England is free, is orthodox and has plenary authority within herself. She has no need to recur to other Churches to direct her what to believe or what to do.'

Of course this is not to say that we should ignore the entreaties and the advice of other Churches, but to quote Wake again: 'The truths of Christianity must not be sacrificed to the peace of Christians.'

Wake was not arguing for some form of Anglican

independency. He was no isolationist in doctrine or sympathies. The European links he established were remarkable for their breadth. What he emphasised, however, is that Anglicanism had preserved the deposit of faith in its loyalty to the scriptures, the creeds, the definitions of the General Councils, the threefold ministry and so on. Developments in its life would flow from those loyalties and be tested by them. The Church of England was no new creation, floating free from the rest of Catholic Christendom.

Faced by the issue of the ordination of women, the irony is that one group of Anglican Catholics now claims that the ordination of women may be a legitimate development within Catholicism while another group declares that it either is not or probably is not! Development, even in Newman's theory, was never achieved painlessly.

There is of course another pain we must recognise. This is the pain of women baptised into Christ who feel disenfranchised, marginalised and unheard. We must recognise the distress of both groups of people – those who feel such a development would call into question our Church's claim to be Catholic, and those who feel they are not included in that catholicity simply because they are female. They believe that Catholics, above all, should witness to the wholeness of humanity in which arbitrary divisions between male and female have no place.

This brings me to a fourth exciting element in the Catholic mosaic – the notion of *wholeness* itself. For many Catholics this is linked with two things. The first is the 'whole' Church. There are many Christians who regard the Church as simply a social entity, but not Catholics. For them it is an extension of God's being and life; part of the givenness of a sacramental understanding of faith. This gives to Catholicism a breadth and depth which invites Christians on a journey towards the fullness of faith. To use a phrase which I have learned from both Gerard W Hughes and Rowan Williams, there is in Catholicism a capacity to be surprised. Catholicism, secure in its faith, has always encouraged speculative thinking. Its devotional life is strong enough to test it out; its traditions are secure enough to allow the Gamaliel principle to work. At its best, Catholicism creates an openness which produces possibilities for development as well as growth. Part of this journey is into the mystery of God himself, revealed as he is in Christ, but still capable of fresh understandings, new insights and undiscovered possibilities.

The other side of this is the 'wholeness' which the individual Christian seeks; the pathway of prayer, contemplation and praise. It comes as no surprise, therefore, to note that the monastic and retreat movements, the Desert Fathers, the great pioneers of mysticism and spirituality, derive almost entirely from the Catholic tradition of the Church. The Catholic style is seen most visibly and experienced most concretely here together with the hunger and drive for holiness without which we shall not see God. Of course, I do not wish to suggest that the tradition that first shaped me is and was incapable of teaching me to pray, to be silent, or to be holy. Far from it; the Evangelical tradition is firmly and passionately committed to a walk with the Lord, to living in the presence of God, to a holy lifestyle as the outworking of sanctification. But most unbiased Evangelicals will freely admit that the very immediacy of Evangelical spirituality seems to close off the growth of spirituality which is such a mark of the Catholic style. Central to that, of course, is the sacrament of the Eucharist which makes available here and now the fruits of redemption as the sacrament of the body and blood of Christ are taken afresh. Such notions as sacramental presence and sacramental adoration are hallmarks of Catholic spirituality and part of the wholeness which the worshipper pursues.

A superficial observer might think that such a tradition would be so other-worldly as to be of no earthly use. Far from it, and this brings me to a fifth part of the mosaic – Catholic social thought. Catholicism encourages a strong social conscience and a commitment to meeting people's material needs. I have already referred to the fine priests of the East End, but one can think also of missionaries, like Bishop Frank Weston of Zanzibar, whose commitment to Christ led them into a radical obedience to his call to live among the poorest and to suffer with them. When a young priest bleated to Bishop Frank that he could not possibly live among savages in Africa,

Frank growled: 'Who said anything about living. You can glorify Christ by your death, you know!' That deeply evangelical Catholic statement is more than a social gospel; it is *the* gospel expressed in dynamic action, and stems from the incarnational and sacramental principle noted earlier. I believe that ministry is still being expressed and lived out in our Church today by some priests, and we thank God for it.

But I would be doing Catholic social thought and action an injustice if I gave the impression that it was limited to the heroic work of a few priests. Catholicism has a social character because it emphasises the corporate. People are saved by becoming members of the saved community, the Church. The individual is saved *in community*. That is why the question 'Are you saved?' is a foreign language among Catholics. 'There is no salvation outside the Church' is not a formula for institutional restriction on God's activity. It points to his grace at work in communities. Catholics believe that Christ's death shows the depth of God's love for every human soul – no matter how unlovely and unresponsive they may be. Christ's love was not theoretical: it was shown in his suffering, in his healings, his battle with all that disabled and handicapped the living of a full human life. Catholic social teachers used to make much of the sacramental principle working in more than one way. Social evils were, they said, the devil's sacraments in which he communicated the deadliest of his poisons to alienate people from God.

The social mission of Anglican Catholicism has never been easy to distinguish from the final element of my mosaic – the evangelical spirit of Catholicism. The two have often been brought together in the life of religious communities: Anglican Franciscans, for example, have long referred to themselves as 'Catholic Evangelicals'. They, and other Anglican communities, have houses in the beautiful English countryside, but also in the midst of our inner cities and anonymous housing estates. Yet I hear few sermons urging the claims of the religious life. The fact that the Church of England has monks and nuns, friars and sisters, is one of our many well-kept secrets. Why keep so quiet about it?

It was largely from our religious communities that the

tradition of parish missions in Anglican Catholicism originated. I hear and see less of them now. The word 'mission' is avoided. Frequently the focus is on renewing the Church congregation before we can evangelise more widely – as if we are ever going to get the gospel right before we preach it to others. If we feel we have succeeded in doing so, the danger is that we think we 'possess' the gospel, and that gives rise to all sorts of terrible possibilities.

I hope that the Decade of Evangelism will help Anglican Catholics recover their evangelical spirit, and I hope too that the religious communities will be at the forefront of this.

So, which way Catholicism? Jeffrey John has remarked that:

The truth is that for years now, since well before the present crisis, Catholicism in the Church of England has been dwindling from a movement into a ghetto. It has become increasingly introverted, negative, fundamentalist and fearful and largely handed over teaching and evangelism – inside and outside the Church – to the Evangelicals.

That perception is uncomfortable but true. But it ought not to be. I want to affirm Catholicism and wish to suggest that you re-examine that mosaic of which I spoke.

If, as I have said, Catholicism has made such an amazing contribution to the Church of England then perhaps the next step is to consolidate its life by affirming Catholicism in the traditions of others. The fullness of Catholicism, I remind you, does not lie in the Church but in the Lord of the Church. The Church only knows of the fullness of Christ. He is the fullness of Catholicism. No genuine Catholicism ever moves away from him but only *into* his fullness. Hans Küng said – and I am passionately committed to this point of view – 'We need to replace a shortsighted and exclusive "Protestantism" and a diffuse and confused "Catholicism" with an "evangelical catholicity" based and centred on the gospel.' Indeed, the challenge confronting Catholicism is whether it is Catholic enough to contain forms of evangelicalism within it; just as the challenge facing Evangelicalism today is whether its gospel is genuinely Catholic.

Think again of the elements of the mosaic – an incarnational faith, the sacramental principle, the commitment to the *regula fidei*, the notion of wholeness, the tradition of social thought and action, and an evangelical spirit. All of them are linked. Catholic worship is in danger of becoming an empty ritual if the ministry which accompanies the celebration of the sacraments has no incarnational dimension. In its ministry, Catholicism must give priority to the pastoring of the unchurched, and avoid betraying its tradition by setting sharp divisions between the Church and the world. If it does not take care it could go in that direction and become a sect, losing its sense of wholeness, bereft of social action, and within an embattled rather than evangelical spirit.

It must not neglect the deposit of faith. My advice is to listen to the strange saints of the desert, those puzzling early Fathers, and the voices of the Apostles. And, above all, attend to the word of scripture. Catholics have always been suspicious of proof texts because they attend to the *whole* message of the scriptures, and pray it in the Psalms and the Offices. The God of the scriptures will always break free of any attempt to close him in a book, just as he will break free of any effort to imprison him in a tabernacle. God will always surprise us by leading us into the fullness of truth, and he will always revive his Church with the waters of new life. In this Decade of Evangelism I pray for a vibrant Anglican Catholicism which will again feed the hearts and souls of God's people and lead our Church deeper into the heart of the glory and mystery of our God.

23

The Ordination of Women

The Church of England is no stranger to days of decision such as we face over the ordination of women to the priesthood. At such times we are caught between faith and fear: between the excitement of a new experience and the fear of the risk involved. We are fearful for the Church's unity, for we know God wills his Church to be one. We may be fearful too that this decision could irretrievably fracture the tradition and character of the ordained priesthood as we have inherited it. But I believe that these fears – which in various ways we all share – are not well-grounded. God calls us to take the risk of faith. I believe God is also calling his Church to ordain women to the priesthood.

We come to the debate on the ordination of women priests well prepared. It is no precipitate measure foisted upon an unwilling Church. It has been on the Synod's agenda for nearly twenty years. We have experienced the ministry of well over a thousand women in the diaconate. Elsewhere in the Anglican Communion, women priests are making an increasingly important contribution. And at diocesan and deanery levels, the voting on this legislation clearly demonstrates that it is looked upon with favour by the majority of people.

We have made haste slowly, because we want as broad a measure of unity as we can manage. We look for a two-thirds majority of all those voting in each House: few secular governing bodies set such a demanding threshold. This is a sign of our care for unity.

Despite all this, some people may still wonder whether ordaining women might be an unprecedented risk for the

Contribution to the Debate on Priests (Ordination of Women) Measure, General Synod, Church House, London, Wednesday 11 November 1992.

Church to take. Let us look back for guidance to one of the key days of decision in the Church's life. In the tenth chapter of the Acts of the Apostles, God challenges Peter's assumption that the gospel is only for the Jews.

First, it begins with what is familiar. Peter repeatedly dreams about the food laws. He thinks he knows all about them. God challenges us to begin in the world we know. Today we are looking at a familiar world – of priests and vicars, Church and society, gifts and leadership. We are being challenged to do something new, but it is in the context of what we already know so well, just as it was for Peter.

Secondly, messengers take Peter to Cornelius the Centurion. Peter finds, to his astonishment, that the Spirit has already been given to the Gentiles. God has been working outside the traditions and categories with which Peter is familiar. We too are being challenged to reconsider what God has been doing outside our familiar world in the light of our changed situation.

The final stage is reached as Peter interprets his vision in the light of his new experience. He sees that God does call the Gentiles into the body of Christ. God has shown that what seems novel and risky is consonant with what has happened in the past. I believe the same dynamic is at work today.

The inclusion of the Gentiles within the body of Christ was not as obvious at the time as it now appears. It seemed to be a major break with tradition. The Church is also facing what some believe to be another break with tradition. That is not the case. We are not departing from a traditional concept of ministry. We are talking about an extension of the same ministry to include women. Christianity is all about God liberating, renewing and drawing out what has been there implicitly from the beginning.

Some argue that the Church of England has no right to make such changes on its own. We know that the Roman Catholic Church and the Orthodox Churches do not at present countenance this change. That, however, cannot be an obstacle to the Church of England determining its own mind. Article twenty makes it clear that the Church of England 'hath authority in controversies of faith'.

I am well aware that there are those who are profoundly troubled by the ecumenical implications of the decision to ordain women. I recognise this, but this consideration is not completely over-riding. I believe that constructive, loving relationships with our sister Churches can and will continue. Significant parts of Christendom do not ordain women to the priesthood, but there are many traditions in which the experience of women in ministry is not a burden but a joy, not a handicap to mission but a strength. We must not look in one direction only.

Beyond all this there lies a wider issue. How do we find God's will in such a matter? My predecessor, Robert Runcie, who patiently guided us through the years of the most heated debate on this subject, comments in his book, *Authority in Crisis?*, that the Anglican way is essentially that of the '*consensus fidelium*'. That is to say, it is the gathering together of a response from as many quarters of the Church as possible. Part of that must be in the voting of our Diocesan Synods which indicate that, for our Church, most people believe that God's moment has come for us on this issue.

Discernment does not come through votes alone, but through the manifestation of gifts. Gifts are God's generosity. We have seen the marks of the Spirit increasingly manifest in the ministry of women as well as that of men. We must draw on all our available talents, if we are to be a credible Church engaged in mission to an increasingly confused and lost world. We are in danger of not being heard if women are exercising leadership in every area of our society's life, save the ordained priesthood.

The Anglican way of deciding such matters inevitably involves pain and conflict. The question of truth matters so much to us that as a Church we do not hide our disagreements. We air them in public. We try to find our way through them in a spirit of love and respect for the views of others.

That is why the legislation on women's ordination takes account of those who, in conscience, have to dissent from it and yet do not wish to leave the Church of England. And the associated financial measure makes provision for those few, and I pray they may be very few, who feel duty bound to leave the ordained ministry over this issue.

I urge those who see the future only in terms of schism to recognise that disputes about the nature of ministry are not regarded in the New Testament as grounds for formal separation from one's fellow Christians. The ordination of women to the priesthood is, I believe, a development in the Church's tradition. It alters not a word in the creeds, the scriptures, or the faith of our Church.

Ours is a Church called to look outwards in mission, to be confident in service, and to be prophetic in preaching and teaching. We are also called to be a comprehensive Church in which those who believe on grounds of conscience that women should not be ordained still have an honourable place among us as bishops, clergy and lay people. I desire that those who oppose the ordination of women on grounds of conscience should continue to play their full part in the life of our Church. This debate is not about excluding anybody, but enlarging the sympathies and generosity of our Church in line with the generosity of God himself. I hope with all my heart that we will affirm the place of women in the priesthood of Christ's Church as confidently as Peter affirmed the place of the Gentiles. Let us say with him: 'God gave them no less a gift than he gave us when we put our trust in the Lord Jesus: how could I possibly stand in God's way?'

24

Christon Our Peace

For he is our peace. EPHESIANS 2:12

On Christmas Day 1991 the world's TV screens witnessed a historic sight. We saw the Red Flag being hauled down from the Kremlin where it had flown for 74 years. The vision of Karl Marx, the intellect of Lenin, the oppression of Stalin – all had come to naught. The revolution which was to have led to a new world order of peace, had collapsed, and millions of men and women had died in the process. It is surely one of the great ironies of history that the Hammer and Sickle should have been lowered for the last time on the very day that Christians celebrate the birth of Jesus Christ. For he was heralded as the Prince of Peace, and it was said of him 'the increase of his government and of his peace there shall be no end'.

What is Christ's peace? Jesus himself was careful to distinguish it from the world's peace. 'My peace I give you', he said, 'but not as the world gives.' His peace is at one and the same time more fragile and more powerful. It is fragile because the peace which Christ brings comes not through weapons of war. It cannot be imposed by force, but comes when networks of people are warmed by encounter with the living God. Christ's peace is constructed from the raw materials of justice and mercy, compassion and forgiveness, humility and trust. That is the new creation that Christ inaugurated. In that stable at Bethlehem he became our peace. The child, asleep in a manger, started a revolution in human relationships which has lasted not 74 years, but two millennia. Ever since the shepherds were

---

Address given to the Church of the Redeemer, Amman, Jordan,
Saturday 4 January 1992.

surprised by the message of the angels, the gospel of peace has been a revolutionary force in human history. It certainly made Herod uneasy, and it will always threaten tyrannical rule. The wise men were told that a new king had been born; they were dimly aware that a new era had begun. The exact shape of it they left to others, but the seeds of it were to be seen in that Bethlehem stable. The new order springs from the holy family, and the person of the infant king.

What then is our understanding of Christ's peace? First, there is *the person of Jesus Christ*. Christ is himself our peace: we preach him, and our lives and the life of our Churches should reflect that. Christianity is rooted in the incarnation. The message of the angels was Emmanuel, God with us. The idea of God taking human nature upon himself is often seen as a scandal by other religions. We understand that, but we do not apologise for it. My predecessor, William Temple, called Christianity 'the most materialistic of all religions'. God identifies himself with us. He commits himself to his people. It was Christ's presence in his people that enabled Christians in the Soviet Union to withstand Stalin's purges, to maintain their faith and their human dignity, to be faithful witnesses. So it has been throughout history. As God emptied himself in Jesus, so it has been with the twentieth-century martyrs.

Secondly, there is *the message of Christ*. As Christ's messengers of peace, we are commissioned to spread his peace throughout the world. There is in all human hearts the yearning for peace, prosperity and freedom. All races have a legitimate right to seek these goals, and to build their own communities on their own land. We are all entitled to live at peace with our neighbours, free from oppression, victimisation and fear.

In the Occupied Territories and Israel, Israelis and Palestinians are struggling to overcome deep divisions. There are no simple solutions. There are, however, fundamental human rights, shared by Jews, Muslims and Christians alike. One right is the right to live in one's homeland. I understand the Jewish desire to live in peace in the Holy Land. We understand the pain, suffering and oppression they have endured over the years – which the Churches were slow to recognise. But there is another parallel suffering, the suffering and pain of the Palestinian people. Muslim and Christian Palestinians have frequently been deprived of their rights, their freedom and their homeland. They too have a right to be heard. Justice and peace require no less, and we long to see Arab and Jew living side by side. We fervently hope and pray that the Peace Process will be crowned with success however long it takes. The whole world is longing to see a new order of mutual respect – of each other's beliefs, of each other's histories, and of each other's experiences and of each other's hopes. As Christians we must work to achieve for others those rights we most cherish for ourselves.

Then, thirdly, there is *the mission of Christ*. Violence is not the Christian way, it is an admission of failure, an abdication of our humanity. It is only as a last resort that Christians would turn to arms. That is why Christians must be in the forefront of reconciliation, working wholeheartedly for justice and peace. 'Blessed are the peacemakers', said Jesus, not the peace-lovers, who stand on one side and hope. Christians are people with a mission. We are to be actively engaged in the struggle – by prayer, by personal involvement and commitment. Let there be no mistake: Christian mission is always costly. You cannot build peace by making others suffer, but nor can you or I build peace unless we are prepared to suffer ourselves. That surely is what we learn from the sacrifice of Christ. He died on the cross to reconcile us to God and to one another, and those who wish to follow his way must learn to love as he did. That is our mission. That is how tragic suffering can be redeemed.

The church in Amman in Jordan is dedicated to Christ the Redeemer. It is a dedication that Christians there have not ignored. The church was built by refugees, and it has ministered to them over many years. I pay tribute to the way they have lived up to their name, for they have played their part in alleviating the suffering of this region. With other Churches they have offered hospitality and relief in the name of Christ. No country has carried a heavier burden of refugees than Jordan; no country has opened its arms more generously or hospitably to the stranger.

Indeed the whole Anglican Communion carries the pain and the anguish of the people of Jordan in its heart. We are members one of another, and we cannot bypass each other's concerns. We hear the cries of the Palestinian people. We want to share your burdens. When you suffer, we suffer too, for we are one body in Christ. Christ's peace is indivisible, and we know that in ministering to one another Christ himself can touch us. In this way the witness of the Churches of the Middle East has strengthened the Churches of the world.

Christ is our peace. At every Eucharist we quote these words at its most central moment. It is not a pious hope, or empty rhetoric. He has broken down the dividing wall – between God and ourselves, and between each other. In studying Christ's words, and following Christ's way, we can discover God's hope for peace in our world. We commit ourselves to his way, and place our trust in the Prince of Peace, believing that 'of the increase of his government and of his peace there will be no end'. May the God of peace fill you with his grace, and enable you to be instruments of his peace in the years to come, and to touch the lives of others with dignity, hope and the blessing of God.

25

Jerusalem: Mission and Joy

The Anglican Church took a risk when, 150 years ago, my predecessor, Archbishop Howley, consecrated Bishop Alexander in Lambeth Palace Chapel and sent him to Jerusalem to be the first Anglican Bishop. The Royal Navy offered a vessel to take the bishop, his wife and party. When the bishop found that the ship was called *Infernal*, he was horrified. He felt that was wholly inappropriate and would only confirm people's worst fears about Christianity, so, reluctantly, the Royal Navy offered another vessel. The second ship was no great improvement – its name was *Devastation*! However the offer was accepted and we now know from the history of the diocese that devastation has not been the result.

Instead we rejoice in 150 years of Christian service to the whole community, 150 years of preaching that has been true to the gospel, and respected the rights and dignities of the surrounding faith communities. We rejoice that the Church in Jerusalem is a truly local indigenous Church rooted in the soil of the Holy Land, a Church come of age. And we not only look *back* with thanksgiving but also *forward* to new challenges and fresh opportunities.

The scriptures offer us several clues about the role of the Church in our world, but I believe two key words go to the heart of it: *mission* and *joy*. The gospel leaves us in no doubt that the Christian faith is all about God's mission to his world. It is a mission born of love; freely and generously given. The gift of Christ takes our breath away as we take in all that Christmas means for us and our world.

Address at the 150th Anniversary Celebration of the Diocese of Jerusalem, St George's Cathedral, Jerusalem, Sunday 5 January 1992.

But what are the *dynamics* of this mission in our day and age?

There is, first of all, the fact of *opposition and hostility*. In the scriptures, Herod the Great figures as a hostile threat to the infant Christ. Herod is of course one of history's greatest villains – as well as one of its greatest builders. Jealousy and pique made him put to death his favourite wife and most of his sons. Indeed, a sick joke at the time was that it was better to be one of the pigs than one of his sons. Herod, however, was right to recognise Jesus as a threat to his regime – the two could never have got along. True religion can never be indifferent to the exercise of political power, and good government will always recognise that true power comes only from God. Christianity cannot tolerate man's inhumanity to man. It will always threaten evil and sin, strife and bickering. The message of Christmas is that God has taken on the powers of evil and darkness. Christians everywhere are called to do the same, to oppose anything that challenges his Kingdom of justice and peace. If human rights are endangered, the weak are oppressed, or religious minorities marginalised – then Christians must protest and, if need be, suffer for Christ's sake. I acknowledge with some sadness that the Church has sometimes fallen short of these ideals. But there have nevertheless been wonderful examples of their being put into action through the ministry of the Anglican Church in its work in schools, in hospitals and clinics as well as its continuing pastoral work. For all that we thank God.

But there is another element in that mission. It is this. Jesus Christ is *God's gift to all people*. The Christian mission is a universal mission. It is a mission to all the world, or it is a mission to none. If Christ does not speak to humanity as a whole he has nothing to say to anyone. This is not a popular claim, but the heart goes out of our mission if as Christians we are not prepared to name the name of Jesus Christ and to speak of him to all people. Evangelism is the Church's proper task. Of course it must be done with sensitivity and love, especially among those who disagree with us. God's way of evangelising arises from a generosity of spirit which is inclusive, not exclusive; welcoming not rejecting; inviting not repudiating. The gospel makes the point that the mission that started in Bethlehem so long ago was universal. The wise men represent the Gentile world and carry the unspoken message that Christ's salvation is for all.

But I pinpointed *two* words: *mission* and *joy*. Joy is at the heart of the gospel message too. When the wise men saw the star, they 'rejoiced with great joy'. Their quest was finished when they entered into the presence of the one they believed to be the real king.

But joy which simply looks back is in danger of becoming nostalgic; it runs the risk of assuming that God only acts in the past and that the days of progress are over. But Christians are Easter people, people of hope – we are always reaching forward, never completely discouraged when difficulties come. The *dynamics* of joy in the gospel story offer a way forward for us today. Note the way that joy is often found alongside *suffering*. The joy of incarnation cannot be separated from homelessness, pain and fear of persecution.

The Holy Family were refugees, fleeing to Egypt from the threat of Herod. In the ministry of Christ we find the same combination of joy with hardship and suffering – even the cross combines the two ingredients. The Church that bears his name – if it is true to him – cannot escape the same tension. There can be no joy without pain. In every land, in every ministry, this combination is found. It is found in the Holy Land. As a visitor to that land for a number of years my heart goes out to its people. I find myself caught up in the pain of different communities. I think of the Jewish people who have passed through so much and who still fear for their security. But I also think of the Palestinian community, often ignored and overlooked. Both communities have a right to belong there, and each community should recognise that right in the other. The whole world hears their cries, and longs to see peace and justice restored.

The second dynamic has to do with *the offering of our gifts.* The wise men responded by offering gifts they had carried from their home lands; they gave their best. But generosity is not restricted to the rich. Those who have very few possessions can give the most precious things of all – their love, their devotion, their commitment. I am aware that Christians in Jerusalem, for example, sometimes feel unsupported by the richer and larger Christian Church. We in the Diaspora must do more to extend our support and love. But God is not limited by our weakness or poverty; if he were, the Diocese of Jerusalem would never have been founded. On the contrary, the sending out of Bishop Alexander I talked about earlier was an act of faith; it could have resulted in failure. But it didn't. It resulted in a new community of faith. The joy of the gospel inspired those pioneer missionaries, and today we thank God for them.

No one can visit Jerusalem today and remain unmoved. Christian pilgrims to this holy city are moved by the world-changing events that took place here. God has made it a holy place. But people are more important than places, and I am moved by its people – by their plight, by their courage, by their commitment to their Lord. The people of Jerusalem are always in my heart as every day I thank God for the grace of Our Lord Jesus Christ first revealed there, for the faith of its Anglican followers, and I pray for its peace in the years to come.

26

Unity with Roman Catholics

Salvation is nearer to us than when we first believed.
ROMANS 13:11

St Paul lived in a dangerous world by any standard. The world of the Roman Empire, the heart of which was in Rome, was a world of uprisings, intrigue, disasters and uncertainties. For the growing, but tiny Christian congregations in places like Rome, Antioch and elsewhere the anchor of their hopes was the certainty of Christ's salvation. The verse above seems to express Paul's feeling that final salvation was imminent. Two thousand years later we still await that final salvation. We long for it with a desire equal to St Paul's, because our world is at least as perilous. We think of the collapse of the Soviet Empire. Even though we may welcome an end to this and other regimes which curtail political and religious freedom, it still reminds us of the precariousness of human institutions. We also see how the fragile aspirations for European unity are being threatened by nationalistic tendencies. Racial tension, sectarian violence and apocalyptic nightmares about the state of our environment place in jeopardy our desire for a tranquil world order.

But in a real way St Paul could say with confidence, 'Salvation is nearer to us than when we first believed', because obviously every day takes us nearer to that time when God will make all things new. But does this verse have anything to say to our ecumenical situation today? I believe it does in three ways: Salvation is rooted in our common baptism; it is made

Address given during the Archbishop's visit to His Holiness
Pope John Paul II and the Church in Italy, St Paul-Within-the-Walls,
Rome, Sunday 24 May 1992.

known in our common search for God's truth, and it is expressed in our common mission. Let us begin with baptism. My meeting with Pope John Paul is anchored in an obvious but crucially important theological point; we recognise one another as fellow Christians and pilgrims. Baptism in the name of the Holy Trinity is a family sign; it is the sacrament of our membership of the family of God.

Although there is a slowing down of ecumenical progress compared with a generation ago, we take a great deal of comfort from what has been achieved. In particular, bearing in mind our history, we rejoice in how Rome and Canterbury have been converging towards that unity which is the will of our Lord. Many coalescing factors have contributed to where we are today. We think of the Second Vatican Council; we think too of the Secretariat for Christian Unity and the many national Roman Catholic and Anglican networks which have helped draw us together; we think of the initiative of Pope Paul VI and Archbishop Michael Ramsey in 1966, on that occasion at St Paul-Outside-the-Walls, which brought the Anglican–Roman Catholic International Commission, ARCIC, to birth. I want to express my admiration for the theologians who have contributed so remarkably to the work of ARCIC. My own longing for unity with the Roman Catholic community emerged with great intensity from two visits which I made to Rome some years ago, when I studied Roman Catholic history and dogma.

Alongside all this, the Anglican and Catholic Churches have grown together so much. We have reached remarkable agreement concerning the nature of the Eucharist; we have acknowledged the priesthood of the ordained ministry without denying the priesthood of all believers. We have reached agreement concerning that most controversial of Reformation doctrines, justification by faith. Although much remains to be done, the gains are enormous. Central to those gains is a recognition of our common baptism. Divided and broken though we may be, separated from one another by the tragic divisions which we personally did not cause, we can still say of one another, 'We are fellow Christians'. Yet, we remain broken at the very point where true unity is manifested in the sacrament of the

Lord's Supper. Well did William Temple once declare, 'the essential scandal of Christian division is the inability of devout Christians to meet at the Lord's table'.

But let me return to our common baptism. For common baptism offers us a challenge as well as hope. It offers a challenge because if we are really members of Christ through this charism, why are we still separated from one another at the table? What have we done to separate the sacraments? How can we reunite them? Theologians from different communions are urging us to make baptism the starting point for unity. They ask us to put on one side issues that divide. Why wait for full communion, they cry? We are already one through our baptism. They have a point. But it is not that simple. Members of the same family who have become separated for hundreds of years, have developed different traditions, different understandings and different liturgies. We cannot simply brush these aside as being of no consequence.

But there is also hope because it is undeniably the case that the recognition of our common baptism means that we meet not as strangers but as fellow pilgrims and brothers and sisters in Christ. So baptism is the sign and seal of our salvation. But it is also the source of our common search for truth.

'What is truth?' was the cynical question that Pilate asked. As he spoke, he looked upon the one who is the epitome of truth, Jesus himself. Of course, theological truth is hard to describe and even harder to achieve. It belongs to each of our Communions to emphasise the importance of truth for doctrine and for living the Christian life. All our Churches are rooted in the faith once delivered to the saints. The search for truth requires humility. The moment one's communion insists on embodying it, we deny it to another. The problem is compounded by the fact that we cannot deny what God has given us. How do we bring together the richness that we have inherited and yet remain willing to be learners again? How may our Communions walk and change together without condemning what has benefited past generations of Christians? Surely the kernel of an answer is to be found in following Christ today. It is not that doctrine is supremely important and that life proves its importance; it is that life is supremely important and doctrine illuminates it. The Lutheran theologian Jürgen Moltmann put it splendidly: 'The nearer we come to Christ, the nearer we come together.'

And that common search for the truth in him may well be the way we shall overcome the remaining issues that divide. I am aware that the ordination of women to the priesthood presents a problem to the Orthodox and Roman Catholic Churches. It does so for many Anglicans as well. But I have to recognise that in parts of the Anglican Communion, the ordination of women has not destroyed the Church but, it could be argued, given it new life. There are other issues – authority and personal ethics, for example – which are equally perplexing. They will not defeat us if the end of our pilgrimage is Christ and we walk with him and to him together. We do know that 'Salvation is nearer to us than when we first believed' since we have already travelled a long way with one another, in our common search for God's truth.

But talk of salvation introduces too the note of mission. For St Paul the task of the Church was to proclaim Christ. Baptism, the gift of salvation, is a sign of the Spirit's empowering for mission. It commissions all the people of God for service in the world. We look out on a divided and confused world; such need and so many problems. The need for the gospel today is as great as it has ever been. But the task is too great for one Christian body to achieve alone.

Mission is thus a challenge as well as an opportunity. That challenge is to share mission together. I have often said that ecumenism in the 1990s is likely to take the form of the sharing of mission. Here is a potential for practical unity. Working from the common baptism of which I spoke earlier, we can share in that mission and service to people everywhere. The challenge is one that has to be addressed to every local church – Anglican, Orthodox, Lutheran, Reformed or Roman Catholic. The challenge is to co-operate, to share in liturgy whenever possible. Our priests already show deep cordiality and affection. Our lay people can learn from one another and appreciate the enormous riches which our different heritages have to offer. In such ways the challenge becomes an opportunity for God's grace to reach those at present outside the boundaries of the Church.

For the Christian, what is undeniable is the reality of God in his Church today; with you and me. It is that reality which gives us the strength to persevere, and which steadies our nerve when the ecumenical pilgrim's journey seems tough. Our common baptism, our common search for God's truth and the urgent and common task to reach all people everywhere with the claims of God's love and care, constantly call us to a fresh commitment and an ecumenical discipleship.

27
Multi-Faith Worship

I would like to put my views about multi-faith worship into a more general reflection on what I believe to be the authentic Christian stance in inter-faith relationships. I will concentrate on four key factors which bear on this question: generosity, surprise, challenge and integrity.

I speak of *generosity* because our God is generous. Salvation is all about God's wonderful generosity to us in Christ. He takes us as we are and makes us what he wants us to be. That generosity is seen in scripture in the way that peoples of other faiths are sometimes seen to be in a special relationship to God. In Michael Nazir-Ali's fine book, *From Everywhere to Everywhere*, he shows that the Bible contains a more generous estimate of the faith of non-Jews and non-Christians than we may think. We are warned not to be too grudging in our appreciation of the faith of others. Our Lord's marvelling words at the faith of the Centurion – 'See, I have not seen such faith in the whole of Israel' – may justly serve as an example of an observation of faith outside the covenanted community.

Since becoming Archbishop, I have had a great deal of contact with people of other faiths. I have been trusted with their confidences, their fears and their hopes. I have entered into a warm friendship with the Chief Rabbi and have already benefited greatly from what we have shared together. I have attended prayers in synagogues and have been moved by the depth of devotion. I can say the same of other traditions also. My growing understanding of other faiths has not been

Speech in the Debate on the Multi-Faith Worship?
report to the General Synod,
Church House, London, Sunday 12 July 1992.

without some significant challenges to my own. Bound up with the challenge has been greater knowledge and greater awareness of what they offer humankind. The main world religions are distinctive and different. Only an uninformed observer would believe they could be reconciled or that they were all different paths to one God. I believe neither of these things. But nor do I believe that the God I worship in Jesus Christ has nothing whatever to do with them.

That is why my second word is *surprise*. As we encounter people of other faiths, we see devout, worshipping people. Their faith in God and their adherence to what they understand are his commands may well rebuke our own half-heartedness and indiscipline in our daily living. A Christian walking by Muslims praying openly to Allah in a public place cannot help but be humbled by such a sight. I believe that the report by the Board of Mission, *Multi-Faith Worship?* gives us encouragement to explore the nature of another person's faith. A faith which may at first seem alien and frightening may lead us into many surprises – not only about the areas where we differ in matters of belief and practice, but perhaps more importantly about where we agree and where co-operation is possible.

This is where we are likely to face *challenge*. I believe it is only fearful, insecure Christians who avoid the positive encounter of dialogue and the sharing of common life. We must move beyond the dismissive and negative view that our only task in relation to other faiths is to bring them to Christ because they have nothing to offer us. I do not waver in my missionary endeavours or in my belief that Christ is for all – that I have made clear in all my encounters with people of other faiths – but I am also convinced that God has not hidden himself from other faiths. His grace is not absent from them. A dismissive attitude to other major world religions is found in different measure in many faith communities. To fail to honour the faith of another person soon leads to a failure to honour them as a human being made in God's image. Our world has seen too many conflicts resulting from such attitudes. We must not add to them.

I find my own faith profoundly challenged by theological

questions that come from other believers. For example, Shabbir Akhtar's criticisms of Christianity in his book, *A Faith for all Seasons*, describes the incarnation as 'cognitively suspect' and the Trinity as suffering from 'conceptual confusion'. Such intellectual challenges we can and must face. I wonder how many doctrine courses in our theological colleges compel students to do their theology in a multi-faith context? But together with this must go the principle of reciprocity. Other faith communities in this country enjoy freedom of worship, of association and, if they wish, they may evangelise. Christians rightly look for the same reciprocal freedoms in lands where they are in a minority, and they hope that other believers here will support them in that desire. This serious problem must be faced in places where severe religious laws restrict Christian freedom to worship and distribute the scriptures.

A further challenge is that of findings ways of deepening co-operation. Religions such as Judaism, Christianity and Islam do have much in common, as Hans Küng's book, *Global Responsibility*, makes plain. The kind of mutual exploration that *Multi-Faith Worship?* is encouraging parishes to do will, I believe, identify areas where real partnership in social care, in combating secularism, and in care for our environment, proves not only possible but is urgently necessary.

My final watchword is *integrity*. Frankly, I do not find that people of other faiths are clamouring to engage in multi-faith worship. Some of them have told me that they are puzzled by this apparent obsession amongst Christians. They have told me with real anger that they object to watering down theological truths in the hope that the lowest common denominator will make the event acceptable to all. It is at this point that I find the *Multi-Faith Worship?* report does not offer quite enough help. It would have been useful, for example, to have had some reflection on whether the options for multi-faith worship within the Jewish–Christian–Muslim tradition are greater than with other religions worldwide. This would have provided a good way of following up the Lambeth Conference document, *Jews, Christians and Muslims: The Way of Dialogue*. Secondly, I would have appreciated a little more work done on the different underlying meanings of multi-faith worship. I believe that the only safe ground for developing multi-faith relationships with integrity is one which begins from a firm base in Christian theology and epistemology. For me and for many here, that means that the finality of Christ in terms of God's revelation is pivotal and definitive. Can there really be common worship together if the content of faith is not agreed and shared? I really have strong doubts that such a thing is possible without there being some major qualifications about the very nature of worship itself. I fully appreciate that in a multi-faith and multi-cultural society the nature of a Civic Service may need to be reviewed. It is also self-evident that sensitivity should guide the preparation of the liturgy and the sermon if a large number of people present are going to be those from other faiths. But I am sure that a single tradition of faith should determine the character of the service. This preserves everyone's integrity. What other people ask of us is integrity and that is what we ask of them. If an unapologetic commitment to Christ is the framework for our dialogue with sincere followers of other faiths, we shall be respected and understood. They will not understand us and they possibly will not respect us either if our expression of faith falls a long way from the historic faith of which we are custodians and to which we bear witness. And we do not wish them to qualify their own distinctiveness simply to accommodate us.

The strength of *Multi-Faith Worship?* is that it recognises the distinctiveness of different world faiths. It is not an encouragement of multi-faith worship; indeed, it is a distinctively Christian piece of writing. But it is urging us to think, study and understand the strong conviction of others. I think if we do that, it will help us to understand and appreciate our own faith also – and may well provide an important ancillary theme in this Decade of Evangelism.

28

Taizé: A Lesson in Simplicity

Peter said to Jesus: 'Lord, it is good to be here.'
MATTHEW 17:4

These words of Peter on the Mount of Transfiguration capture many people's feelings about the Taizé Community
in Burgundy, which has become a centre of pilgrimage for
young people. It is a place which enables people to experience
a real meeting with our Lord. Like the disciples, people are
touched with the presence of Christ – in the singing, in the
praying, in the silence, in study and in the sharing together.
Even in the work and especially in common meals, the presence
of God can be felt. Again, like the disciples, one is able to
look beyond oneself to see 'no one but Jesus only'.

Perhaps this is the essential genius of Taizé. We are taken
out of ourselves and directed to Jesus Christ. That alone earns
our gratitude, although it also makes it tempting for us to
reflect Peter's spontaneous response to his transfigured Lord,
'Lord, it is good to be here. Let us make three tents and stay
here for ever!' Of course, some are called to remain at Taizé
to live the community life. But most are not called to be on the
mount for ever. Just as the Transfiguration gave the disciples a
new sense of direction, so at Taizé one can endeavour to
glimpse that same transfigured Lord and rediscover the truth
that Augustine found so long ago when he said of Christ that:
'Our hearts are restless until they find their rest in you.'

From Taizé, our Lord takes us by the hand and walks with
us down into the valley – back into the world in which sorrow
is mixed with joy, where wars between countries are matched

---

*Address to the Taizé Community, Taizé, Burgundy,
Thursday 27 August 1992.*

by conflicts within our personal lives. The special privilege and vocation of the Brothers is to point us back into the everyday world which must be the focus of reconciliation. What do they give to us?

First, Taizé is a *simple* community. My initial impression was that the buildings were only half-finished. Everything seemed makeshift. But the buildings are not meant to last for centuries. Taizé is not a symbol of permanence. That is deliberate. So simple; so basic. And the liturgy there is like that too – simple songs, simple prayers, short passages of scripture drawing us all into the heart of the gospel – Jesus Christ our Lord. This is the challenge of simplicity. Have we made Church life too complicated and obscured the person of Christ? When the disciples left the mount they 'saw no one but Jesus only'.

Second, Taizé is a *praying* community. My life, like yours, is full of busyness. At home my day begins with prayer. Without it I would be nothing. Taizé has reminded me of the importance of giving space to God. I felt God saying to me: 'Don't be in too much of a hurry. Stay here awhile with me. I am with you. Listen to me.' I found during the haunting singing a time when the worship of others has helped me to meditate and to reflect on my life and ministry. Let us make sure there is always space in our lives for prayer and stillness.

Third, Taizé is an *accepting* community. An international community, the barriers of language and geography are overcome by unity in Christ. Many different Christian traditions come together, but are transcended by oneness in our Lord. That is another of Taizé's challenges: however much we are grateful to the tradition which has shaped us, we need to be humble because no single tradition possesses the whole truth about God. This does not mean that our traditions are useless, valueless or unimportant. Let us cherish what God teaches us in our Churches but let us also value the genuine international and inclusive character of the Church of Jesus Christ.

Finally, Taizé's is a *hopeful* community. It reminds us of what God can do. Many years ago God took Brother Roger's simple obedience and out of it came a miracle. What a parable for us – that God's Church will never die as long as there are Christians who obediently follow the Lord's calling. We live in a world where many seem indifferent to God, but I believe that people are longing for Churches which are obedient to the hope to which they have been called.

I offer the following message to Brother Roger and the Community. It is the same message that the gospel addresses to us all: Keep your eyes fixed on Jesus and his love; stay Christ-centred and prophetic; stay youthful and keep listening to God and his world. And may God bless us all richly as we serve him.

29

European Co-operation

In 1990 the General Synod had a full debate on Europe and on how the Church of England could best contribute to a changing Europe. At a crucial point in that debate a priest from the diocese where I was then bishop made a memorable intervention: 'The Diocese of Europe must give us more guidance', he said. 'After all, the Standing Committee of this Synod do not live in Europe.' As you can imagine his words were drowned in laughter. Such an incident could doubtless reinforce one's worst fears about British insularity. Those fears have frequently been strengthened by the reflections of some British politicians. However, the fact that the Synod saw fit to debate 'The Church of England and Europe' could be interpreted as being encouraging in itself.

It is a fortunate coincidence that early in my time as Archbishop there should be a Conference of European Churches Assembly. Ever since the first Assembly at Nyborg in 1959, CEC has stood for a united Europe. East and West, left and right, could neither divide Christians nor indeed the peoples of Europe. Now, with the Iron Curtain drawn and indeed gone for ever, its prophetic stance has been vindicated. For that we give great thanks.

Britain's geographical position, towards the farthest western extremes of Europe, might suggest a marginal interest in CEC from the Church of England, but that has never been the case. This year marks the 150th anniversary of the Diocese of Gibraltar in Europe and thus of an Anglican presence and commitment in continental Europe. John Arnold's position

---

*Address to the Tenth Assembly
of the Conference of European Churches (CEC),
Prague, Monday 7 September 1992.*

there and his key role in the development of CEC is similarly symbolic of Anglican commitment. Earlier this year I took the opportunity to visit the CEC headquarters in Geneva and talk with the staff. I found that meeting most encouraging, although during our conversations we all acknowledged the great challenges, not to say dangers, facing the peoples and Churches of Europe at this time. Although Europe remains a high ideal in the minds of so many, it still remains a very fragile ideal at this moment in history.

Throughout the existence of CEC there have been two themes which have dominated its work: the unity of God's Church, and peace and unity among the nations. A week in Taizé with one thousand young Anglicans reinforced in my mind and heart how crucial these two themes are within the Christian gospel. The tragedy of the former Yugoslavia presses home on the human level how they cannot be separated. Christian divisions all too easily reinforce basic human divides. In the light of these hopes and dangers I would like to encourage the Churches of Europe to work on three specific matters which I know are already high on the agenda.

First of all, I am convinced that one of the highest priorities of the Church in Europe at present must be to build up trust between fragmented and sometimes opposed communities. Yugoslavia's fate once again says it all. Xenophobia and suspicion between Churches is running high throughout Europe. 'Ethnic and religious cleansing' run completely counter to the message of the Christian gospel. We dare not allow our peoples to return to historic rivalries. In this context, not only ecumenism, but inter-faith co-operation is paramount. A Muslim leader from Bosnia who visited my home at Lambeth recently pressed this home poignantly. 'We are Europeans,' he said. The spirit of trust and generosity must pervade our attempts to come to terms with all that has happened in our Churches and ecumenical bodies during the Cold War era. Such a spirit of trust will require forbearance when we might wish to accuse, and honesty when we might try to forget the difficult past. Now is the time for the healing of memories; reconciliation and not recrimination is the keynote of the gospel we proclaim.

Secondly, we are called to proclaim the gospel. Evangelism must remain at the centre of our priorities. Pope John Paul and also President Jacques Delors of the European Community have both spoken positively of the 'Soul of Europe'. They are right to do so and the commitment of some of our Churches to a Decade of Evangelism underscores this. We need to ask: How can our Churches best express the relevance of worship in a secular world? And secondly, what should be the form of a Christian apologetic for our society? Christianity has been the historic faith of so many people in Europe. We should remain proud of that inheritance and be ready to preach the gospel.

Finally, we cannot afford, or indeed defend, a 'fortress Europe'. The generosity of the gospel requires us to keep our frontiers open. It would be easy for either the dangers which beset us or indeed even our enthusiasm for Europe, to drive us as a continent back into ourselves. The rest of the world, and particularly the developing world desperately needs Europe and we need them. Alongside *their* challenges and difficulties, our own problems almost pale into insignificance.

The CEC has achieved much over the past 30 years.

May it continue to provide the vision and the energy for the tasks which lie ahead.

30

Anglican–Roman Catholic Relations– The Fullness of Truth

There are some places that have a particular resonance within one's heart; often it is names that press the point home. So I look at the plaque on a wall of Malines Cathedral– 'Mercier, Portal, Beaudouin, Halifax, Gore and Frere' – those names mean that this is just one of those places for me. The name Malines, for a student and an enthusiast in Anglican– Roman Catholic relations like myself, echoes down the years in sonorous tones. It was a place in which old men saw visions and young men dreamed dreams.

We dare not be seduced, however, by an other-worldly romanticism. For Malines turned out to be not only a place of visionary dreams, but also a centre of stark realism. In 1926, hopes were to be dashed and, as in the earlier Halifax/ Portal initiative, some 30 years before, all ended in bitter disappointment. Perhaps this is an appropriate starting point for us in our way. Dreams and visions seem to have faded into a mist of disappointment and a mood of resigned realism.

Anglicans cannot pretend to be anything other than disappointed by the Vatican response to ARCIC–I; Roman Catholics are confused and disorientated by the movement throughout Anglicanism worldwide to ordain women to the priesthood. Hopes for organic unity seem to have faded, the Communion for which our Lord prayed sometimes seems as far off as ever. The Church offers to the world a fragmented and flawed facade, battered by the eroding tides of history.

But perhaps the images with which I have been playing in these past few moments are themselves misdirected. Indeed,

---

Address at Malines Cathedral, Belgium, Saturday 13 February 1993.

perhaps we allow for too little richness and diversity when we review God's providence, even in his dealings with his Church. One of the essential features of some of the greatest works of art is the richness of their diversity, the unlimited sense of contrasts. Think, for example, of the different moods expressed in the Flemish school. Think too of the light and darkness, the chiaroscuro of the late Renaissance and the often intense luminosity of medieval painting. Despite all its blemishes, I believe we can see God's Church itself as a great work of art, blessed with an enormous richness of diversity and difference. We have not yet taken this truth seriously enough. We know that from the viewpoint of the Nicene/Constantinopolitan Creed we are already united in one faith. But we have not yet entered into each other's experience, each other's spiritual traditions, each other's historical memories, both bitter and glorious, to a sufficient degree.

I began to perceive something of this during my most memorable visit to the Catholic Church in Italy in 1992. The flamboyance, emotion, colour and mystery of the liturgy in which I took part in the Cathedral in Palermo was in brilliant contrast to much of the austere Protestantism of Northern Europe. This was for me more than an education, it was a fresh baptism into the world of Latin Christianity.

Of course, despite continued divergences and contrasts we should not underestimate how far along the road we have travelled together. We must protect all that has been achieved. The mood of the 1920s went beyond ignorance and misunderstanding to feelings of profound mistrust. Early on in the Malines Conversations one of my predecessors could write to a fellow Anglican bishop of the Halifax/Mercier initiative: 'We must take care not to rush effusively into intercourse in which we have to deal with very clever – I do not want to say crafty – people.' Similarly cynical and suspicious quotations are easily plucked from Roman Catholic annals of the same period.

The ecumenical movement which began early this century, combined with the prophetic changes wrought by Vatican II, have given birth to an earlier unimagined growth in trust and love between our two Communions. Cardinal Mercier's ring, now part of the Mercier Chalice in York Minster, is a symbolic token of this spirit.

The frustration and disappointment of more recent years has, however, taught us that there is still a long way to travel along the road. We have to face together the awkwardness and even unacceptability of believing that baptism unites, but that the Eucharist divides. Why is it that the sacrament which makes us Christian is not sufficient to bring us together around one altar? The instruments of partnership which we have built up remain essential. ARCIC is a vital link and theological dialogue is indispensable. Local Anglican–Roman Catholic committees build more trust. But there remain enormous areas where we must exercise far greater imagination and far greater daring. It may be that it is in those things in which we differ most that we have most to learn from each other.

My own spiritual journey has been enriched beyond measure by my discovery of Catholic spirituality and worship. In ecclesiology, and through the Catholic tradition of peace and justice, Anglicans have become immeasurably the richer through the contemporary experience of ecumenical theology. But I am bold enough to believe that Roman Catholics have something to learn too from our own tradition. The role of representative laity in a synodically governed Church complements the conciliarity of bishops. Our tradition of tolerance, enriched by the Anglo-Saxon intellectual environment, offers a climate in which forms of theology can flourish which are both free and loyal to the tradition. And then our slow, but eventual realisation of the role of women within the Church, both lay and ordained, does, I am convinced, point to a legitimate development within the tradition of Western Christianity.

I would like to challenge the Anglican and Roman Catholic Churches to respond to each other. First of all there is a need for further theological study on the nature of ecclesial and sacramental unity. Within our communions we continue to live separate lives. Our common baptism in the name of the Trinity does not lead to communion at the table of our Lord. We remain estranged at the very heart of our being. But since Vatican II we have recognised the presence of sacramental grace in our churches even where questions remain about the sacramental forms of ministry. How may we build upon this tacit acceptance of the reality of God's grace in our divided communions?

Perhaps we should admit that no one Church exhibits the fullness of the Christian life. It is as we receive from one another that we shall move towards the greater conciliar fellowship which we believe to be the will of God. In saying this I recognise that for Roman Catholics the conviction remains that the true Church 'subsists' in the Roman Catholic Church. Even that, however, accepts the ecclesial status of separated fellowships.

Secondly, a deepening unity may emerge as we learn from each other by what some theologians have called 'the way of exchange'. Three areas are particularly significant: worship, mission and social witness, and the search for a fuller role for women. It is increasingly common for Anglicans and Roman Catholics to worship together in non-Eucharistic celebrations. We should encourage this because as familiarity in prayer together grows, so confidence in one another develops. And we have much to share. Catholicism offers a rich legacy of spiritual devotion gleaned from the saints. It can nourish others who have been separated from that treasury. Anglicans might offer the use of the Bible, particularly in groups.

The area of mission and social witness presents an opportunity for our communions to share their common faith with a needy world. We are confronted with a deepening secularism and with profound moral problems of war and peace, social justice, extreme nationalism and xenophobia. Can ecumenism in the 1990s challenge us to a shared witness to the world around us?

Then there is that fuller role for women. This is not simply to return to the question of the priesthood of women. Above all it is about encouraging the gifts, experiences and insights of women in the service of Christ, both within the life of the Christian community and within the wider human family. Our Churches have failed adequately to affirm the wealth and talent of women.

My third point returns me to my image of the Church as a work of art. Organic unity in art is never achieved through a cheap pastiche, nor through a bland composition of pallid washes. Instead, such organic unity includes vast contrasts and stunning diversity.

It reminds me once again of my time in Italy. During our visit to Venice we were taken in to the astonishing Scuola di San Rocco. There, surrounding us on every side, were 156 breathtaking canvases by Tintoretto. The richness and variety of the paintings was utterly stunning. It forced me to ask, what is the essence of Tintoretto's genius?

That experience may have something to teach us about the nature of truth. Since the Second Vatican Council, we have reflected much on the so-called hierarchy of truths. If we can agree on the nature of the apostolic faith, how can we remain divided by secondary doctrines? I would I think prefer to use a rather different image and talk instead of the fullness of truth. Each of the Tintoretto canvases in itself expressed profoundly an organic unity, a glimpse into the fullness of truth. Not until we had been immersed into the entire array, however, not until we had been offered an appreciation of the form, the texture, the style and the artistic passion of the whole could we begin to appreciate still more fully the perfection, the completeness of Tintoretto's life's work.

Against such a canvas, and using such images, our Churches still have some way to go. There remains much hope and so much enthusiastic commitment. But I remain convinced that only the most daring engagement and partnership can offer us the ultimate hope of seeing the complete work of art in all its glory.

Epilogue: Pressing Towards God's Future

A s the title of this Epilogue suggests, I would like to take
this opportunity to examine the vocation of the Church
of England as we look towards the last years of this century.
Inevitably, one outcome of the current debates, such as the
question of the ordination of women to the priesthood, has
been to raise questions about the nature and authority of the
Church to which we belong. However, that questioning has
been simplistically coupled with other factors. In particular it
has been linked first to the numerical decline in formal or
conventional religious practice in all mainstream denominations in Western Europe, and secondly to the contemporary
development by which nearly all institutions and traditional
models of authority are criticised and attacked in public
debate. By bringing these disparate elements together the conclusion has been drawn that the Church of England has
departed from its roots and is now terminally ill. In this Epilogue I shall dig much deeper into the truth of the matter and
I assure you that I shall come to a quite different conclusion.

Where are we then, and who are we, in the Church of
England? Any institution builds its future from its past and
we shall not understand ourselves or our calling from God as
a Church for the twenty-first century unless we take hold of
the words and ideas which have shaped our past.

What are these words – banners under which so many sons
and daughters of the Church of England have marched, and
sometimes have marched to their death? 'Catholic'; 'Prot-

*Address at the 900th Anniversary of the Consecration of
Winchester Cathedral, Monday 24 May 1993.*

estant'; 'Evangelical'; 'Reformed'; 'Apostolic'. They are all words which can be honourably and gladly owned by members of the Church of England.

I have already given some expression to the strength of continuity in time and place which are a reminder of the 'catholicity' of our Church. The Reformation 're-formed' the Church in this land. It testified to the responsibility of God's people in the light of scriptural teaching, coupled with reason and tradition, to embrace even radical change when it is seen to be necessary. This was the nature of the 'Reformed Catholicism' as taught by Richard Hooker, unquestionably our greatest thinker of the sixteenth century. For him the Reformation made no new Church. Against Roman Catholics of the time Hooker defended the antiquity of the Church: 'We hope that to reform ourselves if at any time we have done amiss, is not to sever ourselves from the Church we were before. In the Church we were, and we are so still.'

But the *via media* Church it became also resulted in a different accusation, this time from Protestant purists, who claimed that the Church of England was afraid to break from Rome. It was said that the Church of England had the frame of a new faith but the furniture of the Church of Rome. Hooker's reply was equally sturdy: 'The customs and ceremonies we have retained are not the property of the Church of Rome but have been handed down to us by our fathers in the faith who had them from the ancient Church.' Hooker's line is uncompromisingly clear – our identity as a Church is one with the Christian Church of the past. We have rejected nothing that would rob us of catholicity. The Church of England did not claim to have its own version of the Christian faith. Rather it claimed to be authentically part of the Body of Christ forming and developing itself in the light of Scripture, Tradition and Reason.

The emerging Church of England, Catholic and Reformed, was committed to witness and evangelism, the words which undergird the concepts of 'Protestant' and 'Evangelical'. For 'Protestant', unravelled from its Latin origin, means not to protest against, but to bear witness to or for. It was in bearing witness that distinctive insights were formed which marked out the emerging Church of England and the ecclesiological tradition which we now know as Anglicanism.

Similarly, the term 'Evangelical' had a long history in Germany and Switzerland before it was adopted and adapted in eighteenth-century England. It means not only an emphasis upon the authentic individual experience of forgiveness and liberation in Christ, but also that the communication of good news is paramount. The Church exists not only to be the ark of salvation for believers, but equally the vessel which is to carry good news to others, everywhere and always.

To gather all these concepts into one, as the English Church did, however uneasily, in the time of Gardiner and Andrewes, was a tremendous adventure. It was a unique achievement, not worked out, of course, as a purely intellectual exercise in theology, but in the politically energetic and dangerous world of Tudor and Stuart monarchs imposing their will on the institutions and people of the land. Thus was brought into the frame another significant element in emergent Anglicanism. The Church is called above all to faithfulness to holy Scripture and obedience to the faith which comes down through the ages. But this commitment has always to be worked out in realistic and effective engagement with the world as it is at the time.

Now, we may be accustomed to calling this whole development the 'Elizabethan Settlement'. It was not a new kind of Church or Christian faith for, as I have already mentioned, it was seen decisively as the continuation of the Church of the Apostles. Its sacramental continuity was deliberately safeguarded. Not a new Church but a Church which had 'washed its face'; a Church that traced its roots to the faith 'once delivered to the saints'.

More important, however, than the achievement of the sixteenth-century Reformation was the pattern of activity which it bequeathed to the Church of England for the future. The Elizabethan Settlement is not a fossilised organism from the past imposing a rigid shape for all time. Rather, it is a particular example of a dynamic form which should shape the work and life of the Church in every generation. Not reformed once and for all, but *semper reformanda* – always involved in a process of reformation; always careful to cherish strong bonds of continuity with the past; always checking the fundamentals of belief against the word and the sense of scripture; always straining to bear witness to an articulation of the gospel which will engage with the minds and hearts of contemporary people.

This Anglican ecclesiology can, of course, be represented as a hopelessly ragged synthesis. So, some critics will latch on to the real engagement with contemporary culture and society, including the State connection, and argue that the Church of England is a body in which real faith has evaporated and individuals of any convictions or none are held together by a merely political compromise to be the State Church. Others will tell us that the Church of England is a mass of irreconcilable theological convictions, tenuously maintained by a common liturgy and only sustainable because those who disagree with one another rarely meet.

I myself firmly believe that the untidiness is essentially, and sometimes gloriously, creative in terms both of theology and spirituality. Our understanding of God is linked as closely to our liturgies as to the Articles of Religion. The very stresses and strains of the Anglican way of doing theology and of self-understanding bear witness to the belief that the truth of Christ transcends every attempt to tie it down to simplistic formulations. In that sense, the word infallibility is not a word in the Anglican vocabulary.

This is a point of some substance, since some critics of the General Synod's decision regarding the ordination of women accuse the Synod of having pretensions to infallibility in such matters. I want to submit there need be no misunderstanding about that. Synod's role is to take decisions about the right ordering of the Church's affairs. It does not claim to be inerrant and is therefore open to debate, discussion and change. It is precisely for that reason that those who are doubtful of the correctness or wisdom of this recent decision need not, and should not, come to believe that they no longer have any place in the Church of England.

The point here is that the claim to ultimate inerrancy, whether lodged in the *magisterium* of the Church, or in a particular understanding of the Bible, distorts and unbalances that dynamic of insights and concepts which characterise Anglican theology. And here I contend with those who have been suggesting recently that because of the decision to ordain women to the priesthood the Church of England has forfeited its claim to catholicity and has become a 'Protestant sect'. Quite apart from the (one hopes unintended) insult here to the Free Churches such as the Methodist Church, the Lutheran and the Baptist Churches which emphasise their Protestant roots, this particular criticism is diametrically opposite to the truth. For the spirit of Sectarianism shows its true identity where there is a desire to see an end to the dynamic of complementary truths, which is the essence of the Anglican faith, and to prefer the triumph of one sector over the whole.

The discomforts and stresses which mark the process of decision-making in the Church of England on important issues at the present time, far from signalling the end of the Elizabethan Settlement, are a continuing contemporary expression of the coming together of aspects of Christian truth which actually created the Elizabethan Settlement and continue to characterise Anglican theology.

Can these varied observations about aspects of the Church of England's past and present attempts to deal with particular eventualities offer us pointers or encouragement for the future?

It is true that so far as the creeds are concerned, Anglicans believe what the universal Church believes. It is true too that we have always been reluctant to resort to too much doctrinal definition. Despite the honoured place that the Thirty-nine Articles have in our polity, the Church of England does not have an equivalent of the Augsburg Confession or the Westminster Confession. In that sense we are not a 'Confessional' Church, but that does not mean that the Church of England is left without a firm identity when wrestling with matters of doctrine. From Jewell and Hooker onwards, the Anglican way has been that of bringing to bear upon matters of truth the threefold criteria of Scripture, Reason and Tradition. This distinctive methodology now needs to be confidently reasserted, so that no one of these three is lost. For those who fear this is a dangerous retreat into a radical liberalism, let me make it clear that classic Anglicanism affirms the place of Scripture as the cornerstone of our way of doing theology. Reason, then, ensures that we do not drift into an unthinking fundamentalism and Tradition prevents us from cutting ourselves off from the past.

It follows that we need not be ashamed or afraid in the Church of England of the freedom to debate openly about matters of faith. This gives maximum liberty to those whose pilgrimage towards the truth leads them into adventurous ways. Of course, just as reliance upon Scripture and Tradition can become exaggerated and exclusive, so can the libertarianism which some might take to be the flowering of the element of rationality. We must be clear that by reason we do not mean a carte blanche to ignore the insights of scripture and tradition. Instead we mean the exercise of a committed and disciplined mind seeking the truth in Christ in a spirit of humble reverence for the inexhaustible insights embedded in holy scripture, and in the subsequent struggles of the people of God to know, to love and to worship him in the Body of Christ. In that context, we should have the courage and the confidence to encourage those who enjoy this gift of God in their search for truth.

What then is the vocation of the Church of England as we face the last decade of this century?

Our task is surely to rise to the challenges with which we are presented and to share those very special insights and practices that characterise Anglicanism. I see no reason for uncertainty, dismay or retreat. Our history, our theology, our resources, our strength are gifts to offer our Lord and all those we serve both in the wider Church and in the nation.

In the remaining half of this lecture I shall enumerate seven areas where I believe Anglicans have something distinctive and important to share.

First, our Anglican tradition of 'diversity-in-unity' is a rich gift we offer to others. I have already alluded to our breadth and comprehensiveness. We have not always been good at recognising this as a strength; various groups in our Church have, from time to time, been anxious to make their own ecclesiologies and belief the *sine qua non* of the Church. We have resisted this as we have resisted attempts to make us a Confessional Church. To be sure there are potential weaknesses as well as strengths about this position. It may lead to woolliness of belief, an accusation which is often made. It may lead to the challenge of A D Gilbert that Anglicanism in England results in, 'a religion demanding minimum commitment, and requiring neither deviation from the generally accepted ethical and social standards of the wider society nor burdensome donation of time, money or energy'. Stephen Neill agrees in part: 'To be a bad Anglican is the easiest thing in the world, the amount of effort required in a minimum Anglican conformity is so infinitesimal that it is hardly to be measured.' He adds however: 'To be a good Anglican is an exceedingly taxing business.' It is taxing because the call to be an open Church which allows others to grow, to think, to dispute, and yet to stay passionately committed to a historic faith in a world of doubt, is very daunting and demanding indeed.

Yet I for one would not have it any other way. We sell the Christian faith short when we minimise life's problems and make our faith fit our interpretation of the world. As the writer R E C Browne wrote: 'To expound doctrine is not to teach a system of thought and then demonstrate that no experience can disturb it. It is not that doctrine is supremely important and that life proves its importance; it is that life is important and doctrine illuminates it.' The Church is compelled to pass on the faith in ways which relate to the real needs of people. Faith must be interpreted in ways which penetrate the consciousness of people in our current culture, yet it must not be circumscribed by what conforms to the fashions of the day.

Anglicanism at its very best seeks to find a way between 'conservative' and 'modernist' polarisations, while respecting the diversity of taste and opinion in non-essential matters among those who share a common commitment to our Lord and his Church. Demanding though this programme is, it is hardly a surprise to students of history to detect that some other traditions are following Anglicanism into broader theologies today. In my view the complex nature of truth requires it.

Secondly, there is our vocation to be a Church *for* the nation. Such an involvement is both prophetic and pastoral. The Church of England with its long rich history and traditions must not shrink from its pastoral calling to serve the nation, accepting its historical establishment as God's gift. Here I use the word 'establishment' in a wide sense. Questions like those surrounding the appointment of bishops are perhaps comparatively unimportant compared with the immense, if inarticulate, volume of goodwill and recognition of the Church of England as 'our Church', and the parson as 'our vicar'. This goodwill has to be built on and is sustained by our commitment to the nation as a whole and not just to the faithful, however we may define them.

Our 16,000 or so parishes offer a ministry to the whole of the nation seven days a week. Time and again in recent years our clergy have been called on to represent the community in times of pain and disaster. The treasures of our cathedrals and our many parish churches are not merely Church treasures but national treasures of inestimable wealth. The many Church of England schools remain pivotal to the education of our land; our Chaplains in universities, colleges of higher education, prisons, the armed services and hospitals provide faithful ministry in a wide variety of situations. What is more, those of other faith communities sometimes look to us to act on their behalf.

Indeed it is our pastoral concern to the nation that inevitably leads us to speak prophetically on occasion. In recent years we have seen the enormous impact made by the thinking of *Faith in the City* and the contribution of the Church Urban Fund which flowed from it. This is but one example illustrating that our Church is continuing to play a vital role in the life of the nation and one, which if we can find ways of communicating it more boldly, could bring greater glory to God.

Thirdly, we are committed to serving the people of this land in conjunction with other Christian denominations. We are committed to that ecumenical task and to the quest for unity. It is a task to which our Church has contributed much in the past. We intend to go on building on those achievements in the future. Though reformed radically in the sixteenth century, we have retained an emphasis on the sacraments and Catholic order. Our liturgy has shaped so much of our theological thinking, giving us natural links with the Orthodox tradition. As a representative of Anglicanism, I have met people from a wide variety of Churches in various circumstances ranging from the Baptist Assembly in Nottingham, to the Norwegian Lutherans in London, the Roman Catholic Church in Tbilisi, and the Armenian Orthodox Cathedral in old Echmiadzin. Anglicanism has a vital role in understanding and interpreting different Churches to one another. Despite setbacks, the Anglican–Roman Catholic International Commission and other dialogues recognise a real convergence between traditions, a convergence of which we are but a part. We have travelled a long, long way since the Reformation fragmented the religious map both of this country and of Europe. We are now travelling together in many ways towards a deeper unity of faith, worship and Christian life with other Christians.

Fourthly, I want to point to our vocation in the Anglican Communion, which has more than 70 million members. As my wife and I visit other parts of this great and developing Communion I cannot but help note with joy and excitement the way in which our life together is embraced. The 'Englishness' which once marked the Communion has long since disappeared. For example, there is nothing English about Korean, Japanese, Malagasy, Tanzanian, Sri Lankan, Spanish or Brazilian forms of Anglicanism. Sturdy, independent Churches, they look to the Church of England as their Mother Church and they look to the Archbishop of Canterbury alongside their own Primates as *primus inter pares*. We are now beginning to see and to learn how much we can learn from the richness of our sister Churches abroad whose suffering and adventurous faith have so much to offer us in our pilgrimage. It is that challenge that needs to be taken further as we approach the end of this century.

A fifth element, linked to our position within the Anglican Communion, stems from the Lambeth Conference of 1988. There it was agreed that the 1990s should be a Decade of Evangelism. Other Churches had also been considering such an initiative and it has now been taken up by them. Once again the Church of England within the Anglican Communion has a vital role to play. Of course the title, Decade of Evangelism, though open to much misunderstanding, is an invitation to a deeper commitment to the gospel with its implications for our day. I have said repeatedly that evangelism is not a cry for one way of presenting the Christian faith. It is rather a challenge to be the Church at the service of others; both to preach the good news and to prove it in authentic Christian living. It will mean many different things but essentially it exists in being a Church confident in its faith, committed to growth, and open to the world around. Evangelism in this sense is a crucial part of our vocation for the years ahead.

Returning to focus on this country in particular, a sixth area of importance is what we can contribute to the current debates about personal and public morality. It is indeed true that there is something very exciting about being members of a society with such a rich cultural mix, but more and more people these days feel increasingly lost where moral and spiritual signposts appear to be missing. The end of the book of Judges concludes with the terrible words, 'Everyone did what was right in his own eyes'. The same sort of individualism prevails today. No objective framework seems discernible. The assertion of personal freedom and the denial of personal responsibility has led to agonising fragmentations in society and family life. But I want to say it has been gratifying to see how in recent months the leaders of all the main political parties have stressed the need for the Churches in general, and the Church of England in particular, to play their part in shaping the nation's morality.

That call is one to which we can, and we should, respond. In this sphere of ethics and morals, I believe the distinctive Anglican mixture of Scripture, Tradition and Reason can continue to make a rich contribution both to our society and to the wider Christian Church. Once again, our wholehearted commitment to holy scripture and the struggle of the universal Church of Christ down the ages to understand and interpret God's will are set beside the responsibility, as we see it, of each individual and of the Church, to continue that struggle in prayer and humility in our own time. Conscience, prayer, openness to the Holy Spirit, the summoning up of our powers of observation and reason, the conscientious testing of resulting opinions in open debate: all these need to play a part in discerning God's will for our Church and society. Much of this we share with other traditions. Anglican moralists have, however, from the seventeenth century onwards offered a distinctive approach rooted in 'holiness'. Morality and spirituality are of one piece. Bishop Jeremy Taylor wrote of 'Holy Living' and 'Holy Dying' and his moral teaching is an integral part of the spirituality for which Bishop Lancelot Andrewes is renowned.

My seventh and final point is that no account of the role of Anglicanism at the end of this century would be complete without acknowledging the continuing significance of the liturgy to our tradition and to which the Bishop of Winchester, Colin James, has contributed so much as Chairman of the Liturgical Commission. For us the patterns of worship have shaped, as I have said already, our understanding of doctrine. The Book of Common Prayer and its successors have been a well-spring of our theological tradition. The knowledge of God and worship are inextricably linked. The New Testament shows that the search for God leads to worship, and worship back to knowing God. What was true of the Apostolic period is true for us today. Once again this represents a rich inheritance we can share with our neighbours. Our understanding of liturgy does not, of course, blind us to any one form. In the range of services now authorised or allowed by Canon, I see something of the genius of Anglicanism working itself out in this generation. These changes have allowed us to give a greater role to the laity and to free us from some of the greater excesses of clericalism. Whether in a quiet 8 a.m. Book of Common Prayer service, or the glories of a Cathedral Eucharist or the freedom of family services there is still something distinctively Anglican about what we do, and on such foundations we can continue to build and develop.

In enumerating these seven areas I do not pretend that I have exhausted the riches of the contribution the Church of England has to make at this part of our history, but I trust they provide sufficient evidence for the strong belief that I have, and many others have, that we can with confidence press forward with hope in God's mission to our people.

We should give thanks to God for those who lived before and after the Reformation: fellow-worshippers divided by history but united in their passion for God and for the souls of their fellow human beings. From the viewpoint of history we see that our problems have a familiar ring about them. It is an age-old battle to maintain identity and faithfulness with the past, whilst coming to terms with the present; it is a constant struggle to keep faith with a God who is always going before and who sometimes does not wait for us to catch up.

A longer perspective encourages us to treat with tolerance, love and respect those who disagree with our own opinions as together we seek God's will. We are also warned against investing with too much significance the ways in which we organise our affairs from one generation to another.

Although I do not want in any way to belittle the present soul-searching going on in our Church – because it does represent much thought and commitment – yet I would urge that it is kept in perspective. Our long-term mission; our commitment to Christian morality and action in our world; our relations with those of other traditions; our joyful, reverent worship of our risen Lord; our proclamation of the glorious news of our redemption and salvation: these must be our priorities and our preoccupations.

Just a few months ago I visited the Esso Refinery at Fawley. There I saw a plant as awesomely complex as the Church of England. In its natural state crude oil is of little practical use, but when broken down into its constituent parts, when it is refined, purified and reformed into new combinations, it becomes the lifeblood of the twentieth century. Through an intricate series of controlled interactions, the raw material emerges transformed as multiple products for use in cars, in homes and businesses.

Our Church bears some resemblance to that extraordinary plant. As human life and aspirations encounter the Church of England, in all its different manifestations, there are innumerable interactions with the riches of Anglicanism. Some of these interactions are in our diverse churches and cathedrals themselves, some in our schools, in prisons and hospitals, in meetings around the desks of government ministers or in the heart of devastated inner cities, in the great institutions of the nation or in the day-to-day rhythm of parish life. The changes wrought through these encounters at so many different levels in the life of our country are far more numerous even than the products of a refinery, and the cumulative effect is, we pray, to the greater glory and service of God.

I am tempted to press the image a little further. God's process of taking people who are 'crude' and making us into his image and likeness is the reason why the Church exists at all. The breaking down and the building up are parts of the same process of renewal. Both as individuals and as a Church, we need to face and acknowledge our many weaknesses and shortcomings. There is never any renewal without penitence and a determined resolution to do better. *Semper reformanda* is a call that comes to God's people at every stage of our pilgrimage.

So there is no reason to collude with those who would have us think that the Church of England is a spent force, or merely the shredded remains of a Church that once was, or a body that is about to disintegrate. Rather, there is a vision to glimpse, a challenge to face, countless opportunities to grasp for a Church of England which is resolved to be faithful to its long and glorious history, to take possession of its own life as Christ's servant, to be a living body in the world, and to take his gospel to our nation in word and deed. *That* is pressing forward towards God's future.